The Blue Book

Jim Branch

This book is for all who seek to know the immense affection of our God — especially Carol, Tim, Michelle, and Hunter. With Much Love.

~JLB.

Preface

This book has been a long time in the making. At its core it is simply a spiritual journal of the themes and seasons of my own journey with Jesus over the past twenty years or so. It is a collection of words and poems and scriptures and prayers that have been spoken into my life by various saints, poets, and pilgrims along the way — most of whom I have never personally met. To each of them I am eternally grateful.

I am also grateful for the loving community of family and friends and coworkers who have surrounded, cared for, and invested in me through the years. Your contribution to the pages that follow cannot be overstated. Special thanks to Rhonda Lowry, whose wisdom, kindness, and tireless efforts have helped make this dream become a reality.

My deepest desire for this book is that it might be helpful in your journey with Jesus. That it might offer space and time and scripture and structure for you to discover the ancient rhythms of God that were whispered into you when he breathed you into being. My prayer is that it would not get in the way of what God wants to do in and through you, but that it might actually encourage and enable it. Thank you for giving me the incredible privilege of accompanying you on this extraordinary adventure into the heart of our God. May you always know the depths of his great affection.

Introduction

Welcome. My guess is that if you have made it this far you are interested in finding a fruitful way of being with God and with his word on a daily basis. Believe me, you are not alone. Years ago I began a search for a tool that would help bring me into the presence of God regularly. God wonderfully directed that search to a book called *Disciplines for the Inner Life* by Michael W. Benson and Bob Benson, which he used to form my inner life over the next 7-8 years in ways that I never imagined. That book, as well as the one that it was modeled after (*A Guide to Prayer for Ministers and Other Servants* by Rueben P. Job and Norman Shawchuck), have served as a model for what you now hold in your hands. My prayer is that it would offer you rich space and time to simply be with Jesus in a way that nourishes your soul and transforms your heart.

Using this book is quite easy and should offer your time with God some structure. Start by using the **prayers** as a means of focus and attentiveness to the theme of the week. Next, pray the **Psalm** every day for the week. If the Psalm is too lengthy for you to pray each day, break it into parts. Praying the Psalms has been a tool of Christians for centuries to commune with God. To pray them, just read them aloud, slowly and reflectively. For the **Scripture** passage each day, read it the same way. In the words of Mme. Jeanne Guyon, a French writer of the seventeenth century, "*Take in fully, gently, and carefully what you are reading. Taste it and digest it as you read. Use the passage to sense the presence of the Lord and stay with the passage until you have sensed the very heart of what you have read...your purpose is to take everything from the passage that unveils the Lord to you.*" Try to read one or two of the **Readings for Reflection** each day as a means of allowing God to speak through some of the great writers of the past and present. Then take time for **reflection** and **listening**. Try to be still and hear what God is saying to you, maybe writing down what you hear in a journal. Next, turn your heart toward God in **prayer**. Pray as you feel led. Remember that Clement of Alexandria once said that prayer is "simply keeping company with God." Use the **song** as an expression of worship and praise to the One that made you. I regret that it was not possible to include the lyrics to all of these songs in the text, but in this day and age it should be easy enough to find them on your own. My prayer is that they might add a beautiful dimension to your daily rhythm with God. Sing them aloud or in your heart, which ever you prefer.

    Finally, know that place and time are important elements of this process. Find a place that is set aside for you and God alone; a place that helps you be attentive to Him, a place that will not be full of distractions or noise. Remember that three main enemies of your spiritual life are crowds, noise, and busyness. Also, pick a time that is a good time for you; a time of day or night when you are at your best, awake and alert. As your time with God unfolds each day try not to keep an eye on your watch, just allow your time to happen. Some days it may take a while and some days it may be relatively short. We're going for quality. Let the Spirit of God be your guide. The key is just to be consistent. Over time you will begin to notice that God is near, be it ever so subtle at times.

    Here's hoping that your time with Him is full and rich.

Jim Branch
12 December 2002

Follow my blogs: BlueBookBlog.com
and jb-coreleadership.blogspot.com

Contents

Made in His Image

I. Opening Prayer
Blessed are you, God of all creation. Let us who are made in your image and are sustained by your hand reflect you in all that we do, that in all things you may be glorified, forever and ever. Amen. —*Work of God* ed. by Judith Sutera

II. Psalm 139

III. Daily Scripture Readings
Monday	Genesis 1:26-31
Tuesday	Romans 8:18-27
Wednesday	Colossians 3:1-17
Thursday	Psalm 8:1-9
Friday	Ephesians 2:4-10
Saturday	2 Corinthians 3:12-18
Sunday	Colossians 1:15-23

IV. Readings for Reflection

V. Reflection and Listening: silent and written

VI. Prayer: for the church, for others, for myself

VII. Song   *I Have a Maker*

VIII. Closing Prayer
Loving Creator, I have no quarrel with the way you have so carefully designed me in your image. Truly I am your work of art. Take me deeper today. Show me my virtues—the wonders of your design for my life. Help me not to be afraid to look into the depths of myself and believe in what I see—for I am the work of your hands. If I can believe in what I see, then I can rejoice in what I see. Precious in your sight, I am your

work of art. Continue to create me in your image.
Amen. — *Behold Your Life* by Macrina Wiederkehr

Readings for Reflection-

Why did God make us? Do you ever wonder about that? I know I do. I mean, God did not have to make us, right? In fact, things appeared to being going along just fine. For before there was anything else there was God — Father, Son, and Holy Spirit — in wonderfully intimate, loving union; three, yet one, dancing the great round dance of love from eternity to eternity. Sounds pretty incredible doesn't it?

But God was so full of love that he simply could not contain himself. He had to create. Maybe not *had to* in the way we normally understand it, but *had to* in the very best sense of the word. He could not *not* do it. His heart was so full of love that creation just spilled out. It was the overflow of his great affection. Out of love he created a world and a people, in order to invite us into this amazing inner circle of joy, intimacy, and infinite delight.

I guess that's why Meister Eckhart once said that we *were created out of the laughter of the Trinity.* I love that image. I love the image of a God so overcome with joy and delight that he cannot keep the smile from his lips as he dreams us into being. And I think the reason I love that image so much is because it's true. It is true in my head and rings true to the depths of my soul, because I was made in his image. I was made to be in intimate union with God. I was made to love and to be loved. That is his great desire for me. That is his great desire for us. Therefore, may we always strive to be exactly who and what he made us to be.

— Jim Branch, January, 2016

In the mysteries of eternity past, God the Father, God the Son, and the Holy Spirit dwelled in unsurpassed union and intimacy. The Holy Three have always existed as a divine dance of romance, a whirlwind of affection and pleasure and love unending. It was from this pulsating intimacy that God created humanity and the natural order. Though we will always remain the creation, He formed humanity to enter into relationship with the Trinity, the Godhead. In His great mysterious heart was a desire to bring human beings into the holy river of affections known between Father, Son, and Holy Spirit, and to share in this Divine communion with them. The Father desired a family, and the Son desired a bride. From this overflow of burning desire, humanity was brought forth. — *Deep Unto Deep* by Dana Candler

I am not sure exactly what all I think we mean when we say that we are made in the image of God. But part of it, I believe, is that the calling voice of God is sounding out in the caves and caverns deep beneath the soil of our souls. And it is by obeying this call we learn who we truly are and what we can become.

So if I do not seem to hear him speak from outside, and if there does not seem to be any message from the sky, then I must listen to the voice that is within me. For that voice, too, is the purposeful, calling voice of God to us.

Not many of us have enough confidence in ourselves to listen to that whispering voice that comes from within. Most of the time, we do not even hear it. But it doesn't matter because we wouldn't trust it. We cannot believe that this inner voice is capable of leading us due north.

We seek advice from friends and professionals, disc jockeys and Dear Abbys. We put out a fleece. We flip coins. We take aptitude tests. We do everything but believe that we could possibly have the answers deep within.

The message of Paul in this place is that the calling indeed comes in the lives of the unlikely and the "foolish." You think you are unlikely; well you're not. You have difficulty believing that God could do great things in you; well, he wouldn't.

Now if God can take a tiny seed and, in the process of giving it his life, endow it with a knowledge of what it is supposed to be; if he can give it the purpose and strength and fruitfulness to not only accomplish it all, but to perpetuate itself as well; and if he can give it an inner calendar to tell it when all of this is supposed to be done, why is it so hard to believe he has done the same for our hearts?

Since he has done this for tomatoes and thistles and beans and dandelions, it shouldn't stretch our credibility so much to believe that his image in us, the image inherent in the life he gives to each of us, is calling us to *be*.

The trick is to hear the voice, to believe it, and to trust it. — *See You at the House* by Bob Benson

These days when someone commits an atrocity, we tend to sigh and say, "That's human nature." But our attitude would seem wrong-headed to the desert monks, who understood human beings to be part of the creation that God called good, special in that they are made in the image of God. Sin, then, is an aberration, not natural to us at all. This is why Gregory of Nyssa speaks so often of "returning to the grace of that image which was established in you from the beginning." Gregory, in fact, saw it as our lifelong task to find out what part of the divine image God has chosen to reveal in us. Like the other early monks, he suggests that we can best do this by realistically determining how God has made us — what our primary faults and temptations are, as well as our gifts — not that we might better "know ourselves," or in modern parlance, "feel good about ourselves," but in order that we might become instruments of divine grace for other people. — *The Cloister Walk* by Kathleen Norris

Our very existence is one of the never-to-be-repeated ways God has chosen to express himself in space and time. Because we are made in God's image and likeness, you and I are yet another promise that he has made to the universe that He will continue to love it and care for it.

    Yet even if we grasp the fact that we are a word uttered by God, we may not grasp what he is trying to say through us. In *Seeds of Contemplation* Merton writes, "God utters me like a word containing a partial thought of himself. A word will never be able to comprehend the voice that utters it. But if I am true to the concept God utters in me, if I am true to the thought in him I was meant to embody, I shall be full of his actuality and find him everywhere in myself, and find myself nowhere. I shall be lost in him." — *Ruthless Trust* by Brennan Manning

You are a special and sacred word-of-God-made-flesh. He loves you as you are. He spoke your name and created you as a unique person. So be who you are as created by God. In prayer say your own word, sing your own song and be true to it. — *A Traveler Toward the Dawn* by John Eagan

In reality, however, the image of Christ is the fulfillment of the deepest hungers of the human heart for wholeness. The greatest thirst of our being is for fulfillment in Christ's image. The most profound yearning of the human spirit, which we try to fill with all sorts of inadequate substitutes, is the yearning for our completeness in the image of Christ. — *Invitation to a Journey* by M. Robert Mulholland Jr.

We need to come to know who we truly are, that uniquely beautiful person that God has made us. And to have the courage to live accordingly. Each of us is a unique expression of the divine goodness and beauty. If we do not live that and express it in our lives, it will never be expressed in this world for the glory of God and the up-building of the whole Body of Christ.
— *Breaking Bread*, Basil Pennington

John Calvin, the sixteenth-century Protestant Reformer, claimed that the image of God remains on our souls; yet because we have so corrupted the image by sin, it is hard to recognize it in us. In silent moments, though, there is still enough of the image left for us to realize that we thirst for something. — *Sacred Thirst* by Craig Barnes

The early church fathers describe the Trinity as a Round Dance in which Love flames forth from one Person to the Other in a flow that never ceases...The Father is One and his Dance is Three: Love flowing out of the Silence of the Secret One to the Son, and returning to Abba in one concurrent, timeless motion—in the embrace of the Spirit. — *Dancing Madly* Backwards by Paul Marechal

What might it mean to live fully and freely in the life of the Trinity, knowing and loving God the Father, Son, and Holy Spirit as they know and love each other?
— *Mansions of the Heart* by R. Thomas Ashbrook

Who Are You?

I. Opening Prayer
Lord God, my Heavenly Father, thank you that in Christ
I am your beloved. Thank you that your love for me
does not depend on my accomplishments, or my
achievements, or my impressive actions. You love me
simply because you made me. You love me because I
am yours. I belong to you. Help that truth guide my
steps and transform my heart this day. Amen. —*Pieces II*
by Jim Branch

II. Psalm 62

III. Daily Scripture Readings
Monday	Isaiah 62:1-12
Tuesday	Matthew 3:13-17
Wednesday	Song of Songs 2:8-17
Thursday	1 Peter 2:9-10
Friday	Deuteronomy 33:12
Saturday	Luke 15:11-32
Sunday	John 15:5-17

IV. Readings for Reflection

V. Reflection and Listening: silent and written

VI. Prayer: for the church, for others, for myself

VII. Song   *Arise* by Ryan Long

VII. Closing Prayer
O God, our Heavenly Father, who created us beautifully
and wonderfully, may we always look to you for our
value and worth, remembering that we are each a
unique expression of your infinite love, care, and
creativity. Help us, O Lord, to see ourselves as you see

us—objects of your extravagant love and tender affection. Through Christ we pray. Amen.

Readings for Reflection-

One of my new favorite words of the spiritual life is the word *bestow*. And I don't mean new in the sense that it just arrived on the scene, but new in the sense that it is brand new to me. I suppose it has been there all along, lying on the page, waiting for me to dig a little and uncover the treasure it holds, but for some reason I have simply passed over it all these years. Then one day I stumbled upon it—and we all know that it wasn't stumbling at all, but God's hand and his leading—and was completely captured by its beauty. For the word *bestow* is indeed a magnificent treasure. And I think the reason I have been so captured by it recently is because of the very thing we are talking about.

You see, *bestow* is not something that can be achieved or accomplished or even earned; by its very nature it is something that can only be given or conferred. It is a gift, something we can never hope to attain on our own, but something that can only be done for us, or to us. *Bestow* focuses all of the attention on the heart of the Giver, and not on the worthiness, or skill, or aptitude of the receiver. It has everything to do with God, and the intricate care with which he made us, and the extravagant love with which he loves us. *Bestow* is all about receiving.

This is especially true when it comes to our identity. A few months ago, as I was meditating on this treasure, I came to a realization. I tend to go through life trying—in futility, I might add—to *create* a self each day rather than to simply *receive* a self each day. And any self that is created by anything or anyone other the Creator, the God that breathed me into being, can only be false. Any *self* that I create or manufacture is a false self because it is just a cheap imitation, adaptation, or distortion of the *me* I was created to be by the One who dreamt me into being before the foundations of the earth.

My true identity can only be *bestowed*, it can never be achieved. So my challenge, each and every day, is to stop the ongoing pattern of trying, in desperation, to create a self that has in fact already been *fearfully and wonderfully made*; and to simply receive my true self in peace and in freedom from the God who made me uniquely and loves me dearly. It is funny how much I strive to make a name for myself, when only he can give me the name I was made to bear—my true name.

How incredibly freeing! It is as if God is saying: "*I have given you your value and your worth. I have bestowed it upon you and it can never be lost. So stop measuring. Stop earning. Stop comparing. Stop performing. Your worth is not hanging in the balance. It does not depend on anything you achieve, or on any accomplishment you attain. So relax. Live in the freedom of knowing you are loved deeply and fully and completely – as well as eternally. Instead of working so hard to prove yourself, just fall in love with Me.*"
— *Becoming* by Jim Branch

What do you do when alone with God? Many of us think, talk, or ask. But when alone with God how vital also to listen! Solitude is the place where you can hear the voice that calls you the beloved, that leads you onto the next page of the adventure, that says, as God said to Jesus early in the Gospels, "This is my son, the Beloved, with whom I am well pleased" (Matthew 3:17)

How vitally that the word *beloved* can resound across our lives! Can you hear it? Everyone hears voices that seem to speak for God: "Prove yourself. Do something that makes you significant and then I will show up in love." Or we hear, "Do something relevant, be sure that people speak well of you. Be sure you gather money and property and influence, then I will love you." In our insecurity we try very hard to respond to such voices. And then we stay busy proving to others that we deserve some attention, that we are good people worth praise, that we merit affection or attention.

We push ourselves to wield influence or make a mark. Often we call that "vocation" but Jesus calls it "temptation." He has no patience with the one who insists that he jump from the temple to show his power or turn stones into bread to prove his ministry credentials. He has heard God speak of his belovedness as God's Son. That forms the basis of what he does and knows himself called to do. He will not be distracted by merely doing superficial good. He bears the very presence of God.

It is hard for us to hear the voice that proclaims that we are loved in Christ, not for our reputation or impressive actions, but because God has loved us with an everlasting love. "I don't hear anything," some say. We are too prone, too conditioned to listen for all the other voices that insist on "success" or "results." I hear only the voices that urge me to go here or do that or get done this mandate, we sometimes think. But then we also long for that other voice.

I do not suggest by this that you or I should not see fruit from our ministries, not own property, or not enjoy any possessions. I am not saying we should not want to find affection and love from others. I am saying, however, that our identity can find its basis only in God's word to us that we are beloved, not on the world's fickle promises. In Christ we live as God's beloved before we were born and after we have died; all the circumstances in between will not negate that. — *Turn My Mourning Into Dancing* by Henri J. M. Nouwen

He is the one who can tell us the reason for our existence, our place in the scheme of things, our real identity. It is an identity we can't discover for ourselves, that others can't discover in us — the mystery of who we really are. How we have chased around the world for answers to that riddle, looked in the eyes of others for some hint, some clue, hunted in the multiple worlds of pleasure and experience and self-fulfillment for some glimpse, some revelation, some wisdom, some authority to tell us our right name and our true destination.

But there was, and is, only One who can tell us this: the Lord himself. And he wants to tell us, he has made us to know our reason for being and to be led by it. But it is a secret he will entrust to us only when we ask, and then in his own way and his own time. He will whisper it to us not in the mad rush and fever of our striving and our fierce determination to become someone, but rather when we are content to rest in him, to put ourselves into his keeping, into his hands. Most delightfully of all, it is a secret he will tell us slowly and sweetly, when we are willing to spend time with him: time with him who is beyond all time. — *Clinging* by Emilie Griffin

The Christian's identity and value do not reside in the fragile order and tenuous control that she or he imposes upon life. Identity and value are found in a vital and living relationship with Christ as Lord. This relationship liberates Christians from dependence upon their little systems of order and fragile structures of control. Not that believers live without order or control, but they are liberated from dependency on those systems and structures for their sense of self. — *Invitation to a Journey* by M. Robert Mulholland Jr.

As long as we keep running around, anxiously trying to affirm ourselves or be affirmed by others, we remain blind to One who has loved us first, dwells in our heart, and has formed our truest self. But we can also open our eyes. We can see a new way forward. — *Turn My Mourning into Dancing* by Henri J.M. Nouwen

So you sit at the feet of the wise and learn what they have to teach, and our debts to them are so great that, if your experience is like mine, even twenty-five years later you will draw on the depth and breadth of their insights, and their voices will speak in you still, and again and again you will find yourself speaking in their voices. You learn as much as you can from the wise until finally, if you do it right and things break your way, you are wise enough to be yourself, and brave enough to speak with your own voice, and foolish enough, for Christ's sake, to live and serve out of the uniqueness of your own vision of Him and out of your own passion. —*A Room Called Remember* by Frederick Buechner

When we are insecure about our own identities, we create settings that deprive other people of their identities as a way of buttressing our own. This happens all the time in families, where parents who do not like themselves give their children low self-esteem. It happens at work as well: how often I phone a business or professional office and hear, "Dr. Jones's office — this is Nancy speaking." The boss has a title and a last name but the person who answers the phone has neither, because the boss has decreed that it will be that way.

There are dynamics in all kinds of institutions that deprive the many of their identity so the few can enhance their own, as if identity were a zero-sum game, a win-lose situation. Look into a classroom, for example, where an insecure teacher is forcing students to be passive stenographers of the teacher's store of knowledge, leaving the teacher with more sense of selfhood and the vulnerable students with less. Or look in on a hospital where the doctors turn patients into objects— "the kidney in Room 410"—as a way of claiming superiority at the very time when vulnerable patients desperately need a sense of self.

Things are not always this way, of course. There are settings and institutions led by people whose identities do not depend on depriving others of theirs. If you are in that kind of family or office or school or hospital, your sense of self is enhanced by leaders who know who they are.

These leaders possess a gift available to all who take an inner journey: the knowledge that identity does not depend on the role we play or the power it gives us over others. It depends only on the simple fact that we are children of God, valued in and for ourselves. When a leader is grounded in that knowledge, what happens in the family, the office, the classroom, the hospital can be life-giving for all concerned. — *Let Your Life Speak* by Parker Palmer

At every moment you choose yourself. But do you choose *your* self? Body and soul contain a thousand possibilities out of which you can build many *I* 's. But in only one of them is there a congruence of the elector and the elected. Only one — which you will never find until you have excluded all those superficial and fleeting possibilities of being and doing with which you toy, out of curiosity or wonder or greed, and which hinder you from casting anchor in the experience of the mystery of life, and the consciousness of the talent entrusted to you which is your *I*. — *Markings* by Dag Hammarskjold

It's true, Lord, that you are always thinking of us.
It's true from the beginning of time, before we existed.
Even before the world existed,
You have been dreaming of me,
Thinking of me,
Loving me.
And it's true that your Love created me,
Not assembly line, but unique,
The first one so made, and the last,

Indispensable to humanity.

It's true, Lord, that you have conceived for my life a
unique destiny.

It's true that you have an eternal plan for me alone,

A wonderful plan that you have always cherished in
your heart, as a father thinks over the smallest details
in the life of his little one still unborn.

It's true that, always bending over me, you guide me to
bring your plan about, light on my path and strength
for my soul.

It's true that you are saddened when I stray or run
away, but that you hasten to pick me up if I stumble
or fall.

Lord, you make bald heads, but above all beautiful lives,

You, the divine Attentive One,

the divine Patient One,

the divine Present One,

See that at no time I forget your presence.

I don't ask you to bless what I have decided to do, but
give me the grace to discover and to live what you
have dreamed for me.

Lord, living in your grace, let me share a little, through
the attention I give to others, your loving care for us.

Let me, on my knees, adore in them the mystery of your
created love.

Let me respect your idea of them without trying to
impose my own.

May I allow them to follow the path that you have
marked out for them without trying to take them
along mine.

May I realize that they are indispensable to the world,
and that I can't do without the least of them.

May I never tire of looking at them and enriching myself
with the treasures you have entrusted to them.

Help me to praise you in their journeying, to find you
in their lives.

And that not an instant of their existence should go by,
Not a hair of their heads fall,
By me, as by you, unheeded.
— *Prayers of Life* by Michael Quoist

O God
help me
to believe
the truth about myself
no matter
how beautiful it is!
— *Seasons of Your Heart* by Macrina Wiederkehr

It takes heroic humility to be yourself and to be
nobody but the man, or the artist that, God intended you
to be. — *New Seeds of Contemplation* by Thomas Merton

Identity does not grow out of action until it has taken
root in belonging. — *Chasing Fireflies* by Charles Martin

Longing

I. Opening Prayer

O God, I have tasted Thy goodness, and it has both satisfied me and made me thirsty for more. I am painfully conscious of my need for further grace. I am ashamed of my lack of desire. O God, the Triune God, I want to want Thee; I long to be filled with longing; I thirst to be made more thirsty still. — *The Pursuit of God* by A. W. Tozer

II. Psalm 63

III. Daily Scripture Readings

Monday	2 Corinthians 5:1-5
Tuesday	Romans 8:18-27
Wednesday	Ecclesiastes 3:1-11
Thursday	Deuteronomy 33:12
Friday	Proverbs 13:12-25
Saturday	Hebrews 11:1-16
Sunday	Psalm 36:5-10

IV. Readings for Reflection

V. Reflection and Listening: silent and written

VI. Prayer: for the church, for others, for myself

VII. Song *Satisfied*

VIII. Closing Prayer

Teach me to seek you, for I cannot seek you unless you teach me, or find you unless you show yourself to me. Let me seek you in my desire, and desire you in my seeking. Let me find you by loving you, let me love you when I find you.

—St. Anselm

Readings for Reflection-

Our souls long to be filled, long to be loved, and long to be known. Therefore, our lives are one continuous movement in the direction of our deepest longings. The problem is that we tend to stop too soon, too near the surface. When we taste something that tastes good to our souls, we assume that *it* is what our souls were made to be filled with. And so we go charging off in the direction of that person, or that thing, or that experience, trying to extract something from them (or *it*) that they were never intended — or able — to fully give us. C. S. Lewis said it so well when he said that these things or people or experiences *"are only the scent of a flower we have not found, the echo of a tune we have not heard, news from a country we have never yet visited."* In other words, the deepest, most wonderful things of this life were never intended to fully satisfy us, but to point us toward God.

—Jim Branch, March, 2016

The whole of the good Christian life is a holy longing. What you desire ardently, as yet you do not see...By withholding of the vision, God extends longing; through longing he extends the soul, by extending he makes room in it. Let us long because we are to be filled...that is our life, to be exercised by longing.

—St. Augustine

Our ability to satisfy one another's deepest longing is so limited that time and time again we are in danger of disappointing one another. Despite all of this, at times our longing can be so intense that it blinds us to our mutual limitations and we are led into the temptation of extorting love, even when reason tells us that we can't give one another any total, unlimited, unconditional love. It is then that love becomes violent. It is then that kisses become bites, caresses become blows, forgiving looks become suspicious glances, lending a sympathetic ear becomes eavesdropping, and heartfelt surrender becomes violation. The borderline between love and force is frequently transgressed, and in our anxiety-ridden times it doesn't take very much to let our desire for love lead us to violent behavior. — *Letters to Marc About Jesus* by Henri J.M. Nouwen

For over the margins of life comes a whisper, a faint call, a premonition of richer living which we know we are passing by. Strained by the very mad pace of our daily outer burdens, we are further strained by an inward uneasiness, because we have hints that there is a way of life vastly richer and deeper than all this hurried existence, a life of unhurried serenity and peace and power. — *A Testament of Devotion* by Thomas Kelly

If I find in myself desires which no experience in this world can satisfy, the most probable explanation is that I was made for another world. If none of my earthly pleasures satisfy it, that does not prove that the universe is a fraud. Probably earthly pleasures were never meant to satisfy it, but only to arouse it, to suggest the real thing. — *Mere Christianity* by C. S. Lewis

Deep within each of us is the urge to know and to be known. It is as central to the core of our being as is the urge to dance in the sunshine or cry at weddings or sing in the shower or laugh at children or fall backward into the snow. It is buried as deeply within us as is the sense that it takes for us to know not to give children stones and serpents instead of bread and fish. It is as much a part of us as hugging a child or tending the sick or walking on the beach.

When we were given the capacity to love, to speak, to decide, to dream, to hope and create and suffer, we were also given the longing to be known by the One who wants to be completely known. It is a longing woven into the very fabric of the image in which we were made. — *Between the Dreaming and the Coming* True by Robert Benson

Only God's purpose can satisfy your longing and leave you nothing to wish for. Adore, walk close to it, see through and abandon all fantasy. — *The Sacrament of the Present Moment* by Jean-Pierre De Caussade

The secret of being in love, of falling in love with life as it was meant to be, is to befriend our yearning instead of avoiding it, to live into our longing rather than trying to resolve it, to enter the spaciousness of our emptiness rather than trying to fill it up. — *The Awakened Heart* by Gerald May

Every day, when Adam and Eve walked by the tree of the knowledge of good and evil, they had to remember they were never created to have it all. There is always something missing in life. This is, in fact, the mark of a created being, for only God is whole and complete, lacking nothing. The missing part of our lives can either drive us crazy to the point where we lose paradise by reaching for more than we currently possess, or it can become the best altar for our prayers, where we remind ourselves of our dependence on God. When we understand how dependent we really are, we become free to enjoy the rest of the garden, as well as the people inside it, without trying to make them our savior. — *Sacred Thirst* by Craig Barnes

Ever since the day I was born I have been trying out loud to get hold of the mystery I find shaping my life. I have been trying to take the step that will lead me to myself. We all seem to carry within us a burning desire to be more than we are. My own explanation of this desire is that it is a call from God to grow. I take all this longing and look at it. I promise to give it every opportunity to mature. There is a crisis upon crisis as I stumble toward myself. It is mystery! It is wonder! It is pain! I am settling for nothing less than heaven these days, but I am discovering that part of heaven is *loving getting there.* — *Seasons of Your Heart* by Macrina Wiederkehr

The books or the music in which we thought the beauty was located will betray us if we trust to them; it was not in them, it only came through them, and what came through them was longing. These things — the beauty, the memory of our own past — are good images of what we really desire; but if they are mistaken for the thing itself they turn into dumb idols, breaking the hearts of their worshippers. For they are not the thing itself; they are only the scent of a flower we have not found, the echo of a tune we have not heard, news from a country we have never yet visited. — *Weight of Glory* by C. S. Lewis

Hunger and Thirst

I. Opening Prayer

You called, You cried, you shattered my deafness. You sparkled, you blazed, You drove away my blindness. You shed your fragrance, and I drew in my breath, and I pant for You. I tasted and now I hunger and thirst. You touched me, and now I burn with longing for your peace. — *Confessions* by St. Augustine

II. Psalm 81

III. Daily Scripture Readings

Monday	John 4:1-26
Tuesday	John 6:25-35
Wednesday	John 7:37-41
Thursday	Isaiah 55:1-5
Friday	Jeremiah 2:11-13
Saturday	Matthew 5:3-12
Sunday	Psalm 42:1-11

IV. Readings for Reflection

V. Reflection and Listening: silent and written

VI. Prayer: for the church, for others, for myself

VII. Song   *All Who Are Thirsty*

VIII. Closing Prayer

O God of tender mercies, I know I've kept you at arm's length. I've kept you safe in heaven. But heaven has leaned down to the earth and I've been touched anew. Like thirsty ground I long for you. Forgive my casualness about your Love. Forgive my shallow life. I am finished with shallowness. I used to pray that I be saved from eternal death, but now I pray to be saved from shallow living. Eternal death? Shallow living? Is there a difference? O God, deliver me from shallow living! —*A Tree Full of Angels* by Macrina Wiederkehr

Readings for Reflection-

Trying to satisfy our thirst can be an incredibly exhausting process, you can hear it clearly in the words of the Samaritan woman, "*Sir, give me some of this water so I won't get thirsty and have to keep coming here to draw water.*" Our hearts seem to be a bottomless pit, in constant need of love and affirmation, significance and value. We just don't seem to be able to get full and stay full. We are always longing for more. It is an endless process of filling and filling and refilling our thirsty souls — over and over and over again. Why? Because ultimately we turn to all the wrong places in our attempt to quench our thirst, places that were never intended to fill the deepest longings of our souls — only God can do that. —*Beginnings* by Jim Branch

Unlike the Samaritan woman, most of us do know who Jesus is. We know all about the cross and the resurrection. We have accepted his gift of forgiveness for our sins, been baptized, and joined the church. We may even serve on a committee or volunteer in church missions. We, at least, are not Samaritans. We even love the temple. But we still yearn for something more. We yearn for something more in our relationships and families. We yearn for something more in our jobs and sense of purpose. We yearn, most of all, for something more in our experience of God.

George Barna, one of the leading researchers on church and religious issues, recently published statistics showing that seventy-five million people attend church every Sunday. But less than one-third of these people believe that they interacted with God during the worship service, and over one-third say they have never experienced God's presence. That is amazing. But one statistic Barna didn't cite is even more striking: one hundred percent of us thirst for more of God than we now have.

Like the woman at the well, sooner or later, perhaps in a quiet, reflective moment, we must all come to terms with the honest truth that we were looking for more than we've found thus far. We certainly don't resemble the Samaritan woman. We keep our marriages to a minimum, and we hold down respectable jobs and pay our bills on time. We may look pretty respectable and orthodox. But still our souls are very thirsty.

Perhaps your prayer life has dried up, or in spite of your best efforts you still are not making much of a difference in anyone's life, or maybe you've lost all the joy, all the passion, in your life. You have the same sadness buried in your soul as all those Samaritans had. You may have a head full of knowledge about God, but you still yearn to experience something sacred, something that will at long last calm the ache from deep within. As this story unfolds, take your place next to this Samaritan woman.

It's part of my pastoral calling to look closely at the lives of those who go to church. They all clean up pretty nicely on Sunday morning. But just below the surface of their navy-blue suits and colorful dresses lie souls that are not nearly so tidy. On a typical Sunday in our church, I sit facing the congregation while the choir sings the anthem before the sermon. I gaze into the faces of people I know and love. I see the elder whose marriage is hanging on by a thread. Next to him is the Sunday school teacher whose daughter was arrested last week for driving under the influence of alcohol. Two pews behind them is the church's newest widow, who is wondering how she will survive sitting in church alone for the first time in forty years. She happens to be sitting next to a young couple who desperately want to be parents, but not a single one of the fertility treatments seem to be helping. The details may change as I look from face to face, but the essential story remains the same. They are all thirsty.

My job is to remember that what we are struggling with is not just our families and jobs. No, the stakes are much higher than that. The real struggle is with our parched souls. We were created with a need to satisfy our physical thirst, and every morning of our lives we are reminded of this thirst. But this physical thirst is a symbol, maybe even a sacrament, that points to the deeper spiritual thirst of the soul. So also is our longing for better families and more satisfying jobs a symbol of our deeper yearning to be a part of the family and mission of God. We simply cannot satisfy the thirst of our souls by pouring on new relationships, experience, achievements, or careers.

As the Samaritan woman discovered, it doesn't matter how many times we may try to rearrange our relationships and reorder our lives. Until we find relief for the soul, everything else will be nothing more than a distraction — a very temporary one at that — from our fundamental craving for living water.

Most of us haven't gone through five spouses, but we have gone through jobs, five moves, five weight-loss programs, or five churches — and still the insatiable thirst continues. We will never find what we are looking for in the things we pick up along the way. Not even the religious things. Not even important things like relationships. All of these things will leave our souls empty if we try to force them to satisfy our thirst. The true object of our search is nothing less than an encounter with the Holy One. — *Sacred Thirst* by M. Craig Barnes

"Are you thirsty?" said the Lion.

"I'm dying of thirst," said Jill.

"Then drink," said the Lion.

"May I — could I — would you mind going away while I do?" said Jill.

The Lion answered this only by a look and a very low growl. And as Jill gazed at its motionless bulk, she realized that she might as well have asked the whole mountain to move aside for her convenience.

The delicious rippling noise of the stream was driving her nearly frantic.

"Will you promise not to — do anything to me, if I do come?" said Jill.

"I make no promise," said the Lion.

Jill was so thirsty now that, without noticing it, she had come a step nearer.

"Do you eat little girls?" she said.

"I have swallowed up girls and boys, women and men, kings and emperors, cities and realms," said the Lion. It didn't say this as if it were boasting, nor as if it were sorry, nor as if it were angry. It just said it.

"I daren't come and drink," said Jill

"Then you will die of thirst," said the Lion.

"Oh dear!" said Jill, coming another step nearer. "I suppose I must go and look for another stream then."

"There is no other stream," said the Lion.

— *The Silver Chair* by C. S. Lewis

"He who is satisfied has never truly craved," said Abraham Heschel, and he said this, I think, because he knew that heaven's richest food does not satisfy our longings but rather intensifies them. — *Windows of the Soul* by Ken Gire

We stand in the midst of nourishment and we starve. We dwell in the land of plenty, yet we persist in going hungry. Not only do we dwell in the land of plenty; we have the capacity to be filled with the utter fullness of God (Eph. 3:16-19). In the light of such possibility, what happens? Why do we drag our hearts? Lock up our souls? Why do we limp? Why do we straddle issues? Why do we live feebly, so dimly? Why aren't we saints?

Each of us could come up with individual answers to all these questions, but I want to suggest here a common cause. The reason we live life so dimly and with such divided hearts is that we have never really learned how to be present with quality to God, to self, to others, to experiences and events, to all created things. We have never learned to gather up the crumbs of whatever appears in our path at every moment. We meet all of these lovely gifts only half there. Presence is what we are all starving for. Real Presence! We are too busy to be present, too blind to see the nourishment and salvation in the crumbs of life, the experiences of each moment. Yet the secret of daily life is this: *There are no leftovers.*

There is nothing—no thing, no person, no experience, no thought, no joy or pain—that cannot be harvested and used for nourishment on our journey to God.

What I am suggesting here is that everything in your life is a stepping-stone to holiness if only you recognize that you do have within you the grace to be present to each moment. Your presence is an energy that you can choose to give or not give. Every experience, every thought, every word, every person in your life is a part of a larger picture of your growth. That's why I call them crumbs. They are not the whole loaf, but they can be nourishing if you give them your real presence. Let everything energize you. Let everything bless you. Even your limping can bless you. —*A Tree Full of Angels* by Macrina Wiederkehr

I speak to thirsty hearts whose longings have been wakened by the touch of God within them. — *The Pursuit of God* by A. W. Tozer

All of us are willing to admit pangs of hunger and feelings of emptiness inside us. We experience half-formed dreams and vague drives for something more than human resources can promise or produce. There is in each of us a dynamic, a mystique or drive that, unless detoured by human selfishness, leads to search for God, whether we know it or not. It is this desire that carries us beyond what we can see into the darkness and obscurity of faith. It is a hunger that can be satisfied in God alone. Obviously, God does not intend to satisfy this desire completely in this world; its function is to draw us closer and closer to God who alone can give us complete satisfaction. This is the truth which St. Augustine discovered, after the discouragement of so many blind alleys: "our hearts were made for you, O God, and they shall not rest until they rest in you."

The experience of God touching and involving the human will in search may come to different men in different ways. There are many avenues of attraction to God. Some are drawn to him through his beauty, others to his peace, and still others are attracted by his power. Most men find themselves drawn to God as the source and wellspring of the very meaning of life, the ultimate ground of human existence. But it may be that the first motion of God within the believer-to-be is one of disturbance. Sometimes we forget that God comes to us, not only to give us peace but also to disturb us. He comforts the afflicted and he afflicts the comfortable. For some men life becomes a hopeless mess, and they find themselves aware of a demand to know what it is all about. This inner restlessness and disquiet can well be God sowing the first seeds of faith in the human heart. — *A Reason to Live! A Reason to Die!* by John Powell

We have to acknowledge that our hunger for God comes from Him and will not be completely satisfied on earth. The deepest pleasures of life don't satisfy — they point us forward. — *Finding God* by Dr. Larry Crabb

Each of us, for instance, carries around inside himself, I believe, a certain emptiness — a sense that something is missing, a restlessness, the deep feeling that somehow all is not right inside his skin. — *The Magnificent Defeat* by Frederick Buechner

The Heart

I. Opening Prayer:
O God, in all ages you have imparted yourself to man and set alight the fire of faith in his heart, grant to me the faith which comes from search. Cleanse my life from all that negates and crushes faith, and fill it with the purity and honesty that foster it. Cleanse me from the evil which makes unbelief its friend, and drive it far from me, so that, being willing in all things to do your will, I may know the truth which shall set me free. Through Jesus Christ, our Lord. Amen. —*Daily Prayer Companion*, Samuel M. Shoemaker

II. Psalm 73

III. Daily Scripture Readings

Monday	Jeremiah 29:4-14
Tuesday	Ezekiel 11:17-21
Wednesday	Isaiah 29:13-16
Thursday	Mark 12:28-34
Friday	Proverbs 4:20-27
Saturday	1 Samuel 16:1-13
Sunday	Psalm 51:10-17

IV. Readings for Reflection

V. Reflection and Listening: silent and written

VI. Prayer: for the church, for others, for myself

VII. Song: *Greater Than Our Hearts*

VIII. Closing Prayer
You, O Lord, set eternity in our hearts and lit the fire of faith deep in our souls. Help us now, we pray, to be all

that you created us to be — living expressions of your
unbridled creativity and unfailing love. Amen.

Readings for Reflection:

deep inside by Jim Branch

way down
under the layers of activity and insecurity
a heart — covered over

longing to be known
to be lived from
to have its truth honored

but the journey to its core is a long one
requiring much time and effort and courage

maybe life on the surface is easier? safer?
or is it? is it really life at all?
or only slow death?

for the true contents of this heart
must be discovered
must be known
must be nurtured
must be released
must be lived
must be

for what is real
and true
and good
is deep inside

Deep within us all there is an amazing inner sanctuary of the soul, a holy place, a Divine Center, a speaking Voice, to which we may continuously return. Eternity is at our hearts, pressing upon our time-torn lives, warming us with intimations of an astounding destiny, calling us home unto Itself. — *A Testament of Devotion* by Thomas Kelly

There is a secret place. A radiant sanctuary. As real as your own kitchen. More real than that. Constructed of the purest elements. Overflowing with the ten thousand beautiful things. Worlds within worlds. Forests, rivers. Velvet coverlets thrown over featherbeds, fountains bubbling beneath a canopy of stars. Bountiful forests, universal libraries. A wine cellar offering an intoxication so sweet you will never be sober again. A clarity so complete you will never again forget. This magnificent refuge is inside you. Enter. Shatter the darkness that shrouds the doorway... Believe the incredible truth that the Beloved has chosen for his dwelling place the core of your own being because that is the single most beautiful place in all of creation. — *Interior Castle* by Teresa of Avila

The key to this home, this heart of God, is prayer. Perhaps you have never prayed before except in anguish or terror. It may be that the only time the Divine Name has been on your lips has been in angry expletives. Never mind. I am here to tell you that the Father's heart is open wide — you are welcome to come in.

Perhaps you do not believe in prayer. You may have tried to pray and were profoundly disappointed . . . and disillusioned. You seem to have little faith, or none. It doesn't matter. The Father's heart is wide open — you are welcome to come in.

Perhaps you are bruised and broken by the pressures of life. Others have wronged you, and you feel scarred for life. You have old, painful memories that have never been healed. You avoid prayer because you feel too distant, too unworthy, too defiled. Do not despair. The Father's heart is wide open — you are welcome to come in.

Perhaps you have prayed for many years, but the words have grown brittle and cold. Little ever happens anymore. God seems remote and inaccessible. Listen to me. The Father's heart is wide open — you are welcome to come in.

Perhaps prayer is the delight of your life. You have lived in the divine milieu for a long time and can attest to its goodness. But you long for more: more power, more love, more of God in your life. Believe me. The Father's heart is open wide — you too are welcome to come higher up and deeper in.

If the key is prayer, the door is Jesus Christ. How good of God to provide us a way into his heart. — *Prayer: Finding the Heart's True Home* by Richard Foster

There is a desire within each of us, in the deep center of ourselves that we call our heart. We were born with it, it is never completely satisfied, and it never dies. We are often unaware of it, but it is always awake. It is the human desire for love. Every person on this earth yearns to love, to be loved, to know love. Our true identity, our reason for being, is to be found in this desire. — *The Awakened Heart* by Gerald May

Find the door of your heart, and you will discover that it is the door of the Kingdom of God.

—John Chrysostom

Though our mind knows a path, our heart is the way. — *Jacob's Journey* by Noah benShea

40

And now here is my secret, a very simple secret: It is only with the heart that one can see rightly; what is essential is invisible to the eye. — *The Little Prince* by Antoine De Saint-Exupery

The heart has its reasons which reason knows not of.

— Blaise Paschal

Your vision will become clear only when you can look into your own heart. Who looks outside, dreams; who looks inside, awakes. — *Psychology and Religion: West and East* by C. G. Jung

Shaped By the Word

I. Opening Prayer

Saving God, you set your heart on us and made us your own. May we listen with the ear of our hearts to the many ways your Word and your love will be present to us and formed in us this day. We ask this through Jesus, the Word made flesh. Amen. — *The Work of God* ed. by Judith Sutera

II. Psalm 1

III. Daily Scripture Readings

Monday	Colossians 3:12-17
Tuesday	Psalm 119:1-16
Wednesday	Joshua 1:1-9
Thursday	Hebrews 4:12-13
Friday	2 Timothy 3:16-17
Saturday	Isaiah 55:6-13
Sunday	Proverbs 3:1-6

IV. Readings for Reflection

V. Reflection and Listening: silent and written

VI. Prayer for the Church, for others, and for myself

VII. Song   *Lord, Speak To Me*

VIII. Closing Prayer

O Lord, Thou didst strike my heart with Thy Word and I loved Thee.

—St. Augustine

Readings for Reflection

In our culture, from our early days on, we are trained to read in a certain way. It starts in grade school and goes all the way through our college years. Simply put, we are taught to read for *information*. There is much material to be learned, and we are bound and determined to learn it. Our grades depend on it. So we read as much as we can, as fast as we can, in order to master whatever material may be in front of us. We study and we analyze. We read with a critical eye, with the text as our object.

It is a good thing, this kind of reading, but when it comes to the Scriptures we need to know that there is another way. When we read the Scriptures we must learn how to read with a different set of eyes. Or, as Eugene Peterson likes to say "we must turn our eyes into ears." For it is through the Scriptures that we hear God's voice. It is through the Scriptures that God reveals himself, and his heart, to us. The Scriptures are not just some sterile, impersonal mass of material, they are an incredibly beautiful love letter written to us from our God.

I don't know about you, but when I get a letter from someone that is dear to me, I do not read it like I would read a text book. I take that letter to a quiet place, where I will not be interrupted, and I read every single line, every single word. As a matter of fact, I read between the lines. I read it slowly, stopping from time to time to consider the depths of what I've just read. I savor it and try to enjoy every single bit of it. I read it in a way that allows me to hear the voice of the one I love in and through the text. And when I am finished reading it, I read it again, and again. I read it not for information, but for *formation*; not to work on the text, but to let the text work on me.

I do this because of the love of the one who wrote it. I want to fully know that love. I want to be captured by that love. I want to hear and experience every bit of that love and affection. So it is for each of us when we read the Word of God. It is God's letter of love and affection to each of us, meant to capture our hearts and kindle our affections.

—Jim Branch, March, 2016

The stories of Scripture are stories about where we come from and where we are going as much as the story of our immigrant past is; and here too, if we are to understand what they mean — what they mean to us, mean for us, mean about us — we have to try to get inside them somehow. Through whatever imagination, intuition, human compassion we can muster, we have to stand where these people stood and feel what they felt: to sail in that little boat as the wind freshened and the waves started to heave; to bury our own faces in our hands before the terrible darkness of that tomb or the sight of that great city being laid waste. — *A Room Called Remember* by Frederick Buechner

Take in fully, gently, and carefully what you are reading. Taste it and digest it as you read. Use the scripture passage to sense the presence of the Lord, you stay with the passage until you have sensed the very heart of what you have read...your purpose is to take everything from the passage that unveils the Lord to you. — *Experiencing the Depths of Jesus Christ* by Jeanne Guyon

My beginning advice to you is this: Always read the Scriptures with a heart ready to repent. Receive the storm that repentance brings. Let the holy winds toss you to and fro. You will be awakened to new depths as you wrestle with the life forces within. What seems like violence at first will lead you gently into the eye of God where all is calm and quiet, like the eye of a hurricane. When you finally surrender and stop fighting the winds, you will be carried by angels into the eye of God. There, you will rest in peace and learn to see like God. It will be the great harvest of contemplation — through the storm into the quiet. — *A Tree Full of Angels* by Macrina Wiederkehr

The Bible is hundreds upon hundreds of voices all calling at once out of the past and clamoring for our attention like barkers at a fair, like air-raid sirens, like a whole barnyard of cockcrows as the first long shafts of dawn fan out across the sky. Some of the voices are shouting, like Moses' voice, so all Israel, all the world, can hear, and some are so soft and halting that you can hardly hear them at all, like Job with ashes on his head and his heart broken, like old Simeon whispering, "Lord, now lettest thy servant depart in peace." The prophets shrill out in their frustration, their rage, their holy hope and madness; and the priests drone on and on about the dimensions and furniture of the Temple; and the law-givers spell out what to eat and what not to eat; and the historians list the kings, the battles, the tragic lessons of Israel's history. And somewhere in the midst of them all one particular voice speaks out that is unlike any other voice because it speaks so directly to the deepest privacy and longing and weariness of each of us that there are times when the centuries are blown away like mist, and it is as if we stand with no shelter of time at all between ourselves and the One who speaks our secret name. *Come,* the voice says. *Unto me. All ye.* Every last one. — *A Room Called Remember* by Frederick Buechner

If we would dance our way into some deeper communion with God, we must stop working on the

Word, wherever it is found, and let the Word begin to work on us. — *Living Prayer* by Robert Benson

If scripture is to become my teacher, I must put on each story like a robe to be worn, identifying with the characters, walking in their shoes, feeling with their hearts. — *Seasons of Your Heart* by Macrina Wiederkehr

We listen to the Word, to the silence of prayer, and to the poem of our own lives, for in all these God is speaking. And if God is speaking, then nothing else matters but listening.

When it comes to listening to God speak, we must always begin with the Word of God, His clearest and most authoritative voice. But, as in all listening, we must learn to allow the other Person to speak. This may sound oversimplified, but in fact it can be a major task. When we find ourselves trying to listen to someone whose speech is slow or deliberate, the great temptation is to finish their sentences for them. The same is often the case when we listen to God's Word, particularly to familiar passages. Adopting a listening stance before the Word means keeping your mind as quiet as possible and letting the Bible finish its own sentences and stories. Allowing the Bible to speak for itself means listening with as few presuppositions as possible.

Often we fail in listening when we read only for theological or doctrinal affirmation. The baptism of Jesus becomes a proof text for immersion and not a scene to which we are transported by our imagination. The crucifixion becomes a necessary piece of the puzzle for redemption, the obligatory final step in a long "holy history," and not a heartbreaking moment of transformation. Parables and visions become codes to break, sponges to squeeze dry and then leave behind. Sometimes my own temptation is to merely use the Bible as a folder for lyrics.

In all these ways and more, we effectively plug our ears to the Voice of Scripture. The simple act (which is sometimes not so simple) of quieting our minds and hearts and allowing the Bible to speak, as if it has never before spoken in its own voice to you, will transform your time with the Word. Be quiet, be patient, and let Scripture say what it has to say! — *The Walk* by Michael Card

The Hebrew word for *meditate* means "to mutter or to mumble, to make a low sound." It is used of the gentle cooing of a dove, the low growl of a lion, and the soft music of a harp. It was the habit of people reflecting on the Scriptures to turn the words over and over in their mind, and they did this by speaking the words, often in a whisper that sounded very much like mumbling. They would do this on an early-morning walk, on a garden bench in the afternoon, or on their bed at night. Going over and over the words worked something like a root stimulator, allowing the words to penetrate their heart more quickly and more deeply. — *The Reflective Life* by Ken Gire

The practice of *lectio divina* guides us to the inner work that brings about transformation. It requires a deep listening to the Word planted in our souls. It summons us to a tender abiding in the hidden mystery of God. It asks of us a patient waiting for God's personal revelation of truth to us. It draws us into a loving romance with the One who rules the world from the throne of our hearts. It encourages in us a joyful expectation of the healing touch of the Beloved. A deep listening! A tender abiding! A patient waiting! A loving romance! A joyful expectation! These are the warm invitations of this gentle way of being with the Word of God. The gift of this intimate way of praying does not come in one sitting. It is a daily discipline requiring faithful practice.

Long ago when I was a novice in monastic life, I would get up before the crack of dawn and trudge sleepily to our monastery chapel to pray the Divine Office with my sisters. Together we would climb through the psalms: praising God, rejoicing, pleading, complaining, yearning, crying out, thanking.

In our daily classes we were assured that if we were faithful to the Word we would be drawn more deeply into relationship with God, making our morning treks to the chapel a delight. In our daily pondering of the Scriptures, we were asked to listen with the *ear of the heart*. It was all very romantic at first, but the crack of dawn began coming too soon. The romance wore off. I am happy to say that now, in my middle years, the romance is returning. I am beginning to see lectio divina as a way to *romance the Word*.

When you romance the Word, you pursue the Word as it pursues you. You ponder it, pray it, sing it, study it, love it. You treasure it as Mary treasured the mysteries unfolding in her life (Luke 2:19-20). Listen to it with the ear of your heart. Cling to it as to a beloved. Cherish it. Become a home for it. — *The Song of the Seed* by Macrina Wiederkehr

Meditation is the activity of calling to mind, and thinking over, and dwelling on, and applying to oneself, the various things that one knows about the works and ways and purposes and promises of God. It is an activity of Holy thought, consciously performed in the presence of God, under the eye of God, by the help of God; as a means of communion with God. Its purpose is to clear one's mental and spiritual vision of God, and let His truth make its full and proper impact on one's mind and heart. — *Knowing God* by J.I. Packer

Scripture is more than a word about God; every word of scripture is always consecrating, always releasing immense energy. It is not simply revealing God to his people but revealing to us who we are in God, and who we are to become. — *Gathering Fragments* by Edward J. Farrell

Before this time my practice had been, at least for ten years previously, as a habitual thing, to give myself to prayer, after having dressed in the morning. Now I saw, that the most important thing I had to do was to give myself to the reading of the Word of God and to meditation on it, that thus my heart might be comforted, encouraged, warned, reproved, instructed; and that thus, whilst meditating, my heart might be brought into experimental communion with the Lord. I began therefore, to meditate on the New Testament, from the beginning, early in the morning.

The first thing I did, after having asked in a few words the Lord's blessing upon His precious Word, was to begin to meditate on the Word of God; searching, as it were, into every verse, to get blessing out of it; not for the sake of the public ministry of the Word; not for the sake of preaching on what I had meditated upon; but for the sake of obtaining food for my soul. The result I have found to be almost invariably this, that after a very few minutes my soul has been led to confession, or to thanksgiving, or to intercession, or to supplication; so that though I did not, as it were, give myself to prayer, but meditation, yet it turned almost immediately more or less into prayer. — *The Autobiography of George Mueller*

It was not easy for Mr. Taylor, in his changeful life, to make time for prayer and Bible study, but he knew that it was vital. Well do the writers remember traveling with him month after month in northern China, by cart and wheelbarrow with the poorest of inns at night.

Often with only one large room for coolies and travelers alike, they would screen off a corner for their father and another for themselves, with curtains of some sort; and then, after sleep at last had brought a measure of quiet, they would hear a match struck and see the flicker of candlelight which told that Mr. Taylor, however weary, was pouring over the little Bible in two volumes always at hand. From two to four A.M. was the time he usually gave to prayer and study; the time he could be most sure of being undisturbed to wait upon God. — *Hudson Taylor's Spiritual Secret* by Dr. and Mrs. Howard Taylor

The Word of Scripture should never stop sounding in your ears and working in you all day long, just like the words of someone you love. And just as you do not analyze the words of someone you love, but accept them as they are said to you, accept the Word of Scripture and ponder it in your heart, as Mary did. That is all. That is meditation...Do not ask "How shall I pass this on?" but "What does it say to me?" Then ponder this Word long in your heart until it has gone right into you and taken possession of you. — *The Way to Freedom* by Dietrich Bonhoeffer

We read Scripture in order to listen again to the Word of God spoken, and when we do, we hear Him speak. Somehow or other these words live. — *Working the Angles* by Eugene Peterson

Scripture is the story of an unwavering love that seeks an answering affirmation. It is a vivid, sometimes parabolic account of God's persistent, unrelenting quest for us and our stumbling, often faithless response. — *The Untamed God* by George Cornell

In our meditation we ponder the chosen text on the strength of the promise that it has something utterly personal to say to us for this day and for our Christian life, that it is not only God's Word for the Church, but also God's Word for us individually. We expose ourselves to the specific word until it addresses us personally. And when we do this, we are doing no more than the simplest, untutored Christian does every day; we read God's Word as God's Word for us. —*Life Together* by Dietrich Bonhoeffer

Devotion

I. Opening Prayer

Late have I loved you, O Beauty, so ancient and so new, late have I loved you! And behold, you were within me and I was outside, and there I sought for you, and in my deformity I rushed headlong into the well-formed things that you have made. You were with me, and I was not with you.

—St. Augustine

II. Psalm 86

III. Daily Scripture Readings

Monday	Acts 2:37-47
Tuesday	2 Peter 1:3-11
Wednesday	Colossians 2:1-7
Thursday	Revelation 3:14-22
Friday	Matthew 25:1-13
Saturday	1 Timothy 4:1-16
Sunday	1 Chronicles 22:17-19

IV. Readings for Reflection

V. Reflection and Listening: silent and written

VI. Prayer: for the church, for others, for myself

VII. Song   *Lord Most High*

VIII. Closing Prayer

Grant me, O Lord, to know what I ought to know, to love what I ought to love, to praise what delights you most, to value what is precious in your sight, to hate what is offensive to you. Do not allow me to judge according to the sight of my eyes, nor to pass sentence according to the hearing of my ears; but to discern with a true judgment between things visible and spiritual, and above all things, always to inquire what is the good pleasure of Your will.

—Thomas À Kempis

Readings for Reflection-

There is an old saying that goes, *"If you aim at nothing, you will hit it every time."* That statement couldn't be more true, especially when we are talking about the spiritual life. One of the biggest enemies of spiritual growth is a lack of intentionality. Spiritual maturity doesn't take place by accident, it must be something that we thoughtfully and prayerfully *aim at* and *plan toward*. If we want to live in an intimate relationship with God, it will not just fall on our heads (as Richard Foster once said). We will have to arrange our lives in certain ways.

The early church knew this. That's why after Peter's sermon, when thousands turned and followed Jesus, they decided to devote themselves to certain things in an effort to move toward a deeper, richer life with him. As a matter of fact, the literal words in the Greek for *devoted themselves to* mean to be *strong toward*. Somehow, somewhere they got together and decided what things they needed to be *strong toward* in order to nurture this new life of faith that they had just begun.

The four things were: the apostles' teaching, the community, the breaking of the bread, and the prayers. These things would be a constant and consistent part of their life together. They would make space regularly for the Word to be spoken to them and take shape within them. They would take special care to make sure they were journeying together in community — having real, authentic, loving, and caring relationships. They would set times and places to take the Lord's Supper together, in order to make sure that the cross of Jesus was a regular focal point of their communal life. And they would gather at appointed times during the day and night (*Seven times a day I will praise you – Psalm 119:164*) to pray. This would be the rhythm their community would operate by to ensure that they were not *aiming at nothing.* — *Being with Jesus* by Jim Branch

Philosopher William James said: "In some people religion exists as a dull habit, in others as an acute fever." Jesus did not endure the shame of the cross to hand on a dull habit. (If you don't have the fever, dear reader, a passion for God and His Christ, drop this book, fall on your knees, and beg for it; turn to the God you half-believe in and cry out for His baptism of fire.) — *The Signature of Jesus* by Brennan Manning

If you are weary of some sleepy form of devotion, probably God is as weary of it as you are.

— Frank Laubach

Oh be generous in your self-surrender! Meet His measureless devotion to you, with a measureless devotion to Him. Be glad and eager to throw yourself headlong into His dear arms, and to hand over the reins of government to Him. Whatever there is of you, let Him have it all. Give up forever everything that is separate from Him. — *The Christian's Secret of a Happy Life* by Hannah Whitall Smith

Watch the things you shrug your shoulders over, and you will know why you do not go on spiritually. First go — at the risk of being thought fanatical you must obey what God tells you. — *My Utmost for His Highest* by Oswald Chambers

O Begin! Fix some part of every day for private exercises. You may acquire the taste which you have not: what is tedious at first will afterward be pleasant. Whether you like it or not, read and pray daily. It is for your life; there is no other way: else you will be a trifler all your days.

—John Wesley

The Christian way is different: harder and easier. Christ says, "Give me All. I don't want so much of your time and so much of your money and so much of your work: I want You. I have not come to torment your natural self, but to kill it. No half-measures are any good. I don't want to cut off a branch here and a branch there, I want to have the whole tree down....Hand over the whole natural self, all the desires which you think innocent as well as the ones you think wicked — the whole outfit. I will give you a new self instead. In fact, I will give you Myself: my own will shall become yours.
— *Mere Christianity* by C. S. Lewis

It is unlikely that we will deepen our relationship with God in a casual or haphazard manner. There will be a need for some intentional commitment and some reorganization in our own lives. But there is nothing that will enrich our lives more than a deeper and clearer perception of God's presence in the routine of daily living. —Ways of Prayer: Designing a Personal Rule by William O. Paulsell

I ask you, Lord Jesus,
to develop in me, your lover
an immeasurable urge towards you,
an affection that is unbounded,
longing that is unrestrained,
fervor that throws discretion to the winds!

The more worthwhile our love for you,
      all the more pressing does it become.
Reason cannot hold it in check,
      fear does not make it tremble,
      wise judgment does not temper it.
   — *The Fire of Love* by Richard Rolle

By participating in Christian disciplines, we live out our desire and intention to cooperate with the Holy Spirit. As we do so, we are encouraged, instructed, healed, challenged, loved, renewed, and beckoned to God and godly living.

While it is true that God is in every when and where and that many other things besides disciplines contribute to our deepening relationship with God, we discover that it makes a meaningful difference in everyday life when we set aside time, space, and ourselves to be more fully present with and attentive and responsive to God. Disciplines are like faithful companions on the way. The benefit we seek and desire most is deepening companionship with God. We come away from other pursuits to listen for the still, small voice that is our best friend, our beloved Savior, the Holy One, God. — *Holy Invitations* by Jeanette Bakke

Practice comes first in religion, not theory or dogma. And Christian practice is not exhausted in outward deeds. These are the fruits, not the roots. A practicing Christian must above all be one who practices the perpetual return of the soul into the inner sanctuary, who brings the world into its Light and rejudges it, who brings the Light into the world with all its turmoil and its fitfulness and recreates it. — *A Testament of Devotion* by Thomas Kelly

Seek

I. Opening Prayer

Father, You alone know what lies before me this day.
Grant that in every hour of it I may stay close to you.
Let me today embark on no undertaking that is not in
line with your will for my life, nor shrink from any
sacrifice which your will may demand. For my Lord
Christ's Sake. Amen. — *A Diary of Private Prayer* by John
Baillie

II. Psalm 24

III. Daily Scripture Readings

Monday	Psalm 63:1-11
Tuesday	Matthew 6:25-34
Wednesday	Matthew 7:7-12
Thursday	1 Chronicles 28:8-10
Friday	2 Chronicles 7:12-22
Saturday	Isaiah 55:6-13
Sunday	Psalm 27:4-14

IV. Readings for Reflection

V. Reflection and Listening: silent and written

VI. Prayer for the Church, for others, for myself

VII. Song   *Abide with Me*

VIII. Closing Prayer

Lord, I am yours; I do yield myself up entirely to you,
and I believe that you do take me. I leave myself with
you. Work in me all the good pleasure of your will, and
I will only lie still in your hands and trust you. Amen.
— *The Christian's Secret of a Happy Life* by Hannah Whitall
Smith

Readings for Reflection-

What does it look like to seek God earnestly? The dictionary tells us that the definition of the word *earnestly* is "serious in intention, purpose, or effort; sincerely zealous." Now that's a pretty weighty definition, particularly when we apply it to seeking God. Do I have serious intention when I seek God, or is it just casual, haphazard, and random? Am I serious in purpose, or am I aimless and adrift? Am I serious in effort, or am I lackadaisical, tepid, and lazy? My guess is that if I indeed want to find him in my seeking, it will depend a good bit on the earnestness of my seeking. At least that's what Jeremiah would tell us: *"You will seek me and find me, when you seek me with all your heart."*

The Hebrew word for *earnestly* is *shachar* which means *to seek diligently,* or *early.* This word gives the definite impression that the thing that is being sought in this manner is the first thing, the most important thing, or, as Jesus said, the *one thing.* When we seek something in this way, all other things take a back seat.

So what does it look like to seek God earnestly? Or, more particularly, what does it look like *for me* to seek God earnestly? And if I am not seeking him earnestly, exactly how I am seeking him? And is that enough? All great questions to ponder.

—Jim Branch, March, 2016

We tend to use God instead of seek Him. We want God to do our bidding more than we want Him. —*When the Pieces Don't Fit* by Glaphre Gilliland

When religion has said its last word, there is little that we need other than God Himself. The evil habit of seeking God-*and* effectively prevents us from finding

God in full revelation. In the *and* lies our great woe. If we omit the *and* we shall soon find God, and in Him we shall find that for which we have all our lives been secretly longing. — *The Pursuit of God* by A.W. Tozer

Let us not amuse ourselves to seek or to love God for the sensible favors (how elevated soever) which He has or may do us. Such favors, though never so great, cannot bring us so near to God as faith does in one simple act. Let us seek Him often by faith; He is within us; seek Him not elsewhere. Are not we rude and deserve blame, if we leave Him alone, or busy ourselves about trifles which do not please Him and perhaps offend Him? It is to be feared these trifles will one day cost us dear. — *The Practice of the Presence of God* by Brother Lawrence

There are no two ways about it. You've got your eyes open or you don't. You're watching at midnight or you're not. You better be ready when it comes flying at you, skimming swiftly over the surface of time.

The cares of this world are no excuse. Not father, mother, wife, nor children. No burials or births or weddings. Not fixing formula, scrubbing toilets, peddling pills or prose. Whatever the great human enterprise currently in hand, the point is to watch. All the rest is addenda. Seeking the kingdom is the essential integer. — *And the Trees Clap Their Hands* by Virginia Stem Owens

That practice which is alike the most holy, the most general, and the most needful in the spiritual life is the *practice of the presence of God*. It is *the schooling of the soul to find its joy in His divine companionship*, holding with Him at all times and at every moment humble and loving converse, without set rule or stated method, in all time of our temptation and tribulation, in all time of our dryness of soul and disrelish of God, yes, and even when we fall into unfaithfulness and actual sin. — *The Practice of the Presence of God* by Brother Lawrence

He can't be used as a road. If you're approaching Him not as the goal, but as a road, not as the end but as a means, you're not really approaching Him at all. — *A Grief Observed* by C. S. Lewis

Pray remember what I have recommended to you, which is, to think often on God, by day, by night, in your business, and even in your diversions. He is always near you and with you; leave Him not alone. You would think it rude to leave a friend alone, who came to visit you: why then must God be neglected? Do not then forget Him, but think on Him often, adore Him continually, live and die with Him; this is the glorious employment of a Christian. In a word, this is our profession; if we do not know it, we must learn it. — *The Practice of the Presence of God* by Brother Lawrence

We must know before we can love. In order to know God, we must often think of Him; and when we come to love Him, we shall then also think of Him often, for our heart will be with our treasure. — *The Practice of the Presence of God* by Brother Lawrence

There is not in the world a kind of life more sweet and delightful than that of a continual conversation with God. Those only can comprehend it who practice and experience it; yet I do not advise you to do it from that motive. It is not pleasure which we ought to seek in this exercise; but let us do it from a principle of love, and because God would have us. — *The Practice of the Presence of God* by Brother Lawrence

God's Voice

I. Opening Prayer

Lord, teach me to listen. The times are noisy and my ears are weary with the thousand raucous sounds which continuously assault them. Give me the spirit of the boy Samuel when he said to Thee, "Speak, for thy servant heareth." Let me hear Thee speaking in my heart. Let me get used to the sound of Thy voice, that its tones may be familiar when the sounds of earth die away and the only sound will be the music of Thy speaking voice. Amen. — *The Pursuit of God* by A. W. Tozer

II. Psalm 29

III. Daily Scripture Readings

Monday	Matthew 3:13-4:11
Tuesday	Matthew 17:1-13
Wednesday	Exodus 3:1-15
Thursday	1 Kings 19:1-13
Friday	Isaiah 43:1-13
Saturday	1 Samuel 3:1-21
Sunday	2 Corinthians 12:7-10

IV. Readings for Reflection

V. Reflection and Listening: silent and written

VI. Prayer for the Church, for others, for myself

VII. Song   *Blessed Be Your Name*

VIII. Closing Prayer

Father, you have taught us that in returning and rest we shall be saved, in quietness and confidence we shall be strengthened: By Your Spirit lift us to Your presence,

where we may be still and know that You are God. —
Living Prayer by Robert Benson

Readings for Reflection-

I don't know about you, but I can tell you from
experience that the voices within and around me that try
to convince me of things other than the truth of who I
am in Christ are loud indeed. And I'm sure they were
loud for Jesus as well. For example, just look at the
temptation in the desert. Right after that amazing
moment in the Jordan when the heavens open up, the
Spirit of God comes upon Jesus like a dove, and the
voice from heaven says to him, "You are my Son, whom
I dearly love, with you I am well pleased," he is quickly
attacked by the voice of the enemy trying to convince
him that it just isn't true.

"If you really are God's Son..." says the voice of the
enemy. It is an attack directed at his core, trying to get
Jesus to either question, or think he has to prove, his
identity. And it is an attack aimed at a place of deep
hunger. Should it be any surprise that the enemy would
attack us in much the same way — in the very places we
are most vulnerable, most hungry? Should it be any
surprise that the enemy would try to convince us that
God is either not willing or not able to meet us in our
deepest places, so that we might take matters into our
own hands and try to feed ourselves? It seems that the
most successful attacks on my heart, soul, and spirit are
those aimed at my identity, trying to make me doubt my
worth and value in the eyes my God. Trying to convince
me that I need to take matters into my own hands and
feed myself in any and every way I can. Trying to make
me believe that I can find satisfaction for my deepest
hunger outside of God, which leads me on a wild goose
chase in search of someone or something to satisfy the

deepest longings of my heart. These voices are loud indeed.

Therefore, I must turn my ear to the true voice, the voice of the God who made me uniquely and loves me dearly. The One who says to me, as he said to Jesus, "You are my beloved son, whom I love, with you I am well pleased." That is the only voice that can give me the fullness and life I was made for.

—Jim Branch, July, 2012

Every once in a while, life can be very eloquent. You go along from day to day not noticing very much, not seeing or hearing very much, and then all the sudden, when you least expect it very often, something speaks to you with such power that it catches you off guard, makes you listen whether you want to or not. Something speaks to you out of your own life with such directness that it is as if it calls you by name and forces you to look where you have not had the heart to look before, to hear something that maybe for years you have not had the wit or the courage to hear. —*A Room Called Remember* by Frederick Buechner

Theological reflection is reflecting on the painful and joyful realities of every day with the mind of Jesus and thereby raising human consciousness to the knowledge of God's gentle guidance. This is a hard discipline, since God's presence is often a hidden presence, a presence that needs to be discovered. The loud, boisterous noises of the world make us deaf to the soft, gentle, and loving voice of God. A Christian leader is called to help people to hear that voice and so be comforted and consoled. —*In the Name of Jesus* by Henri J. M. Nouwen

I need time to listen, to examine, and to confess, time to take off some of the hats I wear. I need time to listen for the Voice, if for no other reason than so I will recognize it more clearly in the ways it speaks into the noise and bustle of the life I lead. —*Living Prayer* by Robert Benson

I believe that we know much more about God than we admit that we know, than perhaps we altogether know that we know. God speaks to us, I would say, much more often than we realize or than we choose to realize. Before the sun sets every evening, he speaks to each one of us in an intensely personal and unmistakable way. His message is not written out in starlight, which in the long run would make no difference; rather it is written out for each of us in the humdrum, helter-skelter events of each day; it is a message that in the long run might just make all the difference.

Who knows what he will say to me today or to you today or into the midst of what kind of unlikely moment he will choose to say it. Not knowing is what makes today a holy mystery as every day is a holy mystery. —*The Magnificent Defeat* by Frederick Buechner

I am convinced that the Voice that whispered us into being still whispers within us and all creation. I am dead certain of it sometimes, terrified of it at other times, longing for it at all times. The silence that so often seems to overcome me is more likely a matter of my not trusting my own ears than it is a matter of the Voice having gone suddenly, inexplicably silent. —*Between the Dreaming and the Coming True* by Robert Benson

There is a story making the rounds right now about a four-year-old girl who was overheard whispering into her newborn baby brother's ear. "Baby," she whispers, "tell me what God sounds like. I am starting to forget."

Little children will lead us, of course, if for no other reason than that in this world of ours it may well be that it is only a little child who is capable anymore of hearing or recognizing or trusting the Voice that calls us. The rest of us may be too busy drowning out the Voice with calls and cries and shouts of our own. Or claiming ignorance when we should be claiming revelation.
— *Between the Dreaming and the Coming True* by Robert Benson

God speaks into our personal lives, if he speaks anywhere at all, and if we were not blind as bats we could hear him.
— Frederick Buechner

There are four ways in which He reveals His will to us — through the Scriptures, through providential circumstances, through the convictions of our own higher judgment, and through the inward impressions of the Holy Spirit on our minds. Where these four harmonize, it is safe to say that God speaks.

For I lay it down as a foundation principle, which no one can gainsay, that of course His voice will always be in harmony with itself, no matter in how many different ways He may speak. The voices may be many, the message can be but one. If God tells me in one voice to do or to leave undone anything, He cannot possibly tell me the opposite in another voice. If there is a contradiction in the voices, the speakers cannot be the same. Therefore my rule for distinguishing the voice of God would be to bring it to the test of this harmony.
— *The Christian's Secret of a Happy Life* by Hannah Whitall Smith

Retire from the world each day to some private spot, even if it be only the bedroom (for a while I retreated to the furnace room for want of a better place). Stay in the secret place till the surrounding noises begin to fade out of your heart and a sense of God's presence envelopes you...Listen for the inward Voice till you learn to recognize it. Stop trying to compete with others. Give yourself to God and then be what and who you are without regard to what others think...Learn to pray inwardly every moment. After a while you can do this even while you work....Read less, but more of what is important to your inner life. Never let your mind remain scattered for very long. Call home your roving thoughts. Gaze on Christ with the eyes of your soul. Practice spiritual concentration. All of the above is contingent upon a right relation to God through Christ and daily meditation on the Scriptures. Lacking these, nothing will help us; granted these, the discipline recommended will go far to neutralize the evil effects of externalism and to make us acquainted with God and our own souls. — *The Pursuit of God* by A. W. Tozer

Let us labor for an inward stillness,
An inward stillness and an inward healing,
That perfect silence where the lips and heart are still,
And we no longer entertain our own imperfect
    thought and vain opinions,
But God above speaks in us,
And we wait in singleness of heart,
That we may know His will,
And in the silence of our spirit
That he may do His will,
And do that only...

— Henry Wadsworth Longfellow

If you will acknowledge, recognize, and pray — if you will commit yourself to this process of listening — you

will begin to realize that the voice you have heard so often across the days of your life has been His voice.
—*He Speaks Softly* by Bob Benson

In recent years I've begun to understand that prayer is more "gift given" than "mission accomplished." Out of his love for me, Jesus makes me the object of his attention and his affection. Out of my love for him, Jesus becomes the object of my attention and affection. Focusing on Jesus is more helpful than placing all of my attention on praying in a particular way. If I am not faithful to the discipline of prayer, in whatever form, bit by bit I will forget God. I must beg God daily for the grace to live a life of unceasing prayer. I must regularly spend time with God speaking and listening, pondering and getting to know God. If I do anything but this, my mind and my heart will be consumed with other interests and concerns. Before long I will fail to recognize the sound of God's voice, and I will stop speaking to God. I know this from hard experience.
—*Running on Empty* by Fil Anderson

Prayer

I. Opening Prayer
Lord, I know not what I ought to ask of you. You only know what I need. You know me better than I know myself. O Father, give to your child what he himself knows not how to ask. Teach me to pray. Pray yourself in me.

—Archbishop Francois Fenelon

II. Psalm 84

III. Daily Scripture Reading
Monday	Matthew 6:5-15
Tuesday	James 5:13-18
Wednesday	John 17:1-26
Thursday	Psalm 131
Friday	Colossians 1:3-14
Saturday	Philippians 1:3-11
Sunday	1 Thessalonians 5:16-24

IV. Readings for Reflection

V. Reflection and Listening: silent and written

VI. Prayer for the Church, for others, for myself

VII. Song   *Praise to the Lord the Almighty*

VIII. Closing Prayer
You stir us so that praising you may bring us joy, because you have made us and drawn us to yourself, and our hearts are restless until they rest in you.
—*Confessions* by St. Augustine

Readings for Reflection-

I've always had a sneaking suspicion that there is much more to most things than meets the eye — prayer for instance. For years I was under the impression that prayer consisted of closing your eyes, bowing your head, and talking to God. The pictures and images of prayer that I carried around in my heart and mind, quite frankly, left much to be desired. Prayer was not an activity I was particularly drawn to or excited about. My guess is that this had much more to do with my definition of prayer than it did with the real practice of prayer. It wasn't until much later in life that I began to see that maybe my definition of prayer was far too small and rigid. Prayer wasn't so much about performing a duty as it was about building a wonderfully intimate relationship. Prayer was not simply throwing all the words I can muster at the unseen God, but it — at its very core — has always been about union with the God who lives within us. I think that's what Jesus is really getting at in Matthew 6:5-15; he is trying to recapture the true meaning and practice of prayer, which is simply being with God.

Don't stand on street corners, don't babble on and on; prayer is much more intimate and personal than that. Instead go into your closet – that space where true intimacy is possible – and shut the door. Leave everyone and everything else on the outside; I want it to be just me and you. I want us to be together in a way and a place where I have your undivided attention. I have so much I want to say to you; so much of me that I want you to know. And this space and time is the place where that is most possible; the place where I can have the deepest desires of my heart fulfilled, which is just to be with you, my Beloved. Come inside where things are still and quiet and you can hear every whisper of my loving Spirit deep within your heart and soul. That's prayer. — Becoming by Jim Branch

To kindle in his heart such a divine love, to unite with God in an inseparable union of love, it is necessary for a man to pray often, raising the mind to Him. For as a flame increases when it is constantly fed, so prayer, made often, with the mind dwelling ever more deeply in God, arouses divine love in the heart. And the heart, set on fire, will warm all the inner man, will enlighten and teach him, revealing to him all its unknown and hidden wisdom, and making him like a flaming seraph, always standing before God within his spirit, always looking at Him within his mind, and drawing from this vision the sweetness of spiritual joy. — *The Inner Closet of the Heart* by St. Dimitri of Rostov, from *The Art of Prayer*, Igumen Chariton of Valamo

How, then, shall we lay hold of that Life and Power, and live the life of prayer without ceasing? By quiet, persistent practice in turning of all our being, day and night, in prayer and inward worship and surrender, toward Him who calls in the depths of our souls. Mental habits of inward orientation must be established. An inner, secret turning to God can be made fairly steady, after weeks and months and years of practice and lapses and failures and returns. It is as simple as Brother Lawrence found it, but it may be long before we achieve any steadiness in the process. Begin now, as you read these words, as you sit in your chair, to offer your whole selves, utterly and in joyful abandon, in quiet, glad surrender to Him who is within. — *A Testament of Devotion* by Thomas Kelly

Prayer is simply keeping company with God.

— Clement of Alexadria

Why should I spend an hour in prayer when I do nothing during that time but think of people I am angry with, people who are angry with me, books I should read and books I should write, and thousands of other silly things that happen to grab my mind for a moment?

The answer is: because God is greater than my mind and my heart, and what is really happening in the house of prayer is not measurable in terms of human success and failure.

What I must do first of all is be faithful. If I believe that the first commandment is to love God with my whole heart, mind, and soul, then I should at least be able to spend one hour a day with nobody else but God. The question as to whether it is helpful, useful, practical, or fruitful is completely irrelevant, since the only reason to love is love itself. Everything else is secondary.

The remarkable thing, however, is that sitting in the presence of God for one hour each morning — day after day, week after week, month after month — in total confusion and with myriad distractions radically changes my life. God, who loves me so much that He sent His only Son not to condemn me but to save me, does not leave me waiting in the dark too long. I might think that each hour is useless, but after thirty, sixty, or ninety such useless hours, I gradually realize that I was not as alone as I thought; a very small, gentle voice has been speaking to me far beyond my noisy place.

So: Be confident and trust in the Lord. — *The Road to Daybreak* by Henri J.M. Nouwen

We pray, and yet it is not we who pray, but a Greater who prays in us. — *A Testament of Devotion* by Thomas Kelly

Prayer tomorrow starts today, or there is no prayer tomorrow. — *Prayer is a Hunger* by Edward J. Farrell

It is a life at attention that I seek, a life in which prayer has woven itself into the very fabric of my days, a life in which prayer has become a constant, as regular as breathing out and breathing in. — *Living Prayer* by Robert Benson

You should have it firm in your mind that prayer is neither to impress other people nor to impress God. It's not to be taken with a mentality of success. The goal, in prayer, is to give oneself away. The Lord loves us — perhaps most of all — when we fail and try again. — *Clinging — The Experience of Prayer* by Emilie Griffin

Prayer is a journey, a path that is created only by walking it. It creates and reveals oneself in the process. — *Prayer is a Hunger* by Edward J. Farrell

We do not create prayer, but merely prepare the ground and clear away obstacles. Prayer is always a gift, a grace, the flame which ignites the wood; the Holy Spirit gives prayer. — *True Prayer* by Kenneth Leech

prayer by Jim Branch

a gentle hand on my face
a soft whisper in my ear
a warm and intimate embrace
a face filled with affection
eyes dancing with delight
a heart overflowing with love
a beautiful song sung over me
a tender kiss upon my lips
prayer

The only way to pray is to pray; and the way to pray well is to pray much. — Dom John Chapman, quoted in *The Road to Daybreak* by Henri J. M. Nouwen

We must pray not first of all because it feels good or helps, but because God loves us and wants our attention. — *The Road to Daybreak* by Henri J. M. Nouwen

Prayer is being loved at a deep, sweet level. I hope you have felt such intimacy alone with God. I promise you it is available to you. Maybe a lot of us just need to be told that it is what we should expect and seek. We're afraid to ask for it; we're afraid to seek it. It feels presumptuous. We can't trust that such a love exists. But it does. — *Everything Belongs* by Richard Rohr

"Painting cannot be taught," said Picasso once, "it can only be found." I think that in many ways that is true of prayer as well. — *Living Prayer* by Robert Benson

When you enter into the spiritual life through the gateway of prayer, you would do well to see yourself as one who has set out to create a garden. This garden is a place wherein our Lord wants to come and walk and take pleasure. But just now, the soil is barren — except for the places that produce clots of weeds. His Majesty wants to uproot the weeds and plant in his garden many fruitful and fragrant blossoming plants. You may take it for granted that the Lord is already afoot, walking in His garden, if you have any desire to seek Him in prayer, for He always calls to us first and it is His voice we hear when we think it is our desire to pray.

   If we want to be good gardeners of this new-sown soul, we must, with God's help, see to it that the good plantings are tended and grow — and I am speaking now of godly virtues. At very least, we must see that these good things are not neglected and die. Rather, we tend our souls carefully so that the first blossoms appear.

These are the spiritual "fragrances" that begin to rise from our lives — the fragrances of faith, goodness, self-control, love, and the like. By them, many, many others are refreshed in spirit and attracted to the Lord (2 Cor. 2:14-16).

Then the Lord, Himself comes to walk in the midst of our garden. And it is all our joy to sense that He is there, taking pleasure in the lovely virtues.

— Teresa of Avila

Prayer is the act by which we divest ourselves of all false belongings and become free to belong to God and God alone. — *Letting Go of All Things* by Henri J. M. Nouwen, *Sojourners,* May 1979

Contemplation is like holding a magnifying glass to God long enough for him to burn his imprint upon you so that you never can forget his presence in your life, so that you become a burning bush. Contemplation is looking so deeply into things and people that you are continually being ignited by the rays and hidden flames emanating from the splendor of God's presence in all creation. — *Gathering Fragments* by Edward J. Farrell

Prayer is the breath of the soul, the organ by which we receive Christ into our parched and withered hearts. — *Prayer* by Ole Hallesby

. . . Keep on beating the path of God's door, because the one thing you can be sure of is that down the path you beat with even your most half-cocked and halting prayer the God you call upon will finally come, and even if he does not bring you the answer you want, he will bring you himself. And maybe at the secret heart of all our prayers that is what we really are praying for. —*Wishful Thinking* by Frederick Buechner

Listening to God

I. Opening Prayer
Speak, O Lord, as we come to You, to receive the food of Your holy word. Take Your truth, plant it deep in us; shape and fashion us in Your likeness, that the light of Christ might be seen today, in our acts of love and our deeds of faith. Speak, O Lord, and fulfill in us all your purposes, for Your glory. — *Speak O Lord* by Stuart Townend and Keith Getty

II. Psalm 19

III. Daily Scripture Readings
Monday	Isaiah 55:1-3
Tuesday	John 10:1-18
Wednesday	Genesis 28:10-22
Thursday	Genesis 32:22-32
Friday	Ecclesiastes 5:1-7
Saturday	2 Chronicles 7:11-22
Sunday	Luke 10:38-42

IV. Readings for Reflection

V. Reflection and Listening: silent and written

VI. Prayers: for the church, for others, for myself

VIII. Song   *I Heard the Voice of Jesus Say*

IX. Closing Prayer
Bless with your presence my life and ministry all this day long and when night comes grant your servant rest and peace. Amen. — *A Guide to Prayer for Ministers and Other Servants* by Rueben Job and Norman Shawchuck

Readings for Reflection-

Come, all you who are thirsty, come to the waters; and you who have no money, come buy and eat! Come, buy wine and milk without money and without cost. Why spend money on what is not bread, and your labor on what does not satisfy? Listen, listen to me and eat what is good, and your soul will delight in the richest of fare. Give ear to me and come to me; listen, that you may live. ~Isaiah 55:1-3

I am becoming more and more convinced that listening to God is one of the most important practices in all of the spiritual life. I am also becoming more and more convinced that it is something we do far too little of. Maybe it's because we are afraid that if we really try to listen to God, he will not say anything, which will lead us to doubt, hopelessness, and despair. Or maybe we are afraid that he will say something, but not the *something* we were hoping to hear. In either case we cannot deny the importance of the practice. It is mentioned so frequently in the Scriptures. For it is in listening, and then in hearing, that we find life.

So one day I asked myself (or, come to think of it, maybe God asked me), "What do you think God is trying to say to you today?" And here was the reply: *"Relax. Stop trying so hard. Find rest in me. Unburden yourself. Live at peace in me. Breathe. Be free."* Now that's something worth listening to!

—Jim Branch, April, 2016

Unless our identity is hid in God we will never know who we are or what we are to do. Our first act must be *prayer*. To be human is to pray, to meditate both day and night on the love and activity of God. We are called to be continuously formed and transformed by the thought of God within us. Prayer is a disciplined dedication to paying attention. Without the single-minded attentiveness of prayer we will rarely hear anything worth repeating or catch a vision worth asking anyone else to gaze upon. — *The Spiritual Life* by John Westerhoff III and John D. Eusden

My life is a listening, His is a speaking.

— Thomas Merton

Prayer is not a matter of my calling in an attempt to get God's attention, but of my finally listening to the call of God, which has been constant, patient, and insistent in my inner being. In relationship with God, I am not the seeker, the initiator, the one who loves more greatly. In prayer, as in the whole salvation story unfolded by Scripture, God is reaching out to me, speaking to me, and it's up to me to learn to be polite enough to pay attention. When I do have something to say to God, I am rendering a response to the divine initiative. So the questions of whether or not and how God answers prayer now seem to me bogus questions. God speaks, all right. The big question is do I answer, do I respond, to an invitation that is always open. — *Speech, Silence, Action* by Virginia Ramey Mollenkott

Prayer is creating a sacred space where you can be overwhelmed with God's uncompromising love and acceptance. — *Living in God's Embrace* by Michael Fonseca

Whenever an awestruck student would ask Dr. Lane how he approached Scripture, he would answer, "I *listen* to the text." His consistent prayer was that God would allow him to hear the Word and be made wise by the wisdom of God.

Bill repeated a few phrases again and again. They were his special discoveries, made over a lifetime of listening to his own life, and he repeated them endlessly, it seemed to me. "Timing is of the Lord," was his response, among many others, to my agonized questions about whom I should marry and when.

"Let it simmer on the back burner of your mind," he would say when we would talk about some prospective topic for a paper. I found, indeed, that his advice was true. When I was perplexed by some exegetical problem, I would often go to sleep with it "simmering," only to wake with the solution.

An idea from one of his phrases is still simmering on the back burner of my mind. "You must ask God for a listening heart," he would often say when we would speak about some difficulty I was having with some person or situation. We must listen to the Word, to the silence of prayer, and to the poem of our own lives, for in all these God is speaking. And if God is speaking, then nothing else matters but listening. — *The Walk* by Michael Card

We must begin to hear, however faintly at first, the rhythm and movement of the One who set it all in motion when the world began. — *See You at the House* by Bob Benson

In Jesus we have a master to whom we do not sufficiently listen. He speaks to each heart the word of life, the only word, but we do not listen. We want to know what he is saying to others, and do not listen to what he is saying to us. We are not sufficiently attuned to that transcendental being imparted to all things by divine action. — *The Sacrament of the Present Moment* by Jean-Pierre De Caussade

For though we begin the practice of secret prayer with a strong sense that we are the initiators and that by our wills we are establishing our habits, maturing experience brings an awareness of being met, and tutored, purged and disciplined, simplified and made pliant in His holy will by a power waiting within us. For God Himself works in our souls, in their deepest depths, taking increasing control as we are progressively willing to be prepared for His wonder. We cease trying to make ourselves the dictators and God the listener, and become the joyful listeners to Him, the Master who does all things well. — *A Testament of Devotion* by Thomas Kelly

Our waiting on God, then, requires ongoing attentiveness if it is to be more than an empty exercise in passivity. When we pay attention, our awareness is sharpened. Then we hear God speak, predictably in sacred settings, but also in wildly unlikely places and circumstances: the subway, the shower, and the messy garage. After all, the Holy Spirit is blowing over us all the time, sometimes as gentle as a baby's breath and sometimes roaring like a Kansas tornado. — *My Soul in Silence Waits* by Margaret Guenther

You must adapt your word to my smallness, so that it can enter into the tiny dwelling of my finiteness — the only dwelling in which I can live — without destroying it. Then I shall be able to understand; such a word I can take in without that agonizing bewilderment of mind and that cold fear clutching my heart. If you would speak such an "abbreviated" word, which would not say everything but only something simple which I could grasp, then I could breathe freely again.

O Infinite God, you have actually willed to speak such a word to me! You have restrained the ocean of your infinity from flooding in over the poor little wall which protects my tiny life's acre from your vastness. Not the waters of your great sea, but only the dew of your gentleness is to spread itself over my poor little plot of earth. You have come to me in a human word. For you, the Infinite, are the God of our Lord Jesus Christ. — *Encounters with Silence* by Karl Rahner

What makes you the worst version of yourself? For me, I have noticed that it has a lot to do with *room* — making *room*, having *room*, occupying *room*. I need *room* to breathe, *room* to move around, *room* to roam. I need *room* to think, *room* to reflect, *room* to pray, *room* to pay attention. I need *room* to be with Jesus. I need *room* "to sit at his feet and to listen to what he says" the way Mary did. I need *room* to allow his word to do its work deep within me.

And when I do not have room, when I am crowded and pressured and hurried, it can get ugly inside really fast. A sense of constant frustration is one of the early warning signs, but if I follow that down a little deeper I quickly run into those old, familiar foes: anxiety and insecurity. I start to feel like *life is living me,* rather than like *I am living life.* Does that sound familiar? Distracted, worried, and upset — hello Martha! And, for me, hello worst self!

The funny thing about *room* is that it doesn't just happen on its own. You have to be intentional. You won't just *find* room, you have to *make* room. Maybe that's part of what Jesus was trying to teach Martha, that if you are not intentional there will be no room, and thus, no peace.

I saw this pattern play out in my life recently. I noticed that I had been living with a constant sense of frustration. Then came the anxiety and insecurity, plus a sleepless night or two. Demands and expectations began getting the best of me. It was a slow, subtle thing. The kind of thing that sucks you into *a way of being* without you even noticing it. And then it occurred to me, "I need more room. I've been spending my time with Jesus, but I haven't been specifically making room to sit at his feet and listen to whatever he might have to say. I've been distracted. I've allowed circumstances and worries to dominate my heart."

And as soon as I began making more room in my day to sit and listen to the One who calls me his beloved, perspective began to return, frustration began to fade, and life began to come back into my soul once again — driving out the fear, the anxiety, the insecurity, and the frustration. My circumstances had not changed, but I had. I had *room* again to hear his voice. Thanks be to God! Pray that it stays that way.

—Jim Branch, April, 2015

Seeing God and Being Seen

I. Opening Prayer
Then run, faithful souls, happy and tireless, keep up
with your beloved who marches with giant strides from
one end of heaven to the other. Nothing is hidden from
His eyes. He walks alike over the smallest blade of
grass, the tallest cedars, grains of sand or rocky
mountains. Wherever you go He has gone before. Only
follow Him and you will find Him everywhere. — *The
Sacrament of the Present Moment* by Jean-Pierre De
Caussade

II. Psalm 11

III. Daily Scripture Readings
Monday	Matthew 6:22-23
Tuesday	John 1:35-51
Wednesday	Mark 9:1-10
Thursday	Job 42:1-6
Friday	2 Chronicles 16:7-9
Saturday	John 9:1-41
Sunday	Mark 8:1-26

IV. Readings for Reflection

V. Reflection and Listening: silent and written

VI. Prayer: for the church, for others, for myself

VII. Song   *Jesus Cast a Look on Me*

VIII. Closing Prayer
O Lord Jesus, I look at you, and my eyes are fixed on
your eyes. Your eyes penetrate the eternal mystery of
the divine and see the glory of God. They are also the
eyes that saw Simon, Andrew, Nathanael, and Levi, the

eyes that saw the woman with the hemorrhage, the widow of Nain, the blind, the lame, the lepers, and the hungry crowd, the eyes that saw the sad, rich ruler, the fearful disciples on the lake, and the sorrowful women at the tomb. Your eyes, O Lord, see in one glance the inexhaustible love of God and the seemingly endless agony of all people who have lost faith in that love and are like sheep without a shepherd.

As I look into your eyes, they frighten me because they pierce like flames of fire my innermost being, but they console me as well, because these flames are purifying and healing. Your eyes are so severe yet so loving, so unmasking yet so protecting, so penetrating yet so caressing, so profound yet so intimate, so distant yet so inviting.

I gradually realize that I want to be seen by you, to dwell under your caring gaze, and to grow strong and gentle in your sight. Lord, let me see what you see — the love of God and the suffering of people — so that my eyes may become more and more like yours, eyes that can heal wounded hearts. — *The Road to Daybreak* by Henri Nouwen

Readings for Reflection-

How we see things is incredibly important. It determines so much about our lives, our attitudes, and our outlooks. If our *eyes are clear*, if we are looking through the lenses of Scripture — seeing ourselves and our world through the eyes of Jesus — our whole body will be full of light. But if our *eyes are bad*, if our vision is clouded and distorted by fear, or insecurity, or depression, or apathy, or greed, or the thousand-and-one other things that can keep us from seeing accurately, then our whole body will be filled with darkness. And O how great the darkness!

So the call each day is to look at everything, no matter what the circumstance, through the proper lenses; for only then will we have the perspective to see things and people and events as they truly are. And only then will we be able to defeat the darkness that tries to overwhelm and overcome us and live in the light and the love — and truth — of Christ.

O Lord, give me good eyes today, that my soul may be filled with light rather than darkness, love rather than need. Do not let my vision get clouded and distorted by the darkness that is around me or within me, but help my eyes to stay pure and clear, seeing as you see, that I might love as you love. Amen.

— Jim Branch, November, 2015

The emphasis is on seeing. Jesus said to Nathanael, "Before Philip came to call you, I saw you under the fig tree," and after Nathanael's response: "You are the Son of God." Jesus remarked, "You believe that just because I said I saw you under the fig tree. You will see greater things than that...you will see the heaven laid open, and above the Son of man, and the angels of God ascending and descending" (John 1:49-51).

The story speaks deeply to me since it raises the questions: "Do I want to be seen by Jesus? Do I want to be known by Him?" If I do, then a faith can grow which proclaims Jesus as Son of God. Only such a faith can open my eyes and reveal such a heaven.

Thus, I will see when I am willing to be seen. I will receive new eyes that can see the mysteries of God's own life when I allow God to see me, all of me, even those parts that I myself do not want to see.

O Lord, see me and let me see. — *The Road to Daybreak* by Henri J.M. Nouwen

For most of my life I have struggled to find God, to know God, to love God. I have tried hard to follow the guidelines of the spiritual life—pray always, work for others, read Scriptures—and to avoid the many temptations to dissipate myself. I have failed many times but always tried again, even when I was close to despair.

Now I wonder whether I have sufficiently realized that during all this time God has been trying to find me, to know me, to love me. The question is not "How am I to find God?" but "How am I to let myself be found by Him?" The question is not "How am I to know God?" but "How am I to let myself be known by God?" And finally, the question is not "How am I to love God?" but "How am I to let myself be loved by God?" God is looking into the distance for me, trying to find me, and longing to bring me home. — *The Return of the Prodigal Son* by Henri J. M. Nouwen

What comes into our minds when we think about God is the most important thing about us. . . . and the most portentous fact about any man is not what he at a given time may say or do, but what he in his deep heart conceives God to be like. — *Knowledge of the Holy* by A. W. Tozer

God our Lord would have us look to the Giver and love Him more than His gift, keeping Him always before our eyes, in our hearts, and in our thoughts.

—St. Ignatius

If there is anyone who is not enlightened by this sublime magnificence of created things, he is blind. If there is anyone who, seeing all these works of God, does not praise Him, he is dumb; if there is anyone who, from so many signs, cannot perceive God, that man is foolish.

—St. Bonaventure

The hardest thing about really seeing and really
hearing is when you really have to do something about
what you have seen and heard.

— Frederick Buechner

It is not enough that we behave better; we must come to
see reality differently. We must learn to see the depths
of things, not just reality at a superficial level. This
especially means we need to see the nonseparateness of
the world from God and the oneness of all reality in
God: the Hidden Ground of Love in all that is. Prayer is
a kind of corrective lens that does away with the
distorted view of reality that, for some mysterious
reason, seems to be my normal vision, and enables me to
see what is as it really is. — *Silence on Fire* by William H.
Shannon

It was only a small wind
rather gentle, like a breeze.
It blew a strand of hair across my forehead
and I knew it was God.

I was awakened by a tiny gleam of light
it slipped through my curtain, onto my face.
It drew me to my feet and on to the window
Drawing back the curtains
dawn stepped softly into my room.
I knew that it was God.

In the middle of my loneliness
the phone rang.
A voice I knew so well, said
"Hello, I love you."
Love stirred in my soul
I knew that it was God.

Rain fell gently on thirsty ground.
　　Slowly, carefully, steadily it came
to an earth parched with waiting.
　　Through those raindrops
I walked, unafraid — without an umbrella.
　　I knew that it was God.

It was only a little bitterness I thought
　　but it wouldn't leave my heart.
It hung around my soul for ages
　　until a storm came, violent and terrifying.
It shook me to the depths of my being
　　and blew all the bitterness away.
I knew that it was God

It was only a Silver Maple
　　but in the morning's sunlight
It was filled with heaven.
　　I stood in a trance
as one touched by angel wings.
　　I knew that it was God.

O God, I cried,
　　Endearing One, I love you!
You cannot hide from me.
　　Between the cracks of daily life
I find you waiting
　　to be adored.
You slip into my life
　　like night and day
　　like stars and sunshine.
I know that you are God.
　　— *Harvest of God* by Macrina Wiederkehr)

The Word Made Flesh

I. Opening Prayer

Almighty God, who came to us long ago in the birth of
Jesus Christ, be born in us anew today by the power of
your Holy Spirit. We offer our lives as home to you and
ask for grace and strength to live as your faithful, joyful
children always. Through Jesus Christ our Lord. Amen.
— *A Guide to Prayer for Ministers and Other Servants* by
Rueben Job and Norman Shawchuck

II. Psalm 85

III. Daily Scripture Readings

Monday	John 1:1-14
Tuesday	Colossians 1:15-23
Wednesday	Colossians 2:9-15
Thursday	Philippians 2:1-13
Friday	Hebrews 1:1-13
Saturday	Matthew 1:18-25
Sunday	Isaiah 53:1-12

IV. Readings for Reflection

V. Reflection and Listening: silent and written

VI. Prayer: for the church, for others, for myself

VII. Song   *Come Thou Long Expected Jesus*

VIII. Closing Prayer

Come, Lord Jesus!

You are my righteousness. You are my goodness, the
cause and the reason for goodness. You are my life and
the light of life. You are my love and all my loving. You
are the most noble language I can ever utter, my words
and all their meaning, my wisdom, my truth, and the

better part of myself. Amen. —*Preparing for Jesus* by Walter Wangerin Jr.

Readings for Reflection-

Before the beginning there was a Heart and this Heart was the substance of God. It came from the very core of who God was and was the very essence of God from before the beginning.

Through His Heart God created all things, without it nothing received the life-blood of God. This Heart was the source of true *shalom*. Its blood gave us the ability to see—to see the depths of the Heart in spite of all darkness because the darkness is unable stop its beating

And God ripped His Heart from His very chest and He transplanted that Heart into one like us, wrapping it in flesh and bones and giving Him a face and a name. And God's Heart lived with us. He walked with us, talked with us, laughed, and cried with us and we saw what God's Heart looked like…it was pumping with the blood of grace and truth.

—Jim Branch, from John 1:1-14

Christ is the human face of God. Jesus is the autobiography of God. In Christ, God was spelling himself out, expressing himself. Jesus was the audible, visible Word who expressed the heart of the inaudible, invisible God. —*Theology, Notes, and News* by F. Dale Brunner

At Trafalgar Square in the city of London stands a statue of Lord Nelson. Resting atop a tall pillar, it towers too high for passersby to distinguish his features. For this reason, about forty years ago a new statue—an exact replica of the original—was erected at eye level so everyone could see him. God also transcends our ability to see; the eyes of our understanding cannot discern divine features. But we have set before us an exact representation, "the image of the invisible God." To know God we must look only at Jesus. — *The Trivialization of God* by Donald W. McCullough

Jesus Christ is the eternal Word who became flesh and lived among us. The personal revelation of God became, in the words of the Chalcedon Creed, "at once complete in Godhead and complete in manhood, truly God and truly man." This act on humility continues, the Word becomes flesh again and again, through the testimony of Scripture. Stated another way, the Holy Spirit who dwelt fully in Jesus Christ and who inspired the apostolic witness to Him now inspires our reading of it: through the dynamic work of the Spirit, God's Word meets us in something that is not dead but "living and active, sharper than any two-edged sword" (Heb. 4:12). — *The Trivialization of God* by Donald W. McCullough

God presents himself to us little by little. The whole story of salvation is the story of the God who comes.

It is always he who comes, even if he has not yet come in his fullness. But there is indeed one unique moment in his coming; the others were only preparations and announcement.

The hour of his coming is the Incarnation.

The Incarnation brings the world his presence. It is a presence so complete that it overshadows every presence before it.

God is made human in Christ. God makes himself present to us with such a special presence, such an obvious presence, as to overthrow all complicated calculations made about him in the past.

"The invisible, intangible God has made himself visible and tangible in Christ."

If Jesus is truly God, everything is clear; if I cannot believe this, everything darkens again. — *The God Who Comes* by Carlo Carretto

"Guide our feet into the paths of peace, that having done Your will this day, we may, when night comes, rejoice and give You thanks. . . ." We begin the work that is before us this day, asking for the grace to do it well and to the glory of God. We dress children and get them to school, we find our places and undertake the tasks for which we have been dreamed into being. We do the work that is before us, the gift of study or play, the tasks and assignments, the places to go and the people to see. We begin to sense that our work can be changed from job and task into service and act of kindness, from struggle for gain into the offering of gift, from slow death into life-giving co-creation. The work itself can become something more as we come to see ourselves as co-laborers rather than pawns, as hands and feet of God rather than merely the shoulders and backs of the marketplace. We keep our eyes open for the One Who Comes among us in our daily rounds.
— *Living Prayer* by Robert Benson

The first verb Mark used to describe Jesus' action is "came." Jesus *came* to be with us. God's first move is to be among us — Immanuel, God is with us. God comes to us long before we come to God. We may think we are in pursuit of God, but in reality we are only responding to a God who has been pursuing us. — *Embracing the Love of God* by James Bryan Smith

While God does not ask any of us to bring Christ into the world as literally as did Mary, God calls each of us to become a Godbearer through whom God may enter the world again and again. — *The Godbearing Life* by Kenda Creasy Dean and Ron Foster

Incarnating
by J. Barrie Shepherd

Becoming
putting on
clothing oneself
assuming flesh
bearing the bone and blood
mortality that bears us all
through what we call
for better or worse
this life
how did he do it?
Was it like
climbing
clumsy
into
heavy clanking armor
slipping on
a skin-tight wet suit
taking on oneself a body-cast
of stiff unyielding clay?
Or
was there more of
taking off
a shedding
of the iridescent skin
of fair eternity
a love-filled
laying to one side
of glory, majesty and power
before the naked plunge into the
depths to seek a treasure long encrusted
by the sifting sands of night?

God in Himself is the transcendent One. As such he exceeds and explodes all of our human thought categories. No human mind can capture Him. He who is light in himself is darkness for the human mind.

How, then, can he communicate himself to fleshbound human beings in a way calculated to grasp us and grip us and lift us up into a lifegiving personal relationship with him?

The first way God chooses to bridge the gap is creation. He creates our universe, the bewildering variety of touchable, seeable, hearable, palpable beings, so that we can stand before star-studded heavens, before sunrise and sunset glories, before Yosemite and Coldwater, the might of the Pacific in storm, before the complexity of the atom and DNA and the human body, and know something of that Maker: his majesty, his intelligence, his beauty, his power. In a real sense, "the world is charged with the grandeur of God." Creation is the first preaching of the good news. The universe is truly a sacramental universe, disclosing Him. He is the radical secret at the heart of the universe. And so it has been for me in my experience.

But he chooses to bridge the gap in a more significant, personal way. He chooses out of many nations one people and in the years of their history discloses — progressively from Abraham and Moses on, but most specifically in Isaiah and Jeremiah and Ezekiel and Hosea — his holiness, his desire for human beings, his longstanding, faithful love for his rational creatures.

And yet this is not enough. He must say it in a way no one can miss. He must lay his heart open to us and give us the supreme argument of love. He must pour out his inmost identity in an ultimate symbol worthy of himself which would convince us even in our cynicism.

Thus the final way he gladly chose to reveal himself is in his own Son, existing before the stars, who would become a limited human being with a body like me, an emotional life like mine, a thinking loving spirit, and a developing identity — consciousness like mine. So Jesus began life as an infant and grows up in a backwater town, takes up the carpentry trade, is called at the Jordan ford and teaches and heals and forms a small group of followers, dies and rises. And precisely through this short life of carpenter and teacher, God the Father is revealed to the world in stunning clarity. Jesus then is the great sacrament, symbol, revelation of the very depths of the incomprehensible God. What Jesus reveals is the Father's love for us humans: a self-giving love unto death, an unconditional love accepting our flawed condition, forgiving endlessly our weakness and malice. — *A Traveler Toward the Dawn* by John Eagan, S.J.

Let the Word, I pray, be to me, not as a word spoken only to pass away, but conceived and clothed in flesh, not in air, that he may remain with us. Let him be, not only to be heard with the ears, but to be seen with the eyes, touched with the hands and borne on the shoulders. Let the Word be to me, not as a word written and silent, but incarnate and living.

— Bernard of Clairvaux

Books of theology tend to define God by what He is not: *im*mortal, *in*visible, *in*finite. But what is God like, positively? For the Christian, Jesus answers such all-important questions. The apostle Paul boldly called Jesus "the image of the invisible God." Jesus was God's exact replica: "For God was pleased to have all his fullness dwell in him."

God is, in a word, Christlike. Jesus presents a God with skin on whom we can take or leave, love or ignore. In this visible, scaled-down model we can discern God's features more clearly. — *The Jesus I Never Knew* by Philip Yancey

Chosen by God

I. Opening Prayer

Almighty God, you have created us, called us, chosen us to be your people. We wait now to receive your word of guidance and blessing. Grant unto us ears to hear, eyes to see, and faith to respond to your love and leadership. In the name of Jesus Christ. Amen. — *A Guide to Prayer for Ministers and Other Servants* by Rueben Job and Norman Shawchuck

II. Psalm 135

III. Reading for Reflection

IV. Daily Scripture Readings

Monday	Matthew 20:1-16
Tuesday	Matthew 22:1-14
Wednesday	Ephesians 1:3-14
Thursday	John 15:9-17
Friday	1 Peter 2:1-10
Saturday	John 6:35-51
Sunday	Romans 8:28-39

V. Reflection and Listening: silent and written

VI. Prayers: for the church, for others, for myself

VII. Song   *Jesus You Are Lord*

VIII. Closing Prayer

You, O Lord, are the fountain of life, and the source of all goodness; You made all things and filled them with Your blessing. Thanks be to God. Amen. — *Venite* by Robert Benson

Readings for Reflection-

I Choose You by Jim Branch

I choose you. Before the foundations of the world, I formed you, and made you my own. You are a work of art, a masterpiece, a never-to-be-repeated way that I, the God of all creation, has chosen to express himself. I made you with great care and intention to be my very own. You are fearfully made and wonderfully unique. You are my beloved, my delight, and the joy of my heart. When you begin to doubt your own value and worth, just remember that I choose you. When you begin to question whether or not you are worth loving, just remember that I choose you. And when you find yourself unsure about the depths of my affection, just remember that I choose you – not once, not twice, but always again. I choose you. You are mine.

This longing that wells up in us, though, does not spring into existence on its own. "God is always previous," is the way the theologian Von Hugel put it. "You would not have called to me unless I had been calling to you," is the way Aslan put it, the lion in the Narnia Chronicles who called Edmund and three other children from England into the magical land of Narnia. The way the apostle John put it was, "We love because he first loved us."

Maybe, too, that is why we long.

"God's yearning for us stirs up our longing in response," says Howard Macy in *Rythms of the Inner Life*. God's initiating presence may be ever so subtle – an inward tug of desire, a more-than-coincidence meeting of words and events, a glimpse of the beyond in a storm or a flower – but it is enough to make our heart skip a beat and to make us want to know more." – *Windows of the Soul* by Ken Gire

"Come here," said the Lion. And she had to. She was almost between its front paws now, looking straight into its face. But she couldn't stand that for long; she dropped her eyes.

"Human Child," said the Lion. "Where is the Boy?"

"He fell over the cliff," said Jill, and added, "Sir." She didn't know what else to call him, and it sounded cheek to call him nothing.

"How did he come to do that, Human Child?"

"He was trying to stop me from falling, Sir."

"Why were you so near the edge, Human Child?"

"I was showing off, Sir."

"That is a very good answer, Human Child. Do so no more. And now" (here for the first time the Lion's face became a little less stern) "the Boy is safe." I have blown him to Narnia. But your task will be the harder because of what you have done."

"Please, what task, Sir?" said Jill

"The task for which I called you and him here out of your own world."

This puzzled Jill very much. "It's mistaking me for someone else," she thought. She didn't dare to tell the Lion this, though she felt things would get into a dreadful muddle unless she did.

"Speak your thought, Human Child," said the Lion.

"I was wondering—I mean—could there be some mistake? Because nobody called me and Scrubb, you know. It was we who asked to come here. Scrubb said we were to call to—to Somebody—it was a name I wouldn't know—and perhaps the Somebody would let us in. And we did, and then we found the door open."

"You would not have called to me unless I had been calling to you," said the Lion.

"Then you are Somebody, Sir?" said Jill

"I am."

— *The Silver Chair* by C. S. Lewis

98

To live a spiritual life, we have to claim for ourselves that we are "taken" or "chosen." Let me try to expand a bit on these words. When I know that I am chosen, I know that I have been seen as a special person. Someone has noticed me in my uniqueness and has expressed a desire to know me, to come closer to me, to love me. When I write to you that, as the Beloved, we are God's chosen ones, I mean that we have been seen by God from all eternity and seen as unique, special, precious beings. It is very hard for me to express well the depth of the meaning of the word "chosen" has for me, but I hope you are willing to listen to me from within. From all eternity, long before you were born and became a part of history, you existed in God's heart. Long before your parents admired you or your friends acknowledged your gifts or your teachers, colleagues and employers encouraged you, you were already "chosen." The eyes of love had seen you as precious, as of infinite beauty, as of eternal value. When love chooses, it chooses with a perfect sensitivity for the unique beauty of the chosen one. — *Life of the Beloved* by Henri J. M. Nouwen

We do not "find" God as a result of our search for him. We are found by him. The search for God does not end in conversion; it begins at conversion. It is the converted person who genuinely and sincerely seeks after God. Jonathan Edwards remarked that seeking after God is the main business of the Christian life. — *Grace Unknown* by R. C. Sproul

When you lose touch with your chosenness, you expose yourself to the temptation of self-rejection, and that temptation undermines the possibility of ever growing as the Beloved....When we claim and constantly reclaim the truth of being chosen ones, we soon discover within ourselves a deep desire to reveal to others their own chosenness. — *Life of the Beloved* by Henri J. M. Nouwen

I have always enjoyed the part of the prayer that suggests to us that we are taken by God, that we are chosen. "You did not choose me, I chose you," we are told Jesus said to His friends once, and I claim it for myself as often as I feel I can get away with it. I remind myself of the hope of it when the darkness comes, and celebrate the astonishment of it when the Light is all around me. — *Living Prayer* by Robert Benson

An adventure is, by its nature, a thing that comes to us. It is a thing that chooses us, not a thing that we choose. — *Orthodoxy* by G. K. Chesterton

Thirsty hearts are those whose longings have been wakened by the touch of God within them. — *The Pursuit of God* by A. W. Tozer

Whether a man arrives or does not arrive at his own destiny — the place that is peculiarly his — depends on whether or not he finds the Kingdom within and hears the call to wholeness — or holiness, as another might say. The man who hears that call is chosen. He does not have to scramble for a place in the scheme of things. He knows that there is a place which is his and that he can live close to the One who will show it to him. Life becomes his vocation. — *Journey Inward, Journey Outward* by Elizabeth O'Connor

The Grace of God

I. Opening Prayer

We are sure that there is in us nothing that could attract the love of One as holy and just as Thou art. Yet Thou hast declared Thine unchanging love for us in Christ Jesus. If nothing in us can win Thy love, nothing in the universe can prevent Thee from loving us. Thy love is uncaused and undeserved. Thou art Thyself the reason for the love wherewith we are loved. Help us to believe the intensity, the eternity of the love that has found us.
— *The Knowledge of the Holy* by A. W. Tozer

II. Psalm 32

III. Daily Scripture Readings

Monday	John 1:14-18
Tuesday	Ephesians 2:1-10
Wednesday	Titus 3:1-7
Thursday	2 Corinthians 12:7-10
Friday	2 Corinthians 8:1-9
Saturday	Romans 3:21-26
Sunday	Luke 7:36-50

IV. Readings for Reflection

V. Reflection and Listening: silent and written

VI. Prayer: for the church, for others, for myself

VII. Song: *Amazing Grace*

VIII. Closing Prayer

Father, there is no reason for you to love us, but you do. There is no reason for you to be merciful to us, but you are. There is no reason for you to offer us your grace, but still you constantly pour it out upon us. Thank you.

May we do the same to those in our lives and in our world. For your sake. Amen.

Readings for Reflection

Grace. What a great word! In the Greek (*charis*) it means *unmerited favor*; a favor done without any expectation of return. It comes from the word *chairo*, meaning *full of cheer, gladness, or joy*. Thus, grace is God's joyful gift given to us, though we do not deserve it.

—Jim Branch, September, 1999

For Paul, the church is simply the custodian of grace. "Grace" is how he started all his letters. Normally Greek letters started with the word *chairein*—"Greetings." It was a throw-away, a cliché, much as we start letters by saying, Dear...," whether the addressee is dear to us or not.

Paul changed this custom by starting with a new word for "grace," similar in form, *charis*, but radically different in meaning. "May grace be sent to you."
—*Love Beyond Reason* by John Ortberg

Grace is the good pleasure of God that inclines Him to bestow benefits upon the undeserving. It is a self-existent principle inherent in the divine nature and appears to us as a self-caused propensity to pity the wretched, spare the guilty, welcome the outcast, and bring into favor those who were before under just disapprobation. Its use to us sinful men is to save us and make us sit together in heavenly places to demonstrate to the ages the exceeding riches of God's kindness to us in Christ Jesus. —*The Knowledge of the Holy* by A.W. Tozer

We try to live so that He will love us, rather than because He has already loved us.

— Lloyd Ogilvie

Grace means that there isn't anything you can do to make God love you any less. What will drive you crazy is the discovery that there isn't anything you can do to make him love you any more, either. — *Hustling God* by Craig Barnes

Grace is something you can never get but only be given. The grace of God means something like: Here is your life. You might never have been, but you are because the party wouldn't have been complete without you. — *Wishful Thinking* by Frederick Buechner

The more we immerse ourselves in grace, the more likely we are to give grace. — *In the Grip of Grace* by Max Lucado

The greatest saints are not those who need less grace, but those who consume the most grace, who indeed are most in need of grace — those who are saturated by grace in every dimension of their being. Grace to them is like breath. — *Renovation of the Heart* by Dallas Willard

The first movement toward God is itself the gift of God. — *Soul Keeping* by Howard Baker

God has infinite treasures to give us. Yet a little tangible devotion, which passes away in a moment, satisfies us. How blind we are, since in this way we tie God's hands, and we stop the abundance of His grace! But when He finds a soul penetrated with living faith, He pours out grace on it in abundance. God's grace is like a torrent. When it is stopped from taking its ordinary course, it looks for another outlet, and when it finds one, it spreads out with impetuosity and abundance. — *Practicing the Presence of God* by Brother Lawrence

Grace is the presence and action of Christ in our lives inviting us to let go of where we are now and to be open to new values that are born every time we penetrate to a new understanding of the Gospel. — *Awakenings* by Thomas Keating

The Bible often portrays the grace of God as a thin stream of refreshing water that perseveres in a desert land. The only way our parched souls can survive in a spiritually desolate society is to stay close to that stream. That is why we come to worship, read our Bibles, serve others, and pray without ceasing throughout the day. It's all a way of drinking in the grace that keeps us spiritually alive. The more time we spend by that stream, the more deeply our lives become rooted in God (Psalm 1).

Those roots are pretty important because sometimes we get more grace than we want. It doesn't happen often, but when the storms come, the thin stream can suddenly turn into a raging river, washing away everything that is not firmly planted. We never want to get too sentimental about grace. While most days it is God's gentle refreshment to our souls, some days it comes as a terrifying reminder that our lives are out of control.

On the stormy days, we may wonder if it was such a good idea to live so close to the stream. We may even wish God would just leave us alone. Yet if the torrent sweeps away the things that are not spiritually rooted, then even that is a grace. Remember, the point of God's grace is not to be nice to us. Grace does what we cannot do for ourselves. It carries us home to God. Sometimes on a gentle stream. Sometimes on a raging river. Yet always back to God. — *Extravagant Mercy* by M. Craig Barnes

I do not at all understand the mystery of grace — only that it meets us where we are but does not leave us where it found us. It can be received gladly or grudgingly, in big gulps or in tiny tastes, like a deer at the salt. I gobbled it, licked it, held it down between my little hooves. — *Traveling Mercies* by Anne Lamott

Loved by God

I. Opening Prayer

I feel your love as you hold me to your sacred heart, my beloved Jesus, my God, my Master, but I feel, too, the need I have of your tenderness, and your caress because of my infinite weakness.

— Charles de Foucauld

II. Psalm 36

III. Daily Scripture Readings

Monday	Zephaniah 3:14-20
Tuesday	Romans 5:1-8
Wednesday	1 John 4:7-21
Thursday	Song of Songs 7:10-12
Friday	Ephesians 3:14-21
Saturday	Lamentations 3:19-24
Sunday	Psalm 131:1-3

IV. Readings for Reflection

V. Reflection and Listening: silent and written

VI. Prayer: for the church, for others, for myself

VII. Song   *Jesus Lover of My Soul*

VIII. Closing Prayer

O Thou who ordered this wondrous world, and who knowest all things in earth and heaven: So fill our hearts with trust in thee that by night and day, at all times and in all seasons, we may without fear commit all that we have and hope to be to thy never-failing love, for this life and the life to come; through Jesus Christ our Lord. Amen.

— *The Book of Worship*

Readings for Reflection-

"Jim, my son, you are my Beloved. I know how much insecurity and doubt fills your heart and it makes me so sad. It hurts me deeply to see you doubting your value, your worth, and your calling. I know how much you compare yourself with others, and how much (in your mind anyway) you come up woefully short in that comparison. I long for you to know your own beauty, value, and worth. You have something to offer that no one else in all creation has ever had, or ever will have. You are a wonderfully unique expression of my love, care, and creativity, and it gives me such joy to see you be who I made you to be and give what I gave you to give. You are incomparable; beyond compare. You are of infinite worth. Come to me and allow me to celebrate over you daily. Allow me to convince you of my extravagant love. Allow me to convince you that you are worthy of being celebrated. And allow me to remind you that I celebrate you every minute of every day. You are mine!!! And I love you!!!" — *Being with Jesus* by Jim Branch

Aren't you, like me hoping that some person, thing or event will come along to give you that final feeling of inner well-being you desire? Don't you often hope: "May this book, idea, course, trip, job, country or relationship fulfill my deepest desire." But as long as you are waiting for that mysterious moment you will go on running helter-skelter, always anxious and restless, always lustful and angry, never fully satisfied. You know that this is the compulsiveness that keeps us going and busy, but at the same time makes us wonder whether we are getting anywhere in the long run. This is the way to spiritual exhaustion and burn-out. This is the way to spiritual death.

Well, you and I don't have to kill ourselves. We are the Beloved. We are intimately loved long before our parents, teachers, spouses, children and friends loved or wounded us. That's the truth of our lives. That's the truth I want you to claim for yourself. That's the truth spoken by the voice that says," You are my Beloved."

Listening to that voice with great inner attentiveness, I hear words that say: "I have called you by name, from the very beginning. You are mine and I am yours. You are my Beloved, on you my favor rests. I have molded you in the depths of the earth and knitted you together in your mother's womb. I have carved you in the palms of my hands and hidden you in the shadow of my embrace. I look at you with infinite tenderness and care for you with a care more intimate than that of a mother for a child. I have counted every hair on your head and guided you at every step. Wherever you go, I go with you, and wherever you rest, I keep watch. I will give you food that will satisfy all your hunger and drink that will quench all your thirst. I will not hide my face from you. You know me as your own and I know you as my own, You belong to me....wherever you are I will be. Nothing will ever separate us. We are one." —*Life of the Beloved* by Henri J.M. Nouwen

Yes, there is that voice, the voice that speaks from above and from within that whispers softly or declares loudly: "You are my Beloved, on you my favor rests." It certainly is not easy to hear that voice in a world filled with voices that shout: "You are no good, you are ugly; you are worthless; you are despicable, you are nobody — unless you can demonstrate the opposite."

These negative voices are so loud and so persistent that it's easy to believe them. That's the great trap. It is the trap of self-rejection. —*Life of the Beloved* by Henri J. M. Nouwen

Let me talk very intimately and very earnestly with you about Him who is dearer than life. Do you really want to live your lives, every moment of your lives, in His presence? Do you long for Him, crave Him? Do

108

you love His presence? Does every drop of blood in your body love Him? Does every breath you draw breathe a prayer, a praise to Him? Do you sing and dance within yourselves, as you glory in His love? Have you set yourselves to be His, and *only* His, walking every moment in holy obedience? I know I'm talking like an old-time evangelist. But I can't help that, nor dare I restrain myself and get prim and conventional. We have too long been prim and restrained. The fires of the love of God, of our love toward God, and His love toward us, are very hot. "Thou shalt love the Lord thy God with all thy heart and soul and mind and strength." Do we really do it? Is love steadfastly directed toward God, in our minds, all day long? Do we intersperse our work with gentle prayers and praises to Him? Do we live in the steady peace of God, a peace down at the depths of our souls, where all strain is gone and God is already victor over the world, already victor over our weaknesses? This life, this abiding, enduring peace that never fails, this serene power and unhurried conquest over ourselves, outward conquest over the world, is meant to be ours. It is a life that is freed from strain and anxiety and hurry, for something of the Cosmic Patience of God becomes ours. Are our lives *unshakable*, because we are clear down on bed rock, rooted and grounded in the love of God? This is the first and greatest commandment. — *A Testament of Devotion* by Thomas Kelly

Living in an awareness of our belovedness is the axis around which the Christian life revolves. Being loved is our identity, the core of our existence. — *The Rabbi's Heartbeat* by Brennan Manning

This inexhaustible love between the Father and the Son includes and yet transcends all forms of love known to us. It includes the love of a father and mother, a brother and sister, a husband and wife, a teacher and friend. But it also goes far beyond the many limited and limiting human experiences of love we know. It is a caring yet demanding love. It is a supportive yet severe love. It is a gentle yet strong love. It is a love that gives life yet accepts death. In this divine love Jesus was sent into the world, to this divine love Jesus offered himself on the cross. This all-embracing love, which epitomizes the relationship between the Father and the Son, is a divine Person, coequal with the Father and the Son. It has a personal name. It is called the Holy Spirit. The Father loves the Son and pours himself out in the Son. The Son is loved by the Father and returns all he is to the Father. The Spirit is love itself, eternally embracing the Father and Son.

This eternal community of love is the center and source of Jesus' spiritual life, a life of uninterrupted attentiveness to the Father in the Spirit of love. —*Making All Things New* by Henri J. M. Nouwen

We spend most of our lives trying to make things happen for ourselves and for people we love. But life is not reduced to what you give or know or achieve. Nor is it reduced to your mistakes, your failures, or your sin. Life isn't even defined by whom you love. Rather, it is defined by the God who loves you. In other words, you are not the central character—not even of your own life's story. This is not meant to demean you; it is meant to set you free. —*Sacred Thirst* by M. Craig Barnes

God loves us deeply. In fact, He delights in us. His love for us is the thing that is meant to give us our deepest and truest sense of joy and identity. If we are ever tempted to doubt our worth or our value, all we have to do is look at the immense love and delight that God has in his heart for us and be convinced once again that we are priceless to the One who made us uniquely and loves us dearly. — *Beginnings* by Jim Branch

God loves each of us as if there were only one of us.

—Saint Augustine

Just as a weaned child on its mother's breast seeks no physical nourishment but enjoys the riches of unspoken Love given and received (Ps. 131), so the soul in quiet adoration lays its head against the heart of Love and absorbs all that Love yearns to bestow. This Love draws out what is truest and best in all it touches, shapes all things toward the wholeness proper to them, is quietly victorious amid the strident self-importance of the world.

—John S. Mogabgab

Undone

I. Opening Prayer

Here, Lord, I abandon myself to you. I have tried in every way I could think of to manage myself, and to make myself what I know I ought to be, but have always failed. Now I give it up to you. Do take entire possession of me. Work in me all the good pleasure of your will. Mold and fashion me into such a vessel as seems good to you. I leave myself in your hands. Amen.
— *The Christian's Secret of a Happy Life* by Hannah Whitall Smith

II. Psalm 51

III. Daily Scripture Readings

Monday	Isaiah 6:1-8
Tuesday	Luke 5:1-11
Wednesday	2 Samuel 12:1-25
Thursday	Job 42:1-6
Friday	Hosea 6:1-6
Saturday	Revelation 1:9-18
Sunday	Lamentations 3:1-29

IV. Readings for Reflection

V. Reflection and Listening: silent and written

VI. Prayer: for the church, for others, for myself

VII. Song   *Rain Down on Me*

VIII. Closing Prayer

Lord Jesus Christ, Son of God, have mercy on me, a sinner.

Readings for Reflection-

undone by Jim Branch

years and years of hard work
diligently putting it all together
piece by piece
thinking all is well
progress is being made

but then you
come and scramble the whole picture
leaving pieces scattered everywhere

you smile lovingly
as I sit in the middle of the mess
knowing that I don't know
knowing that I'm undone
and thinking to yourself
now that's progress

So now the house is in place, shiny and bright. I have
applause and esteem. They congratulate me for my
flexibility and leadership and enthusiasm and what I've
done and am doing. But this house of mine is somehow
askew: it's my house, not the Lord's house. "In vain do
the builders build." And yet I know in my heart that
each step was taken because it was right and seemed to
be the Lord's way. Yes, it was, but he had something
else in mind for it.

Then another image rose spontaneously as I walked
along. It was the Lord as an artillery captain who came
in front of my fine house dragging his cannon and
proceeded deliberately and systematically to shoot the
whole damn thing apart. Story by story, wall by wall,
brick by brick he gunned down the house that took me

twenty-five years to build until only rubble was left, pieces of masonry on the ground, and I'm standing there with the debris of my life at my feet looking at the ruins.

The strange thing was this big wide grin on the Lord's face as he gunned it apart in high glee. It's as though he said to me: now watch the top story while I blow it apart. There! Now watch the second story: there it goes! Isn't that great? Now watch the back wall: hooray! Now the side walls, now finally the front and it's all gone. Isn't that marvelous! And he turned to me with joy and warmth and smiled on me with much encouragement. — *A Traveler toward the Dawn* by John Eagan

To guide us toward the love that we most desire, we must be *taken* where we could not and would not go on our own. And lest we sabotage the journey, we must not know where we are going. Deep in the darkness, way beneath our senses, God is instilling "another, better love" and "deeper, more urgent longings" that empower our willingness for all the necessary relinquishments along the way. — *The Dark Night of the Soul* by Gerald G. May

Sin is the refusal of spiritual life, the rejection of the inner order and peace that come from our union with the divine will. In a word, sin is the refusal of God's will and of his love. It is not only a refusal to "do" this or that thing willed by God, or a determination to do what he forbids. It is more radically a refusal to be what we are, a rejection of our mysterious, contingent, spiritual reality hidden in the very mystery of God. Sin is our refusal to be what we were created to be — sons of God, images of God. Ultimately sin, while seeming to be an assertion of freedom, is a flight from the freedom and the responsibility of divine sonship. — *Life and Holiness* by Thomas Merton

In solitude I get rid of my scaffolding: no friends to talk with, no telephone calls to make, no meetings to attend, no music to entertain, no books to distract, just me—naked vulnerable, weak, sinful, deprived, broken—nothing. It is this nothingness that I have to face in my solitude, a nothingness so dreadful that everything in me wants to run to my friends, my work, and my distractions so that I can forget my nothingness and make myself believe that I am worth something. But that is not all. As soon as I decide to stay in my solitude, confusing ideas, disturbing images, wild fantasies, and weird associations jump about in my mind like monkeys in a banana tree. Anger and greed begin to show their ugly faces. I give long, hostile speeches to my enemies and dream lustful dreams in which I am wealthy, influential, and very attractive—or poor, ugly, and in need of immediate consolation. Thus I try again to run from the dark abyss of my nothingness and restore my false self in all its vainglory. — *The Way of the Heart* by Henri J.M. Nouwen

The man of broken spirit is one who has been emptied of all vain-glorious confidence, and brought to acknowledge that he is nothing. The contrite heart abjures [gives up] the idea of merit, and has no dealings with God upon the principle of exchange. Where the spirit has been broken (Psalm 51:17) and the heart has become contrite, through a felt sense of the [holiness] of the Lord, a man is brought to genuine fear and self-loathing, with a deep conviction that of himself he can do or deserve nothing, and must be indebted unconditionally for salvation to Divine mercy. — *Heart Aflame* by John Calvin

Conversion, the desert ascetics assure us, is forged in such a place, a place of listening awareness where one becomes attentive to the silence of God. There in the vast stillness of desert solitude, we are gradually converted, unmade, and remade. We become a fresh beginning. — *The Time Between* by Wendy M. Wright

The Cross

I. Opening Prayer

By your cross O Lord, you show the extravagance of your love for us. Love than knows no limits...no boundaries. Love that pours down upon us from every wound of your beloved Son. More love than we could ever ask for or imagine. When we are tempted to doubt the depths of your heart for us, let our eyes immediately look to Jesus crucified — and may all doubt be taken away. In His name. Amen.

II. Psalm 22

III. Daily Scripture Readings

Monday	John 18:1-19:37
Tuesday	Matthew 26:17-75
Wednesday	Matthew 27:1-56
Thursday	Mark 14:1-72
Friday	Mark 15:1-41
Saturday	Luke 22:1-71
Sunday	Luke 23:1-49

IV. Readings for Reflection

V. Reflection and Listening: silent and written

VI. Prayer: for the church, for others, for myself

VII. Song *You are My King*

VIII. Closing Prayer

Our God and Father,

We thank You that You have delivered us from the dominion of sin and death, and brought us into the kingdom of Your Son: Grant we pray that, by his death he has recalled us to life, so by his love he may raise us to eternal joy. In the name of Jesus. Amen. — *Venite* by Robert Benson

Readings for Reflection-

"It is finished." Jesus' final words. And what incredible words they are! *"It is finished"* means that the entire reason Jesus came to earth has been fulfilled — his mission has been accomplished. There is nothing else that needs to be done. Jesus has taken care of it all. All of our sin has been paid for in its entirety: past, present, and future. All of our punishment, every single ounce, has been placed upon him at the cross. *"It is finished"* means that we are totally justified — clean, holy, and free. *"It is finished"* means that our sin is taken away, we may go in peace.

But *"It is finished"* also means so much more than that. Because *"It is finished"* is not just about what God has taken away, but also about what he has given us. Jesus not only takes all of our mess — our sin, our brokenness, our death — upon himself, but he also gives us all that is his to give. He gives us his righteousness, he gives us his holiness, and he gives us his peace. He also gives us all of the love and affection of the Father. He gives us his inheritance, he gives us his place in the family of God, and he gives us the right to become God's beloved sons and daughters. So *"It is finished"* not only says "you may go, your sin is taken away," but it also says, "you may come and enjoy all of the intimacy of the Godhead." Because of the cross, this is now what God says to us: *My child, my delight, the joy of my heart, I wish you knew yourself the way I know you. I wish you saw yourself the way that I see you. And I wish that, deep down in your heart, you knew the truth that, because of the cross, all I have is yours and all you have is mine. Knowing this one truth at your very core will change everything about you. Now, all of my love is yours, all of my affection is yours, and*

118

*all of my delight is yours. In fact, you have completely
captured my heart. And not only that, but you also have all of
my righteousness, all of my holiness, and all of my
purity. Everything I have belongs to you.*

*And all that you have is mine. Your joys are mine and
your wounds are mine, your strengths are mine and your
weaknesses are mine, your gifts are mine and your
inadequacies are mine; so are your insecurities, your anxieties,
your fears, your struggles, your burdens, yes, and even your
sin – all mine. Come to me, my child, with all that you are,
and let me give you all that I am in return. Be mine.*
— *Being with Jesus* by Jim Branch

God's most profound self-revelation is seen in the
cross. We usually think of the cross as something God
'did' to 'solve' the sin problem that alienates us from
God. But in reality, the cross reveals who God is, not
what God did as an action separate from God's nature.
— *For the Sake of Others* by M. Robert Mulholland Jr.

The more we lack everything the more we resemble
Jesus crucified. The more we cling to the cross, the
closer do we embrace Jesus who is nailed to it. Every
cross is a gain, for every cross unites us to Jesus.
— *Meditations of a Hermit* by Charles de Foucauld

The heart of Christianity is a cross, the sign of a love
unto death, and beyond into resurrection. I am
beginning to understand that there is no way of
following Jesus except by undergoing what he
underwent. Unless I die, I can never bear fruit.

No one in this world can escape suffering, but not all
suffering is the cross. Suffering cannot be avoided, but
one can escape the cross. The cross must be a choice, a
free decision, or it is not the sign of Jesus' love. The
cross is an invitation; each person must say yes. No one

becomes a disciple without saying yes to Jesus taking us, blessing us, breaking us open, and passing us around.
—*Gathering the Fragments* by Edward J. Farrell

Take this to heart and doubt not that you are the one who killed Christ. Your sins certainly did, and when you see the nails driven through his hands, be sure that you are pounding, and when the thorns pierce his brow, know that they are your evil thoughts. Consider that if one thorn pierced Christ you deserve a hundred thousand.
—Martin Luther

Reflect carefully on this, for it is so important that I can hardly lay too much stress on it. Fix your eyes on the Crucified and nothing else will be of much importance to you. If his Majesty revealed his love to us by doing and suffering such amazing things, how can you expect to please him by words alone? —*The Interior Castle* by Teresa of Avila

You might like to read one of the gospel accounts of the crucifixion, allowing the text to stimulate your imagination. Or you may find the following prompts helpful:

> * *Build up in your mind's eye the scene of the crucifixion. There is a small hill outside the walls of Jerusalem. There are three crosses. Focus on the middle one, and see Christ stretched out on it. He is there for you.*
> * *Now fill in the fine detail. He is crowned with thorns, which are tearing his skin. Blood is dripping down. See his face, contorted with pain. Let your eyes move to his hands, nailed to the cross. The ugly wounds of the nails are slowly dripping with blood. It is a terrible sight, and you find it difficult to take in.*

* Hear the crowds shouting out "Come down from the cross! Save yourself!" Yet he stays there and saved us instead. There is no limit to his love for us. He gave everything so that we might live.

Once you have built up this mental picture, ask why this is taking place. *He is doing this for us.* He didn't have to; he chose to. We matter so much to him. Anyone who suffers from low self-esteem needs to take this insight to heart. *You matter to the greatest one of all!* For Luther, meditating on the wounds of Christ was a superb antidote for any doubt we might have concerning the love of God for us. *He was wounded for us.* Each of those wounds is a token of the loving care of a compassionate God. Can you see how this changes the way we think about ourselves? We are of such importance to him that he chose to undertake that suffering, pain, and agony.

Form a mental picture of those wounds. Cherish them. It is by them that we are healed. Each of them affirms the amazing love of God for us. Each nail hammered into the body of the savior of the world shouts out these words—"He loves us!" How can we doubt someone who gave everything for us? — *The Journey* by Alister McGrath

The cross, the primary symbol of our faith, invites us to see grace where there is pain; to see resurrection where there is death. The call to be grateful is a call to trust that every moment can be claimed as the way of the cross that leads to new life. — *Turn My Mourning Into Dancing* by Henri Nouwen

For Jesus the call of God had the shadow of the cross upon it. Surely Jesus' sacrifice on the cross, made for us, makes our sacrifice on the cross unnecessary. Can we then expect to escape the shadow of the cross on our journey? Probably not. But we can pray for and receive guidance and strength that will take us safely and victoriously through the dangers and risks we encounter in saying yes to the call of God in our time. — *A Guide to Prayer for All Who Seek God* by Rueben Job and Norman Shawchuck

No picture more clearly illustrates the love of God than the death of Jesus on the cross. As Brennan Manning has said, the cross of Jesus is the signature of Jesus. It's the ultimate expression of God's love for the world. By dying on the cross, Jesus made it possible for our twisted hearts and minds to be in harmony with his.
. . . . God wants to meet us in some exacting way that shows how deep is the love in his heart for us.
— *Running on Empty* by Fil Anderson

In the winter of 1968-69, I lived in a cave in the mountains of the Zaragosa Desert in Spain. For seven months I saw no one, never heard the sound of a human voice. Hewn out of the face of the mountain, the cave towered 6,000 feet above sea level. Each Sunday morning a brother from the village of Farlete below dropped off food, drinking water, and kerosene at the designated spot. Within the cave a stone partition divided the chapel on the right from the living quarters on the left. A stone slab covered with potato sacks served as a bed. The other furniture was a rugged granite desk, a wooden chair, a sterno stove, and a kerosene lamp. On the wall of the chapel hung a three-foot crucifix. I awoke each morning at two A.M. and went in there for an hour of nocturnal adoration.

On the night of December 13, during what began as a long and lonely hour of prayer, I heard in faith Jesus Christ say, "For love of you I left My Father's side. I came to you who ran from Me, fled Me, who did not want to hear My name. For love of you I was covered with spit, punched, beaten, and affixed to the wood of the cross."

These words are burned on my life. Whether I am in a state of grace or disgrace, elation or depression, that night of fire quietly burns on. I looked at the crucifix for a long time, figuratively saw the blood streaming from every pore of His body and heard the cry of His wounds: "This isn't a joke. It is not a laughing matter to Me that I have loved you." The longer I looked the more I realized that no man has ever loved me and no one ever could love me as He did. I went out of the cave and stood on the precipice, and shouted into the darkness, "Jesus, are you crazy? Are You out of Your mind to have loved me so much?" I learned that night what a wise old man had told me years earlier: "Only the one who has experienced it can know what the love of Jesus Christ is. Once you have experienced it, nothing else in the world will seem more beautiful or desirable."

The Lord reveals Himself to each of us in myriad ways. For me the human face of God is the strangulating Jesus stretched against a darkened sky, vulnerable to the taunts of passersby. In another of his letters from prison, Bonhoeffer wrote, "This is the only God who counts." Christ on the cross is not a mere theological precondition for the achievement of salvation. He is God's enduring Word to the world saying, "See how much I love you. See how much you must love one another." — *The Signature of Jesus* by Brennan Manning

We have to be willing to acknowledge and expose our wounds to the healing balm that flows from the pierced hands and feet and side. We need humbly and gratefully to accept this healing, with a gratitude that impels us to seek to sin no more. Then our looking upon him who has been pierced will be for us a saving glance.
— *Seeking His Mind* by M. Basil Pennington

Risen

I. Opening Prayer
Power of Love, shining through the risen Jesus,
radiantly shine in the dark places of my pain. Let their
power to infect me be broken and drawn into your heart.
— *Feed My Shepherds* by Flora Slosson Wuellner

II. Psalm 80

III. Daily Scripture Readings:

Monday	John 20:1-18
Tuesday	John 20:19-31
Wednesday	Luke 24:1-12
Thursday	Luke 24:13-34
Friday	Matthew 28:1-20
Saturday	Mark 16:1-8
Sunday	John 21:1-25

IV. Readings for Reflection

V. Reflection and Listening: silent and written

VI. Prayer: for the church, for others, for myself

VII. Song   *Arise My Soul Arise*

VIII. Closing Prayer
O God, who by your One and only Son has overcome
death and opened to us the gate of everlasting life; grant,
we pray, that those who have been redeemed by his
passion may rejoice in his resurrection, through the
same Christ our Lord. Amen.

— Gelasian Sacramentary

Readings for Reflection:

easter by Jim Branch

the silence was deafening
that early morning as she stood,
gripped by a love that would not release her
everyone else was gone
back to their homes and their families

    "how could they forget so quickly?" she
thought
      as she stood in the first light of dawn,
      tears streaming down her cheeks
      "did they not feel it too…the love?"
      "if they did, how could they leave?"

her heart would not allow her to go
so she stayed — as near to him as she knew how
was she waiting?
was she hoping?
or was she simply doing the only thing she
could —
to be near the place he was last near
she would rather be near him than anyone or
anything
so she stayed…and cried
longing to hear her name from his lips once
more

and then suddenly the voice…it startled her
looking through the tears she could not see who
it was

    "have you seen him?" she asked
    "do you know where he is?"

it wasn't until he uttered her name
that she recognized his voice
and at its sweet sound
everything in her was raised to life again
it was easter you see…and he had risen
and because of that
so had she

Why did Jesus still have wounds on His risen body?
The traditional answer is that the wounds proved it was
really he and not an imposter. Carrying and revealing
the wounds were acts of swift, discerning mercy for his
friends who were in a condition of mixed confusion and
suspicion. But I believe the wounds had a deeper
meaning with radically transforming implications that
affect us through the ages. I believe the wounds were
the sure sign that the eternal God through Jesus has
never and will never ignore, negate, minimize, or
transcend the significance of human woundedness. The
risen Jesus is not so swallowed up in glory that he is
beyond our reach, beyond our cries. He is among us,
carrying wounds, even in a body of light. His every
word and act shining forth the meaning and heart of
God means that God's heart carries our wounds. God
suffers with us. — *Feed My Shepherds* by Flora Slosson
Wuellner

There was one resurrection; there are four narratives of
it. Matthew, Mark, Luke, and John tell the story, each in
his own way. Each narrative is distinct and has its own
character. When the four accounts are absorbed into the
imagination, they develop rich melodies, harmonies,
counterpoint. The four voices become a resurrection
quartet.
    Yet many people never hear the music. The reason, I
think, is that the apologetic style for years has been to

"harmonize" the four resurrection stories. But it never turns out to be harmonization. Instead of listening to their distinctive bass, tenor, alto, and soprano voices, we have tried to make the evangelists sing the same tune. Differences and variations in the resurrection narratives are denied, affirmed, doubted, and "interpreted."

There is a better way. Since we have four accounts that supplement one another, we can be encouraged to celebrate each one as it is, and to magnify the features that make it distinct from the others. Instead of melting them down into an ingot of doctrine, we can burnish the features that individualize them.

When we do that, our imagination expands, and the resurrection acquires the sharp features and hard surfaces of real life. Through the artistry of the four evangelists, the particularity and detail of local history, the kind we ourselves live in, becomes vivid.

—*Subversive Spirituality* by Eugene Peterson

> *Long, long, long ago;*
> *Way before this winter's snow*
> *First fell upon these weathered fields;*
> *I used to sit and watch and feel*
> *And dream of how the spring would be,*
> *When through the winter's stormy sea*
> *She'd raise her green and growing head,*
> *Her warmth would resurrect the dead.*
>
> *Long before this winter's snow*
> *I dreamt of this day's sunny glow*
> *And thought somehow my pain would pass*
> *With winter's pain, and peace like grass*
> *Would simply grow. The pain's not gone.*
> *It's still as cold and hard and long*
> *As lonely pain has ever been,*
> *It cuts so deep and far within.*
>
> *Long before this winter's snow*

I ran from pain, looked high and low
For some fast way to get around
Its hurt and cold. I'd have found
If I had looked at what was there,
That things don't follow fast or fair.
That life goes on, and times do change,
And grass does grow despite life's pains.

Long before this winter's snow
I thought that this day's sunny glow,
The smiling children and growing things
And flowers bright were brought by spring.
Now, I know the sun does shine,
That children smile, and from the dark, cold, grime
A flower comes. It groans, yet sings,
And through its pain, its peace begins.
    – *Resurrection* by Mary Ann Bernard

But the proclamation of Easter Day is that all is well. And as a Christian, I say this not with the easy optimism of one who has never known a time when all was not well but as one who has faced the Cross in all its obscenity as well as in all its glory, who has known one way or another what it is like to live separated from God. In the end, his will, not ours, is done. Love is the victor. Death is not the end. The end is life. His life and our lives through him, in him. Existence has greater depths of beauty, mystery, and benediction than the wildest visionary has ever dared to dream. Christ our Lord has risen. — *The Magnificent Defeat* by Frederick Buechner

One of the consequences of having been sick enough to die once myself is that I am now much more interested in any celebrations regarding being raised from the dead than I once was.

For some years, I prepared for Easter by attending a Good Friday service and watching the cross go out the back door, its ominous and unsettling black veil flowing in the breeze, trying to summon up the courage to imagine and to face some semblance of the sense of loss the disciples must have felt on that day, trying to come to grips with what it means if there is another word after good-bye and what it means if there is not. Being close to being draped in black and carried out the same door myself has, shall we say, made the whole thing a bit easier for me to imagine.

I was in the hospital around Easter, and the doctors gave me a pass to go to church on Easter morning. My sister came to pick me up and help me get there. Sitting in the pew that morning, barely two blocks from the hospital where I was told I might well have been dead instead of alive on this Easter morning, it came to me that the resurrection is a theological concept that may well be ignored unless one's death cannot be.

It then follows that forgiveness is not much of a concept without something for which to forgive and be forgiven. Healing has no meaning in the absence of illness. Peace is no treasure at all to those who have known no war and no strife. Saying hello has no joy in it without the saying of good-bye.

I am coming to believe that the thing God said just before "Let there be light" was "Good-bye, dark." And that Noah could not say hello to the rainbow without first having said good-bye to the world as it disappeared beneath the waters of the flood. And that something deep and mysterious about saying good-bye from the bottom of the pit made the hello that Joseph spoke to his father all those years later all the more wondrous. "Good-bye, Egypt" turned out to be another way for the Israelites to say "Hello, Canaan."

"Good-bye, Jesus of Nazareth," whispers Mary through her tears at the foot of the cross on Friday afternoon. "Hello, Lord of the Universe," she murmurs to the one she mistakes for a gardener, on Sunday

morning. — *Between the Dreaming and the Coming True* by
Robert Benson

the stone lies
on its side
rolled away
easter has
uttered an
invitation *Rise Up! Come out! Enjoy the light of*
new life! but instead we sit befriending the dark
tomb content with despairing — inertia or gravity
has taken
hold so we
sit and mope
in the dark
even though
the stone lies
on its side
rolled away
— by Jim Branch

It is not enough to say that God is on the cross, sharing
our pain — unique and redemptive though that sharing
is. God is also the God of resurrection. In fact, the
Resurrection not only followed the crucifixion but was
inherent in it all along. This inherency is what Jesus
explains to the two disciples on the road to Emmaus.
(See Luke 24:13-27.) The wounds of Christ are not
swallowed up and forgotten; they become radiant
centers of deep love and healing. Within the Christian
experience, the cross and the Resurrection cannot be
divided. — *Feed My Shepherds* by Flora Slosson Wuellner

Faith

I. Opening Prayer:

O Lord, help me to really believe. Help me to really believe that your heart for me is good. Help me to really believe that nothing can separate me from your love. Help me to really believe that you will do what you say you will do. Help me to take you at your word. In the name of Jesus. Amen.

II. Psalm 89

III. Daily Scripture Readings

Monday	John 4:43-54
Tuesday	Hebrews 11:1-6
Wednesday	Hebrews 11:7-28
Thursday	Hebrews 11:29-40
Friday	2 Corinthians 5:1-10
Saturday	Matthew 14:22-33
Sunday	Luke 17:1-19

IV. Readings for Reflection

V. Reflection and Listening: silent and written

VI. Prayer: for the church, for others, for myself

VII. Song   *In Christ Alone*

VIII. Closing Prayer

"For I know the plans I have for you," declares the Lord, "plans to prosper you and not to harm you, plans to give you a hope and a future. Then you will call upon me and come and pray to me, and I will listen to you. You will seek me and find me when you seek me with all your heart. I will be found by you," declares the Lord. —Jeremiah 29:11-13

Readings for Reflection-

What does the word *faith* mean? Many have tried to define it. As you have seen this week, the writer of the book of Hebrews says it is "being sure of what we hope for and certain of what we do not see" (Hebrews 11:1). A. W. Tozer once said that faith is *the gaze of the soul on a loving God.* Martin Luther called faith *the yes of the heart.* And Frederick Buechner said that faith is *the direction your feet start moving when you find that you are loved.*

But maybe there is no better definition of the word *faith* than the one offered in the fourth chapter of John (verse 50). It says the royal official "took Jesus at his word." What a great definition of faith. Believing that what God has said is true. Being convinced. Convinced that he loves us the way he says he does. Convinced that he is in control and can be trusted with our lives. Convinced that he will truly care for us and those we love. Convinced that his heart for us is good. Convinced.

Is there a place in your life right now where you are having to walk by faith? A place where you are having to believe that God's heart for you is good even though you have a hard time seeing it in the circumstances? What does it mean for you to "take Jesus at his word" right now? — *Beginnings* by Jim Branch

Faith as it ripens turns into an almost insatiable appetite, and the awake lion must prowl for God in places it once feared.
                                    —John of the Cross

Faith is the word that describes the direction our feet start moving when we find that we are loved. Faith is stepping out into the unknown with nothing to guide us but a hand just beyond our grasp. — *The Magnificent Defeat* by Frederick Buechner

Faith is the only way of knowing that is patient with also not knowing. — *Everything Belongs* by Richard Rohr

"Your faith has saved you," Jesus said (Luke 7:50). Faith in what? Faith in the divine goodness that is ready to forgive everything and everyone *who comes.* Faith in the infinite mercy of God which is not concerned with numbers, since it is infinite, but with gratitude and self-surrender. By entrusting herself to divine love she received complete forgiveness and was empowered to prove her gratitude by the extent of her courtesy. — *Awakenings* by Thomas Keating

Faith is a way of seeing. It is a way of opening our eyes to see the world as God sees it. That is the spiritual journey we are taking — a journey to ask God to open our eyes so we may see what is there — spiritual forces of power that are mighty and invincible, but invisible to the human eye. We read in Hebrews 11:1 that "faith is the assurance of things hoped for, the conviction of things not seen." Faith isn't blind — it is the opposite. Faith is a spiritual way of seeing what our physical eyes alone will never see on their own. "By faith we understand that the worlds were prepared by the word of God, so that what is seen was made from things that are not visible" (Hebrews 11:3). — *Spiritual Mentoring* by Keith R. Anderson and Randy D. Reese

There are two peculiar characteristics of pure faith. It sees God behind all the blessings and imperfect works which tend to conceal Him, and it holds the soul in a state of continued suspense. Faith seems to keep us constantly up in the air, never quite certain of what is going to happen in the future; never quite able to touch

a foot on solid ground. But faith is willing to let God act with the most perfect freedom, knowing that we belong to Him and are to be concerned only about being faithful in that which he has given us to do for the moment.
— *Let Go* by Francois Fenelon

Faith is the gaze of a soul on a loving God. — *The Pursuit of God* by A. W. Tozer

Faith is the *yes* of the heart, a confidence on which one stakes one's life.
— Martin Luther

Christians are used to talking about faith as if it were a possession. We speak of "having faith," or sometimes, "keeping faith," and the last thing we want to do is "lose our faith." Thus, by holding on to faith we assume that we have another tool with which to pursue our goals in life. The Bible, however, rarely speaks of faith as if it were something we own. It is more typical of the Bible to describe faith as something that owns us.

Actually, faith is quite similar to another virtue called love. We usually don't say a person has love for somebody else; rather, we say that someone is in love. The difference is more than semantics. By claiming that we are in love we admit that we have been overwhelmed by a great commitment to another person. Sometimes it hits us at first sight, and at other times it develops slowly, but at no time could we claim to be in perfect control of the love. More honestly, we know that love has the power to control us.

Similarly, faith in God is a wonderful commitment. It may come slowly or in a moment, but once it truly gets hold of us it changes just about everything.
— *Extravagant Mercy* by M. Craig Barnes

Faith is the courage to accept acceptance. — *The Rabbi's Heartbeat* by Brennan Manning

May today there be peace within. May you trust God that you are exactly where you are meant to be. May you not forget the infinite possibilities that are born of faith. May you use those gifts that you have received, and pass on the love that has been given to you. May you be content knowing that you are a child of God. Let this presence settle into our bones, and allow your soul the freedom to sing, dance, praise and love. It is there for each and everyone of you .

—Teresa of Avila

Story

I. Opening Prayer

Dear Jesus, speak to me during this day about the story you are telling, the story I was made for. Open my eyes, O Lord, to the ways that story is being lived out in the events and circumstances of this day. Show me how all that happens to me this day echoes your larger Story if only I will keep my heart focused on you. In your name I pray. Amen.

II. Psalm 107 (Read a part each day: v.1-9; 10-16, 17-22, 23-32, 33-38, 39-43)

III. Daily Scripture Readings

Monday	Galatians 1:11-24
Tuesday	Luke 1:1-4
Wednesday	Luke 15:11-32
Thursday	Luke 7:36-50
Friday	2 Corinthians 3:1-4
Saturday	Luke 10:25-37
Sunday	Psalm 126:1-6

IV. Readings for Reflection

V. Reflection and Listening: silent and written

VI. Prayer: for the church, for others, for myself

VII. Song   *Step By Step*

VIII. Closing Prayer

Father, write yourself upon my heart and life — that I may be an open book about you, so that others might read of your unending love on every page. In the name of Jesus, the author of our faith. Amen.

Readings for Reflection-

Immediately after my calling — without consulting anyone around me and without going up to Jerusalem to confer with those who were apostles long before I was — I got away to Arabia. Later I returned to Damascus, but it was three years before I went up to Jerusalem to compare stories with Peter. (Galatians 1:16-18, The Message)

I love that the first thing Paul and Peter did when they got together for the very first time was tell stories. Can you imagine being a fly on the wall? There is something about the telling of our stories (or of God's story in us) that is very rich and life giving. It's almost like the stories must be told in order to have their fully desired effect in our hearts, lives, and souls. And the funny thing is that I'm not sure who they have the biggest impact on, the hearer or the teller.

Obviously there is something wonderful about hearing stories of how God grabbed someone's heart or made someone whole, but there is also this strange and wonderful dynamic that takes place in the heart of the teller, even as the story is being told. It is as if somehow the story is continuing to move and to grow in his heart and soul even as he shares what he has seen or heard. Do you know what I'm talking about? It's those times when you are in the middle of telling some incredible story of God's Spirit and God's work and you actually begin to hear what you are saying and are totally captured by it. It is almost as if you don't completely realize what is going on until you begin to tell the story. And, as you open your mouth, it is almost as if the story begins to tell itself and is just using your mouth as its vehicle.

After all, it is not your story, or mine, or even theirs for that matter. The story is God's and something about its quality tells us that. Somehow if the story was only about me or you, it wouldn't carry the same weight, it wouldn't have the same impact. It would fall lifeless to the ground and die. So many of my stories have suffered that fate through the years, simply because I didn't yet understand that the story wasn't about me, but about God. Stories about him have life, they live on and produce fruit long after their telling. And it is a beautiful thing.

—Jim Branch, January, 2012

I love the way Luke begins his gospel. It reminds me that with God there is always a *narrative* being *compiled*, both within me and around me. It is something that I must pay careful attention to, especially during this season, or else I can easily miss it altogether. What exactly is the story God is writing within me these days? What is he doing deep in my heart and soul? How is he drawing me to deeper and deeper places with himself? How is he trying to disrupt or disturb me in order to make me more fully his own? What is he inviting me to? What is he asking of me? How is he being born anew within and around me? Am I living his story for me in every way possible? Or am I somehow resisting, refusing, ignoring, or denying it?

Because there are other narratives within me that compete with his—ones that make the story I end up living each day much darker, much uglier, much less heroic. They are *false narratives* that go deep into my soul; planted there long ago by the arrows that have pierced my heart along the way, as well as what I've interpreted those arrows to mean as far as my value, worth, and identity are concerned. They are the tool of the enemy to keep me living in a bad, dark, hopeless story, rather than the good, beautiful, heroic one that God so deeply longs for *me to live in*. As well as the story he so desperately wants *to live in me*.

So I guess the truth of the matter is that every day I have to choose which story I'm going to be about, which story I am going to live. Am I going to be like Luke and be about *compiling a narrative* of all that God is doing in and through me? Or am I going to live a story that is much less than the story He has imagined for and with me? Doesn't sound like much of a choice, does it? —*Watch and Wait* by Jim Branch

Of the six million species on the planet, only man makes language. Words. What's more — in evidence of the Divine — we string these symbols together and then write them down, where they take on a life of their own and breathe outside of us. Story is the bandage of the broken. Sutures of the shattered. The tapestry upon which we write our lives. Upon which we lay the bodies of the dying and the about-to-come-to-life. And if it's honest, true, hiding nothing, revealing all, then it is a raging river and those who ride it find they have something to give — that they are not yet empty.

Critics cry foul, claiming the tongue is a bloody butcher that blasphemes, slices, slanders, and damns — leaving scars, carnage, the broken the beaten. Admittedly, story is a double-edged scimitar, but the fault lies not in the word but in the hand that wields the pen. Not all stories spew, cower, and retreat. Some storm the castle. Rush in. Stand between. Wrap their arms around. Spill secrets. Share their shame. Return. Stories birth our dreams and feed the one thing that never dies. — *Unwritten* by Charles Martin

The rabbis guide their people with stories; ministers usually guide with ideas and theories. We need to become storytellers again, and so to multiply our ministry by calling around us the great witnesses who in different ways offer guidance to doubting hearts.

One of the remarkable qualities of the story is that it creates space. We can dwell in a story, walk around, find our own place. The story confronts but does not oppress; the story inspires but does not manipulate. The story invites us to an encounter, a dialog, a mutual sharing.

A story that guides is a story that opens a door and offers space in which to search and boundaries to help us find what we seek, but it does not tell us what to do or how to do it. The story brings us into touch with the vision and so guides us. Wiesel writes, "God made man because he loves stories." As long as we have stories to tell to each other there is hope. — *The Living Reminder* by Henri J. M. Nouwen

"You're writing another book about yourself?" Jordan asked. He was sitting at the counter in the kitchen eating a bowl of cereal. He had his laptop open and was choosing the starting lineup for his college fantasy basketball team. He'd been playing the game for a year and finally had a division one team. He said he was going to start his best defense, because defense wins championships.

"I'm not writing a book. I'm not talking about a book. I'm talking about me. I don't think I'm telling a good story."

"I think you tell good stories. Lots of people think so."

"I tell good stories in books. I don't live good stories."

Jordan poured more milk in his cereal. He was looking at me while pouring the milk. He was squinting his eyes a little and furrowing his brow. He stopped pouring the milk. He kept looking at me for ten seconds or more, like he was studying me.

"You're right," he finally said. "You aren't living a good story."

"That's what I was saying."

"I see," he said.
"What do I do about that?"
"You're a writer. You know what to do."
"No, I don't."
Jordan looked at me with his furrowed brow again. "You put something on the page," he said. "Your life is a blank page. You write on it."
—*A Million Miles in a Thousand Years* by Donald Miller

When we submit our lives to what we read in Scripture, we find that we are not being led to see God in our stories but our stories in God's. God is the larger context and plot in which our stories find themselves.

—Eugene Peterson

The first time he saw her was across a bonfire at a friend's house after a football game. She was there with a friend of a friend and caught his eye right off the bat. As a matter of fact, he just couldn't take his eyes off of her. It wasn't just because she was beautiful—which she absolutely was—but it was so much more than that. It was more of a quality about her: the way she smiled, the way she laughed, the way she carried herself. She had *it*, whatever *it* was. And whatever *it* was, *it* came from somewhere deep within her, almost as if there was an inner well bubbling up from her very heart and soul. He could see *it* in everything she did: in the way she listened, in the way she talked, and in the way she cared for people—treating them as if they were the only person in the world at that moment. There was just something about her, a depth and beauty that he had never seen in anyone else.

It took him about thirty minutes, but he finally worked up the nerve to go over and talk to her. And when he did, it was like talking to someone he had known all of his life, the conversation was so easy and comfortable — so good. He got her number and asked if he could give her a call sometime, and when she said *yes* something leapt deep within him. Well one call led to another, and another, and before he knew it he had asked her out. Their first date was the most amazing he'd ever had, not so much because of what they did, but because of the way she seemed to bring out the very best in him. It was almost like he had come home, to a home he had never known before but had been searching for his entire life. In fact the only word that could come close to describing the way she made him feel was *full*, she just brought him to life inside.

Well one date turned into three, and then to five, and before he knew it they had been dating for six months. It was different than any relationship he'd ever had. They talked for hours at a time about things that really mattered; no games, no pretense, no drama. And the most amazing thing was that they were also able to just be together without feeling the need to talk at all, comfortable with just being together in silence. He had never felt that way with anyone before — much less a girl. This relationship was just different, in the very best sense of the word.

One night, as winter was turning to spring, they were lying on the trampoline in her back yard looking up at the stars and enjoying just being together, when she asked him a question: "What do you think it means to be in love?" The question surprised him with its innocence and honesty. It wasn't something that he had not wondered about himself from time to time, especially since he had met her. For a moment he was silent, not really knowing what to say, until he uttered the classic male response, "Uh, I don't know." He then quickly recovered by adding, "What does it mean to you?" She thought for a moment, looking far off into the stars, and said, "I think it means that you are willing to give that person, and that person alone, all of you, every bit of yourself, your whole heart—no holding back. When I tell someone I love them it means that I am committing my entire heart, soul, and life to them completely—forever. And if they want to be with me, if they are really in love with me, I expect them to do the same."

As she spoke, he knew at his core that what she was saying was right and true, it was the kind of love he most deeply longed for and dreamt about, but something about it also scared him to death. "Am I really capable of loving someone like that? Do I really have what it takes?" he wondered. And even if he did, was he willing to enter into that type of relationship with someone—forever? Something in him desperately wanted to believe that he could, and something in him wanted to run away.

Then she turned to him with one of the purest and most innocent looks he had ever seen, so pure and innocent that he knew he was not worthy of it. And as her eyes looked deeply into his, she uttered the words, *"I love you."* He was in complete shock. She immediately put her hands to his lips and said, "Don't say a word. I don't want you to say anything right now. I just wanted you to know how I feel."

A few minutes later he was in his car on the way home, trying to process all that had just happened. It was so confusing, so scary. He didn't know what to say or what to do, so he made his typical decision, he did nothing. He didn't text. He didn't call. He didn't go to see her. He was paralyzed. Before he knew it a week had gone by and he still hadn't communicated with her at all. He just didn't know what to say, so he said nothing.

It had now been two weeks since the conversation on the trampoline, and he was out with some friends at an outdoor concert downtown, when he ran into an old girlfriend. In fact, she was the girl he had been dating before he went to that fateful bonfire. This old girlfriend was nothing particularly special. He didn't love her. He never had, but she was easy—comfortable to be around and never really demanding anything of him. From the day he broke up with her she had wanted to get back together, always promising him that if he would start seeing her again she would not require or expect anything of him. In fact, she would allow him to go wherever he wanted and do whatever he desired, even go out with other girls. She just wanted to get back together and told him so again on this night. So now he had a decision to make: to go with the one that brought him to life like no one ever had but demanded all of his love in return, or go with the one that he didn't love, but was easy to date and demanded nothing from him.

A couple more weeks went by and he was sitting at the mall thinking about all that had happened over the past eight months, when suddenly he got a text from *her*. It said: *"i still luv u. i can forgive and forget the past, but nothing has changed. i still want all of you, or nothing at all.* As soon as he finished reading the text he looked up and there she was, standing right in front of him. She looked deeply into his eyes and asked him THE question, "Do you love me?"

I would love to tell you what he said to her, but I can't. Only you can do that, because he is *you*. You see, this story is a parable, and that's what a parable is all about. It is meant to draw you into a larger story, the story of you and God. The story of a God who is wildly and passionately in love with you, a God that made you for relationship with himself and stands before you this day with that very same question: *"Do you truly love me?"* A God who says, *"You are my Beloved, am I yours?"* His love is totally free, but loving him back requires all of your heart and soul. What is your answer?
—*Pieces II* by Jim Branch

I grew up in Fort Worth, Texas and attended Arlington Heights High School in the late 60's, when the Beatles, the Doors, the Rolling Stones, and anybody else with a drum and an electric guitar produced a lot of powerful music. I heard that music throbbing out of car windows from 8-tracks in the parking lot and reverberating from oversized speakers at school dances. But that was not the music that liberated me.

The music that liberated me was softer, quieter. I heard it one day on campus at the end of my junior year. On that spring day in 1968, Christ showed up.

He showed up in a pair of Converse All-Stars, gym shorts, T-shirt, a handshake, and a smile. Several of us on the basketball team were playing a pickup game in the gym, and this young seminary student from Southwestern Baptist Theological Seminary worked his way into the game. Over the weeks ahead he kept showing up. At lunch. After school. In the parking lot. And before long, he worked his way into our lives.

His name was Scott Manley.

He talked several of us into going to summer camp, and it was, as he promised, the best week of our lives. The following year I got more involved with Young Life, attending weekly club meetings, a Bible study called Campaigners, and the next summer I went to a Young Life college prep camp at Star Ranch.

There, during a 20-minute quiet time after the last message, I gave what little I knew of my life to what little I knew of Christ's. It wasn't much, I told Him, but what I had was His, if He wanted it, or if in some way He could use it.

In the fall I attended Texas Christian University, where I got involved with Young Life leadership. By my sophomore year I was leading a Young Life club and was involved in weekly leadership meetings. From that leadership group came many of my dear friends. And one who is my dearest.

Her name is Judy.

She had been introduced to Christ by a classmate who had become a Christian through her Young Life leader, who had become a Christian through my Young Life leader, Scott Manley.

I don't recall any of the talks Scott gave at club meetings or in Campaigners. I don't remember the lyrics, but the music, the music I'll never forget.

The music streamed into my ears, saying, *I love you. I care about you. You matter. Your pain matters. Your struggles matter. Your life is sacred and dear to God. He has a future for you, plans and hopes and dreams for you, and blessings for you.*

My wife had never met Scott, although she had heard the stories from several of us who had been touched by him. She had thought a long time about what she would say if and when she ever did meet him. She had rehearsed it in her mind over and over again.

Two years ago, she finally met him. We were attending a conference with some friends and three of our four children. He had been introduced by the speaker, who had come to Christ in high school through Scott. After the meeting, Judy gathered the children and searched him out in the crowd.

When she found him, she said: "You don't know me, but I'm Judy Gire, Ken Gire's wife." They hugged, then she continued. "There's something I've been wanting to tell you for a long time." Years of waiting emotion welled inside her. "Scott, you were instrumental in leading my husband to Christ. You led my Young Life leader to Christ. My Young Life leader led a friend of mine to Christ. And this friend told me about Christ. You are my spiritual heritage. These are three of our four children. This is Kelly, and she knows Jesus. This is Rachel, and she knows Jesus. This is Stephen, and he knows Jesus. And Gretchen, our oldest, she isn't here, but she knows Jesus, too. All of us know Jesus because of Scott Manley. Thank you so much. Thank you."

Scott threw his arms around her, and together and for a long time they wept. — *The Reflective Life* by Ken Gire

Following and Being Led

I. Opening Prayer

Dear Lord Jesus,

I am still so divided. I truly want to follow you, but I also want to follow my own desires and lend an ear to the voices that speak about prestige, success, popularity, pleasure, power, and influence. Help me to become deaf to those voices and more attentive to your voice, which calls me to choose the narrow road to life. — *The Road to Daybreak* by Henri J.M. Nouwen

II. Psalm 77

III. Daily Scripture Readings

Monday	John 21:18-25
Tuesday	John 1:35-51
Wednesday	Luke 9:57-62
Thursday	Luke 18:18-30
Friday	Luke 14:25-34
Saturday	Mark 8:31-38
Sunday	Mark 1:14-20

IV. Readings for Reflection

V. Reflection and Listening: silent and written

VI. Prayer: for the church, for others, for myself

VII. Song   *He Leadeth Me*

VIII. Closing Prayer

Drive far from us all wrong desires and incline our hearts to keep Your ways: Grant that having cheerfully done Your will this day, we may, when night comes rejoice and give you thanks; through Jesus Christ our Lord. Amen. — The Book of Common Worship

Readings for Reflection-

Feed my sheep. Stretch out your hands. Follow me. That is what our lives are to be about: minister, surrender, and follow. That's it. It's not very complicated. But obviously we do complicate it. Maybe that's because our regular default mode is not to minister, surrender, and follow, but to feed ourselves, desperately try to control our world, and set our own agenda. We are not much for that whole *led to where you do not want to go* thing. But I guess that's the reason we have to be reminded that this life is not about us, but about him. It was a lesson the disciples had to learn over and over. And it was the simple truth that Jesus was trying to teach Simon Peter as they walked on the beach, *"You only truly love me when this is what your life looks like. Otherwise, you are just loving yourself in a clever disguise."*

—Jim Branch, November, 2015

He leads us step by step, from event to event. Only afterwards, as we look back over the way we have come and reconsider certain important moments in our lives in the light of all that has followed them, or when we survey the whole progress of our lives, do we experience the feeling of having been led without knowing it, the feeling that God has mysteriously guided us.
—*Reflections* by Paul Tournier

I am growing in the awareness that God wants my whole life, not just part of it. It is not enough to give just so much time and attention to God and keep the rest for myself. It is not enough to pray often and deeply and then move from there to my own projects.

As I try to understand why I am still so restless, anxious, and tense, it occurs to me that I have not yet given everything to God. I especially see this in my greediness for time. I am very concerned to have enough hours to develop my ideas, finish my projects, fulfill my desires. Thus, my life is in fact divided into two parts, a part for God and a part for myself. Thus divided, my life cannot be peaceful.

To return to God means to return to God with all that I am and all that I have. I cannot return to God with just half of my being. As I reflected this morning again on the story of the prodigal son and tried to experience myself in the embrace of the father, I suddenly felt a certain resistance to being embraced so fully and totally. I experienced not only a desire to be embraced, but also a fear of losing my independence. I realized that God's love is a jealous love. God wants not just a part of me, but all of me. Only when I surrender myself completely to God's parental love can I expect to be free from endless distractions, ready to hear the voice of love, and able to recognize my own unique call.

It's going to be a very long road. Every time I pray I feel the struggle. It is the struggle of letting God be the God of my whole being. It is the struggle to trust that true freedom lies hidden in total surrender to God's love. — *The Road to Daybreak* by Henri J. M. Nouwen

The call to follow implies that there is only one way of believing in Jesus, and that is by leaving all and going with the incarnate Son of God. The first step places the disciple in the situation where faith is possible. If he refuses to follow and stays behind, he does not learn how to believe.

So long as Levi sits at the receipt of custom, and Peter at his nets, they both pursue their trade honestly and dutifully, and they might both enjoy religious experiences, old and new. But if they want to believe in God, the only way is to follow His incarnate Son. Until that day, everything had been different. They could remain in obscurity, pursuing their work as the quiet in the land, observing the Law and waiting for the coming Messiah. But now He has come, and His call goes forth. Faith can no longer mean sitting still and waiting — they must rise and follow Him. The call frees them from all earthly ties, and binds them to Jesus Christ alone.

The road to faith passes through obedience to the call of Jesus. Unless a definite step is demanded, the call vanishes into thin air. — *Selections from the Writings of Dietrich Bonhoeffer*

The Gospel today reveals that Jesus not only had good, faithful friends willing to follow him wherever he went and fierce enemies who couldn't wait to get rid of him, but also many sympathizers who were attracted, but afraid at the same time.

The rich young man loved Jesus but couldn't give up his wealth to follow him. Nicodemus admired Jesus but was afraid to lose the respect of his own colleagues. I am becoming more and more aware of the importance of looking at these fearful sympathizers because that is the group I find myself mostly gravitating toward.

I love Jesus but want to hold on to my own friends even when they do not lead me closer to Jesus. I love Jesus but want to hold on to my own independence even when that independence brings me no real freedom. I love Jesus but do not want to lose the respect of my professional colleagues, even though I know that their respect does not make me grow spiritually. I love Jesus but do not want to give up my writing plans, travel plans, speaking plans, even when these plans are often more to my glory than to the glory of God.

So I am like Nicodemus, who came by night, said safe things about Jesus to his colleagues, and expressed his guilt by bringing to the grave more myrrh and aloes than needed or desires.

. . .Nicodemus deserves all my attention. Can I stay a Pharisee and follow Jesus too? Doesn't that condemn me to bringing costly spices to the grave when it is too late? — *The Road to Daybreak* by Henri J.M. Nouwen

Jesus says (John 21:18) that maturity means a growing willingness to be led — even to places we might not eagerly choose. — *Turn My Mourning Into Dancing* by Henri J. M. Nouwen

If we had strength and faith enough to trust ourselves entirely to God; and follow Him simply wherever he should lead us, we should have no need of any great effort of mind to reach perfection.

— Francois Fenelon

Meister Eckhart wrote: "There are plenty to follow our Lord half-way, but not the other half. They will give up possessions, friends, and honors, but it touches them too closely to disown themselves." It is just this astonishing life which is willing to follow Him the other half, sincerely to disown itself, this life which intends *complete* obedience, without *any* reservations, that I would propose to you in all humility, in all boldness, in all seriousness. I mean this literally, utterly, completely, and I mean it for you and for me — commit your lives in unreserved obedience to Him. — *A Testament of Devotion* by Thomas R. Kelly

To fall in love with God is the greatest romance; to seek Him the greatest adventure; to find him, the greatest human achievement.
— Saint Augustine

Lord I so want to make all of me ready and attentive and available to you. Please help me to clarify and purify my intentions. I have so many contradictory desires. I get preoccupied with things that don't really matter or last.

I know that if I give You my heart whatever I do will follow my new heart. In all that I am today...all that I try to do...all my encounters, reflections, even the frustrations and failings and especially in this time of prayer...in all of this...may I place my life in Your hands. Lord I am Yours...make of me what you will.

—Ignatius of Loyola

The Road goes ever on and on
Down from the door where it began.
Now far ahead the Road has gone,
And I must follow, if I can,
Pursuing it with eager feet,
Until it joins some larger way.

—J R. R. Tolkein

Lord God, there are so many times and so many places in my heart and life where I am still resistant to you and unwilling to let you have your way with me. I am unwilling to follow you to uncomfortable or unknown places. I am unwilling to set aside my own convenience and comfort to embrace your desire and direction for my life. I am unwilling to let go of the many things, patterns, and agendas I am constantly pursuing in order to fully pursue you. O Lord, forgive me for my unwillingness. Change my heart. Lord, have mercy! Amen. —*Journey to the Cross* by Jim Branch

Following Jesus is a wonderfully unique adventure; one that rarely ever looks the same for each of us. We can never be quite sure exactly where it will take us.

Therefore, we must stay close behind him. We must listen carefully and watch closely. For at times following him may mean going and at others it may mean staying. At times following him may mean speaking and at others it may mean remaining silent. At times following him may mean initiating and at others it may mean waiting. It is a wild and unpredictable journey. It is a journey that requires us to pay careful attention to his voice and his movement. So let us, each day, make time and space to be with him. Otherwise we might totally miss the adventure he has marked out for us.

—Jim Branch, May, 2016

The Breath of God

I. Opening Prayer

O Loving God, who breathed me into being, breathe your Divine Breath in me again this day — that I might be filled with your life and guided by the winds of your Spirit. For the sake of your Son. Amen.

II. Psalm 104

III. Daily Scripture Readings

Monday	Romans 8:12-17
Tuesday	John 20:19-23
Wednesday	Ezekiel 37:1-14
Thursday	John 3:1-21
Friday	John 14:15-21
Saturday	Acts 2:1-13
Sunday	1 Kings 19:9-13

IV. Readings for Reflection

V. Reflection and Listening: silent and written

VI. Prayer: for the church, for others, for myself

VII. Song   *Breathe on Me, Breath of God*

VIII. Closing Prayer

Father, you alone know what lies before me this day, grant that in every hour of it I may stay close to you. Let me today embark on no undertaking that is not in line with your will for my life, nor shrink from any sacrifice which your will may demand. Suggest, direct, control every movement of my mind; for my Lord Christ's sake. Amen. — *A Diary of Private Prayer* by John Baillie

Readings for Reflection-

I love the fact that one of the Spirit's main jobs is to remind us that we are sons and daughters of God. That is no easy task, especially given our tendency to forget the truth and begin to think that our identities can be achieved by what we do, or by how we look, or by what we have. In our culture it is such an easy trap to fall into. So it is good to know that God has placed his Spirit within us for the purpose of reminding us of both who we are and what makes us valuable. I don't know about you, but that gives life and breath to my soul.

—Jim Branch, March, 2016

Even to the last visible moment and beyond, Jesus continues to feed the soon-to-be shepherds. He feeds them with renewal when he comes to the disciples behind their locked doors that Easter night and breathes on them the Holy Spirit. The Hebrew word *ruach* means "spirit" as well as "breath" and ""wind." With this breathing of the Spirit, Jesus renews and empowers them to fulfill the great mandate to love and lift the burdens from others (John 20:19-23). — *Feed My Shepherds* by Flora Slosson Wuellner

We preach, yes, but that does not define us. We visit hospitals, teach classes, counsel, write books, lead retreats, but these activities do not define us. We work among the poor and champion social justice, but these acts in themselves are not our ultimate definition or identity. These acts are among our manifold tasks, but they do not in themselves become the core of our identity. What deeper roots underlie these activities? Who are we?

It is an exciting adventure to reread the scriptures, to reflect on Jesus' relationship with his disciples —

156

especially within the Resurrection narratives — with this one question in mind: Who are we? In response, one major image and phrase kept surfacing for me: *We are the breathed upon.*

> Jesus said to them again, "Peace be with you. As the Father has sent me, so I send you." When he had said this, he breathed on them and said to them, "Receive the Holy Spirit." (John 20:21-22)

Recently I saw the movie version of C. S. Lewis's *The Silver Chair*, the fourth book in The Chronicles of Narnia series. One of the most powerful and symbolic scenes occurs when Aslan the lion (representing Christ) sends the two children Jill and Eustace to Narnia to find and release the captive prince of that country. Aslan blows them there with his gentle, powerful breath. One at a time, they are held in the air and slowly blown over oceans, mountains, chasms, and forests — sustained only by his breath. To me, this scene portrayed a marvelous image of ministry and of all Christian leadership. We too are the breathed upon; we are sent forth and sustained by the breath of that Spirit. — *Feed My Shepherds* by Flora Slosson Wuellner

I feel the winds of God today; today my sail I lift,
Tho' heavy oft with drenching spray,
　　　　　and torn with many a rift...
It is the wind of God that dries my vain, regretful tears,
Until with braver thoughts shall rise the purer,
　　　　　brighter years...
Great Pilot of the onward way, Thou wilt not let me drift;
I feel the winds of God today, today my sail I lift.
— A hymn by Jessie Adams, 1863

"Can a person really start over again from the beginning?" Nicodemus asks. "I'm not sure you realize what that would entail — trying to wipe the slate clean and start all over from scratch. You may as well expect to climb back into your mother's womb. How can these things be?" The Pharisee looks at the younger man, so earnest and confident, and shakes his head. "Take an old man like me. I've spent a lifetime learning, studying, working to get where I am. Surely you're not suggesting I'd be better off scrapping all our heritage and starting all over again?"

"It depends if you want to live in God's kingdom," the young rabbi reports, undaunted by the older man's years and experience. "That's the essential question. Scholarship doesn't get you an entrance ticket. And the only reward for following the rules is a reputation for respectability. If that's enough for you, then fine. But if you want to live with God — in his kingdom — then you have to undergo a radical restructuring, as drastic as being formed again in your mother's womb. But first you have to give up the old life. That's what the ritual water is for — to wash away the old you. . . . Just as your body grows gradually — and without your direction — inside your mother's womb, your spirit must take shape within God's spirit. When you are born into that kingdom, then you're living God's own life, breathing God's own breath. It becomes your very heartbeat."

Now Nicodemus sits back and frowns, shaking his head. God's own breath — what can this young fellow possibly know about the Spirit of the Eternal One? God's life isn't like human life. Far from it. The kingdom of the Eternal will arrive on this earth when people learn to do their duty, not when rash enthusiasts try to turn the system topsy-turvy. Wait till this youngster has lived in this troubled world a little longer. He'll find out what life is really like — a long chain, each link forged by hard work and difficult compromise.

What would become of God's people if it weren't for men like himself who would work to make the weight of the chain bearable?

The young rabbi, as if discerning Nicodemus's objections, holds up a hand. "Don't be put off by my talk about being born a second time. I know it sounds wild — scary even. Especially if you've dedicated your life to judicious management, diplomatic mediation. But life comes from God's spirit, and that's outside our control. Living in God's kingdom means getting blown about by his spirit. You never know what direction the wind will come from next. It's totally unpredictable. Its power comes from something we can't even see. An invisible force fuels the new life I'm talking about. You can't hope to corner it or fence it in. You simply surrender to it. — *Looking For Jesus* by Virginia Stem Owens

When ancient man confronted the mystery of death, which is also the mystery of life — when he looked at the body of a dead man and compared it with himself as a living man and wondered at what terrible change had come over it — one of the first things that struck him apparently was that whereas he himself, the living man, breathed, the dead man did not breathe. There was no movement in his chest. A feather held to his lips remained unstirred. So to be dead meant to have no breath, and to be alive — to have the power to rise up and run and shout in the world — meant to have breath. And the conclusion, of course, was that breath was not just the little wisps of air that men breathe in and out, but that it is the very animating power of life itself. Breath is the livingness of those who are alive. This is why in so many languages the word for breath comes to mean not only the air that fills the lungs but the Mystery and power of life itself that fills a living man. Such is the

Latin word *spiritus*, from which our word "spirit" comes. — *The Magnificent Defeat* by Frederick Buechner

At this point you may be wondering, what about *God's* role in spiritual growth? After all, the Bible speaks of transformation as the work of God. It's always a miracle when it happens. To speak of spiritual growth only as a product of training could make it sound like something *we* can engineer. Anytime a frog is turned into a prince — or even just a gentler, kinder frog — there is always something mysterious and awesome at work. In spiritual growth that "something mysterious" is the work of the Spirit. So another analogy from scripture is helpful. "The wind blows where it chooses," Jesus said, "and you hear the sound of it, but you do not know where it comes from or where it goes. So it is with everyone who is born of the Spirit."

Consider the difference between piloting a motorboat or a sailboat. We can run a motorboat all by ourselves. We can fill the tank and start the engine. We are in control. But a sailboat is a different story. We can hoist the sails and steer the rudder, but we are utterly dependent upon the wind. The wind does the work. If the wind doesn't blow — and sometimes it doesn't — we sit still in the water no matter how frantic we act. Our task is to do whatever enables us to catch the wind.

Spiritual transformation is that way. We may be aggressively pursuing it, but we cannot turn it on and off. We can open ourselves to transformation through certain practices, but we cannot engineer it. We can take no credit for it.

It is profitable to see this. This truth saves us from pride and misdirected effort. Fist-clenching, teeth-gritting exertion is usually not productive. Indeed, feeling a constant sense of strain or burden probably indicates that we are off course. Jesus offered his yoke — his way of life — to tired people because he said his way of life involved ease and lightness and "rest for your souls." This theme is echoed by many of his followers. Frank Laubach writes, "The sense of being led by an unseen hand which takes mine...grows upon me daily. I do not need to strain at all to find opportunity...strain does not seem to do good."

Another analogy from sailing concerns the fact that wise sailors know that their main task is being able to "read" the wind – to practice discernment. An experienced sailor can simply look at the lake and tell where the wind is blowing strongest, or look at the sky and give a weather forecast. A wise sailor knows when to raise and lower which sails to catch the wind most effectively.

Spiritual growth requires discernment. We must learn to respond to the fresh wind of the Spirit. Moses didn't ask or arrange for the burning bush. But once it was there, he had to make a choice: whether to turn aside and pay attention to the work of God.

God's responsibility is to provide the burning bush. Our responsibility is to turn aside. Often I forget this.

Sometime ago I bought a devotional book and set a goal of finishing it by the end of the year. Several times as I read, it was clear that something was happening in my heart; I felt I should stop and study a certain passage for a while. But such delays would have kept me from my goal of finishing the book. So I kept going.

I should have realized that getting through the book "on time" was not, as I thought, the way to demonstrate my devotion. The purpose was to put myself in a place where transformation could happen. If God should speak to me through one passage – if I am being convicted or healed or challenged – them my role is to stay there until the wind dies down. Then it's time to move on. I was motorboating instead of sailing. I failed to turn aside.

Take another example. A friend of mine was at a retreat center recently where a group of people were spending a day in the practice of silence. One of them, not watching where she was walking, bumped into my friend and nearly knocked her over. But because the woman was engaged in silence, she didn't say a word, not even a simple "Excuse me." Yet, the whole purpose of practicing silence is not to see how long we can go without speaking; the goal is to make space for Jesus in our lives so we learn to live like him. Living like him in part involves responding with grace and civility when we bump into people.

Our primary task is not to calculate how many verses of Scripture we read or how many minutes we spend in prayer. Our task is to use these activities to create opportunities for God to work. Then what happens is up to him. We just put up the sails: The wind blows where it chooses..." — *The Life You've Always Wanted* by John Ortberg

Holiness

I. Opening Prayer:
Gracious and loving God, you know the deep inner patterns of my life that keep me from being totally yours. You know the misformed structures of my being that hold me in bondage to something less than your high purpose for my life. You also know my reluctance to let you have your way with me in these areas. Hear the deeper cry of my heart for wholeness and by your grace enable me to open to your transforming presence in this time. Lord, have mercy. — *Invitation to a Journey* by M. Robert Mulholland Jr.

II. Psalm 99

III. Daily Scripture Readings

Monday	1 Peter 1:13-16
Tuesday	Isaiah 61:10-11
Wednesday	Colossians 1:19-23
Thursday	1 Thessalonians 4:1-8
Friday	Isaiah 6:1-8
Saturday	Hebrews 10:1-14; 12:14
Sunday	Revelation 4:1-11

IV. Readings for Reflection

V. Prayer: for the church, for others, for myself

VI. Reflection: silent and written

VII. Song   *Holy, Holy, Holy*

VIII. Closing Prayer
Thank you Lord, that you see me as holy because of the gift of your Son. Help me to celebrate the holiness

you have given me by being wholly yours this day. Amen.

Readings for Reflection-

Is *holy* something to *do* or something to *be*? It seems to me that how we answer this question will make a significant difference in how we end up living our lives. For if holiness is something to *do,* we will, I'm afraid, never arrive at our desired destination. We will live in constant frustration, depression, and despair. We just can't "do" *holy,* no matter how hard we try.

Holiness is something that must be given to us. Holiness is something *we are* because of what God has done for us in Christ Jesus. In fact, he has declared us holy. Therefore, all we have to *do* is *be* who we are, who God has declared us to be. If we are God's *chosen people, holy and dearly loved,* then all we have to *do* is live like it. I don't know about you, but that seems way more possible.

—Jim Branch, March, 2016

Holiness only appears to be abnormal. The truth is, holiness is normal, to be anything else is to be abnormal. Being a saint is simply being the person God made me to be. —*Servants, Misfits, and Martyrs* by James C. Howell

If we are called by God to holiness of life, and if holiness is beyond our natural power to achieve (which it certainly is) then it follows that God himself must give us the light, the strength, and the courage to fulfill the task he requires of us. He will certainly give us the grace we need. If we do not become saints it is because we do not avail ourselves of his gift. —*Life and Holiness* by Thomas Merton

So when God says, "You shall be holy, for I am holy," (1 Peter 1:16) he is not giving us an imperative. He is making us a promise. In Jesus Christ, we *shall* be holy. We do not become holy by trying to obey Jesus' teachings. Instead, we are made holy by allowing the Holy Spirit to draw us so close to Jesus that his love begins to flow through our veins, changing our hearts, renewing our minds, and making us holy in every aspect of life. — *Sacred Thirst* by M. Craig Barnes

So be open to the ministry of Jesus, and allow Him to strip self-love of every adornment, until it stands barren and exposed. Then you may renounce self and receive the robe whitened by the blood of the Lamb, which is the purity of Jesus. And happy is the soul that no longer possesses anything of its own, not even anything borrowed, and abandons itself to Jesus, desiring no glory but His. A soul, purified in this manner, is like a bride about to be married. How beautiful she is when she lays everything aside, and comes to the marriage alter bringing nothing but herself. And, oh, Holy Bride, how beautiful are you when you come to Jesus with nothing of your own. The Bridegroom will be more than pleased with you when he sees you clothed in His beauty. There will be no limit to His love for you, because you are clothed in His holiness. — *Let Go — The Spiritual Letters* by Francois Fenelon

We must hide our unholiness in the wounds of Christ as Moses hid himself in the cleft of the rock while the glory of God passed by. We must take refuge from God in God. Above all we must believe that God sees us perfect in His Son while He disciplines and chastens and purges us that we may be partakers of His holiness. — *The Knowledge of the Holy* by A. W. Tozer

For the Christian, therefore, holiness is the fruit of our association with Jesus. It seems to set us apart, not in the sense of being other-worldly, but rather in the sense of being grasped by the Kingdom vision that formed the center of Jesus' life and message. The call to holiness is a call to live in this world, but not of it—meaning that as we open ourselves to the relationship Jesus offers, we are more and more able to live from a perspective and a vision that transcends what we normally experience.
—*Invitation to Holiness* by James Fenhagen

In holiness and righteousness: these are characteristics of God's covenant people. The righteous are those who stand in right relationship with God, trusting him above every created thing (above parents, spouses, one's own abilities, money) and performing with joy the requirements that come with this particular covenant (loving one another as Jesus loved us). The holy, likewise, are those whose relationship with God separates them (even as God is separate) from the godless world. They neither serve the world nor take their identity from the world's standards, judgments, opinions, delights, behaviors. They are strangers here. But they are also, therefore, free and fearless! —*Preparing for Jesus* by Walter Wangerin Jr.

Holiness in human life is a reflection of the holiness of God and, therefore, has always been associated with the religious experience. Holiness is a special word that suggests not so much a particular quality of the divine, as the essence of the transcendent mystery which for the believer stands at the center of human existence. The word holiness carries with it connotations of the numinous, and therefore includes the experience of awe and wonder and power—all of which cannot be clearly defined. Holiness always implies something more— pointing to that mystery which can never be contained.

More than any other word in the history of the language, it speaks of the essence of religious experience.
—*Invitation to Holiness* by James Fenhagen

The way of holiness is a way of confidence and love. The true Christian lives "in the Spirit" and drinks from the hidden fountains of divine grace, without being obsessed with any special need for complicated and marginal practices. He is concerned above all with essentials — with frequent moments of simple prayer and faith; attention to the presence of God; loving submission to the divine will in all things, especially in his duties of state; and above all the love of his neighbor and brother in Christ. —*Life and Holiness* by Thomas Merton

The purpose of salvation is to make whole that which is broken. The Christian spiritual journey settles for nothing less than such wholeness. But genuine wholeness cannot occur apart from holiness. In *The Holiness of God* R. C. Sproul notes that the pattern of God's transforming encounters with humans is always the same. God appears; humans respond in fear because of their sin; God forgives our sins and heals us (holiness and wholeness); God then sends us out to serve him. This means that holiness and wholeness are the interrelated goals of the Christian spiritual journey. Holiness is the goal of the spiritual journey because God is holy and commands that we be holy (Leviticus 11:44).

Holiness involves taking on the life and character of a holy God by means of a restored relationship to him. This relationship heals our most fundamental disease — our separation from our Source, our Redeemer, the Great Lover of our soul. The relationship is therefore simultaneously the source of our holiness and of our wholeness.

Human beings were designed for intimate relationship with God and cannot find fulfillment of their true and deepest self apart from that relationship. Holiness does not involve the annihilation of our identity with a simple transplant of God's identity. Rather, it involves the transformation of our self, made possible by the work of God's Spirit within us. Holiness is becoming like the God with whom we live in intimate relationship. It is acquiring his Spirit and allowing spirit to be transformed by Spirit. It is finding and living our life in Christ, then discovering that Christ's life and Spirit are our life and spirit. This is the journey of Christian spiritual transformation. This is the process of becoming whole and holy. — *Sacred Companions* by David G. Benner

Holiness has been defined, at times, as meaning "set apart." No! Holiness means wholeness. Holy persons have achieved (through Christ) a certain integrity. In them there is consonance between who they are, as images of God, and the way they hold themselves. Always true to their inner reality, they need not be apart. They can be in the midst without fear. Where there is not love, they bring love. Where there is not innocence, they bring innocence. They are instruments of peace. — *Breaking Bread* by Basil Pennington

Naked

I. Opening Prayer

O Lord my God, how I long to recapture the purity and
joy of the Garden and be able to stand before you, and
others, naked and unashamed. That, indeed, is what I
was made for. But this side of heaven that is not my
reality. My reality is filled with fear and shame, hiding
and covering — terrified that I will be exposed, found
out, not enough. How I genuinely long for true
communion with you, for total vulnerability, and for
deep trust — to be fully known and fully loved. Have
mercy on me! Amen.

II. Psalm 30

III. Daily Scripture Readings

Monday	Genesis 2:18-25
Tuesday	Genesis 3:6-13
Wednesday	2 Corinthians 5:2-5
Thursday	Hebrews 4:13-16
Friday	Ezekiel 16:1-14
Saturday	Hosea 2:1-23
Sunday	Romans 13:8-14

IV. Readings for Reflection

V. Reflection and Listening: silent and written

VI. Prayer: for the church, for others, for myself

VII. Song   *Just As I Am*

VIII. Closing Prayer

Lord Jesus, give me the grace and the strength and the
courage to take off that which I use to cover myself, and
to clothe myself only and always in you alone. Amen.

Reading for Reflection-

Naked. How does that word make you feel? What is the first response that comes up from within you? Does it illicit feelings of terror? Does it cause your face to turn red with embarrassment? Does it create anxiety? Does it bring shame? Or does it bring about more positive feelings? Does it give you a true sense of freedom? Does it make you long for intimacy? Does it cause your soul to dance with delight?

I'll have to admit that my first response to the word is closer to terror than anything else. Even the mention of the word *naked* makes me want to run for cover, because at my fearful core being naked means being exposed and uncovered, which seems so unsafe. It means being seen for who and what I really am, not just who I project myself to be. And surely if anyone were ever to see the real me, completely naked, it would most certainly lead to rejection. Thus, the very idea of being naked leads to overwhelming amounts of fear and insecurity.

But there is another side to this story. Because somewhere deep within me (and within all of us, I believe) there is a longing for nakedness — a nakedness that we were created both in and for. It is the kind of nakedness mentioned in Genesis where we are told that the man and woman *were both naked and unashamed.* They were totally known and yet totally loved. What a beautiful picture of our deepest hopes and wildest dreams — total vulnerability and total acceptance. This is the kind of nakedness we were made for. This is the kind of nakedness that gives us a hint of relationship God longs for with each of us, as well as the type of relationship he longs for each of us to offer one another.

—Jim Branch, January, 2010

Lord, I am stripped bare of all things, as you alone can strip us bare, whose fearful care nothing escapes, nor your terrible love. — *A Diary of a Country Priest* by Georges Bernanos

I'm too alone in the world, yet not alone enough
to make each hour holy.
I'm too small in the world, yet not small enough
to be simply in your presence, like a thing —
just as it is.

I want to know my own will
and move with it.
And I want, in the hushed moments
when the nameless draws near,
to be among the wise ones —
or alone.

I want to mirror your immensity.
I want never to be too weak or too old
to bear the heavy, lurching image of you.

I want to unfold.
Let no place in me hold itself closed,
for where I am closed, I am false
I want to stay clear in your sight.

I would describe myself
like a landscape I've studied
at length, in detail;
like a word I'm coming to understand;
like a pitcher I pour from at mealtime;
like my mother's face;
like a ship that carried me
when the waters raged.
— *The Book of Hours* by Rainer Maria Rilke

To God obscenity is not uncovered flesh. It is exposed intention. Nakedness is just a state of heart. Was Adam any more unclothed when he discovered shame? Yes.
— *The Singer* by Calvin Miller

bare by Jim Branch

the covering is gone
shed its leaves
all that is left is what is
the true essence
of the thing itself
in all of its twistedness
and all of its beauty
like a tree in winter
this heart
laid bare

In the stripping of the dark night we encounter God in a deeper way than we may ever have allowed ourselves before...The outward elements of our life which used to bring a sense of fulfillment are often gone or drained of meaning. The techniques of prayer which used to be so meaningful are no longer so. We cannot control God's presence. In fact, our "self" has no material with which to work. As a result we feel as if the self has been broken.

In a deep sense, this is just what has happened. The old self cracks open, we discover not the annihilation we had feared but a deeper "I." This deeper "I" is not a possession that can be remade through all our efforts at self-improvement. This deepest self is a gift from God.
— "Dark Night," by Sandra Cronk

We must have a real living determination to reach holiness. "I will be a saint" means I will despoil myself of all that is not God; I will strip my heart of all created things; I will live in poverty and detachment; I will renounce my will, my inclinations, my whims and fancies, and make myself a willing slave to the will of God. —*A Gift for God* by Mother Teresa of Calcutta

It is jarring to learn that what He went through in His passion and death is meant for us too; that the invitation He extends is *Don't weep for me! Join me!* The life He has planned for Christians is a life much like He lived. He was not poor that we might be rich. He was not mocked that we might be honored. He was not laughed at so that we would be lauded. On the contrary, He revealed a picture meant to include you and me.

> *It makes me happy to be suffering*
> *for you now, and in my own body*
> *to make up all the hardships that*
> *still have to be undergone by Christ*
> *for the sake of His body, the Church.*
> Colossians 1:24 NJB)

By extinguishing the spirit that burns in the gospel, we scarcely feel the glow anymore. We have gotten so used to the ultimate Christian fact—Jesus naked, stripped, and crucified—that we no longer see it for what it actually is. We are to strip ourselves of earthly cares and worldly wisdom, all desire for human praise, greediness for any kind of comfort, spiritual consolations included. The gospel is a summons to be stripped of those fine pretenses by which we manage to paint a portrait of ourselves for the admiration of friends. —*The Furious Longing of God* by Brennan Manning

If there are a few contemplatives in our parishes it is because most are content to remain "conventional

Christians." Conventional Christians secretly assure themselves that if they attend to the prescribed externals, go regularly to church, and don't go off the deep end, they are pleasing to God (although in fact they are pleasing mostly to themselves). Nonetheless, we are called to "go off the deep end" by abandoning ourselves to the Lord's care and to risk everything by letting go of everything. We are invited (though never demanded) to hang over an *interior abyss* in dark trusting faith where our security blanket of control is stripped away and we stand naked and defenseless before our Creator. —*Why Not Be a Mystic?* by Frank X. Tuoti

real by Jim Branch

i thought i knew me
but the me i thought i knew
wasn't really me at all
just another clever disguise—an illusion
a person that really doesn't exist
a creation of my own deepest needs and fears

it was the person i thought i needed to be
in order to be valued
in order to be worth loving
but how does someone
who really does not exist
hold any value at all
except from this fickle and fleeting world

living a lie
to gain applause and approval
the false for the false
under the guise of true
why is it so hard to tell the difference?
to see and recognize what is real

174

and what is not real?

as long as the false is present
the true is hidden
it can't be lived
and what is the process of discovery?
how is the imposter unmasked?
how do i see the real face underneath?
the naked truth?

wear a mask long enough
and you forget you have it on
it becomes who you are
or you become who it is
until you realize
until you are awakened
come home to yourself

isn't that what this life is really about?
becoming
undressing
letting go of all you thought you knew
in order to discover the true
the real
the beautiful
waiting underneath.

But our moment of solitude is precisely a moment in which we want to be in the presence of our Lord with empty hands, naked, vulnerable, useless, without much to show, prove, or defend. That is how we learn to listen to God's small voice. — *Making All Things New* by Henri J. M. Nouwen

Grasping

I. Opening Prayer

Lord Jesus, forgive me when my bleeding and wounded heart causes me to grasp for life and relief from any and every source available. Instead, help me to reach only for you — that I might touch the fringe of your robe and find healing and wholeness for the brokenness of my heart and soul. In Your Name I pray. Amen.

II. Psalm 16

III. Daily Scripture Readings

Monday	Mark 5:24-34
Tuesday	Mark 10:17-31
Wednesday	Matthew 6:19-34
Thursday	Luke 12:13-21
Friday	Romans 7:14-25
Saturday	Isaiah 55:1-13
Sunday	Philippians 2:1-11

IV. Readings for Reflection

V. Reflection and Listening: silent and written

VI. Prayer: for the church, for others, for myself

VII. Song *Tender Mercy*

VIII. Closing Prayer

Lord God, give me open hands and not clenched fists as I walk with you and for you in the midst of this day — that I might be able to live with a true sense of freedom from the need to grasp desperately for love and value from those I come into contact with. For Jesus' sake. Amen.

Readings for Reflection-

grasping by Jim Branch

something is terribly wrong within her
a long slow bleeding of her heart and soul
has been her constant companion
for as long as she can remember
so many things
she has tried
to make the bleeding stop
or to make her feel better
for at least a moment
but the long line of solutions
have failed her
so here she stands
even worse off than she was before
desperately grasping
for wholeness
or healing
or even a glimmer of hope

maybe Jesus…
maybe He will…
be able
to stop the bleeding
of her weary heart
"if only I can get near enough
to reach and touch"

and when she finally
grasps for him
the bleeding stops
the wound is healed
the broken is made whole
relief streaks down
her tearstained cheeks

freedom
finally

he turns and looks
his eyes meet hers
she falls to her knees
in fear and confusion

"daughter"
He tenderly whispers
to the depths of her heart and soul
indescribable intimacy
in the middle of a crowded street

"go in peace"
with a gentle smile upon his lips
knowing
this is what she most deeply longs for

"be freed from your suffering"
and indeed she is
no more bleeding
no more grasping
only love

and in the midst of
her bleeding
and grasping
and healing
i am reminded
of my need
for the same
reminded
of the open wound
of my insecurity
of my grasping
for value and affection

when only One
offers the touch
that will bring wholeness
and freedom

so there is an invitation
for me
to a new life
of indescribable intimacy
and freedom
with the One
who calls me his "son"
with the One
that whispered me into being
and longs for
wholeness
and freedom
for me
if I will let go
of all of the ways
of my grasping heart
and just reach out
for the edge of his robe

pray that I have the courage
 to reach out
like the woman

We mostly spend our lives conjugating three verbs: to
Want, to Have, and to Do. Craving, clutching, and
fussing, on the material, political, social, emotional,
intellectual — even on the spiritual — plane, we are kept
in perpetual unrest: forgetting that none of these verbs
have any ultimate significance, except so far as they are
transcended by and included in, the fundamental verb,
to Be: and that Being, not wanting, having and doing, is

the essence of a spiritual life. — *The Spiritual Life* by Evelyn Underhill

Greed is often associated with a ravenous appetite that devours anything within reach—a noisy, uncouth vice. Yet it is more often known in the quietly insistent urge that nudges us from wanting to "needing," then to grasping what we now "need" so others cannot deprive us of it. Jesus addressed this grasping, clinging mind when he counseled that we cannot serve God and mammon, and Aramaic word denoting ill-gotten gain (Matthew 6:24).

"In your minds you must be the same as Jesus Christ: His state was divine, yet he did not cling to his equality with God..." (Phil.2:6, JB). The spiritual life is one in which we grow out of the grasping, clinging mind into the mind of Christ. The Christ-mind releases us from our compulsion to associate personal worth with what we have accumulated, taming what nineteenth-century professor Adolphe Gratry calls "the exuberant desire to rise by a borrowed power."

—John S. Mogabgab

Praying is no easy matter. It demands a relationship in which you allow someone other than yourself to enter into the very center of your being, to see there what you would rather leave in darkness, and to touch there what you would rather leave untouched. Why would you really want to do that? Perhaps you would let the other cross your inner threshold to see something or to touch something, but to allow the other into the place where your most intimate life is shaped—that is dangerous and calls for defense.

The resistance to praying is like the resistance of tightly clenched fists. The image shows a tension, a desire to cling tightly to yourself, a greediness which betrays fear. A story about an elderly woman brought to a psychiatric center exemplifies this attitude. She was wild, swinging at everything in sight, and scaring everyone so much that the doctor had to take everything away from her. But there was one small coin which she gripped in her fist and would not give up. In fact, it took two people to pry open that squeezed hand. It was as though she would lose her very self along with the coin. If they deprived her of that last possession, she would have nothing more, and be nothing more. That was her fear.

When you are invited to pray you are asked to open your tightly clenched fists and give up your last coin. But who wants to do that? A first prayer, therefore, is often a painful prayer, because you discover you don't want to let go. You hold fast to what is familiar, even if you aren't proud of it. — *With Open Hands* by Henri J. M. Nouwen

It is a long spiritual journey of trust, for behind each fist, another one is hiding, and sometimes the process seems endless. Much has happened in your life to make all those fists, and at any hour of the day or night you might find yourself clenching your fists again out of fear. — *With Open Hands* by Henri J. M. Nouwen

To pray means to open your hands before God. It means slowly relaxing the tension which squeezes your hands together and accepting your existence with an increasing readiness, not as a possession to defend, but as a gift to receive. Above all, therefore, prayer is a way of life which allows you to find a stillness in the midst of the world where you open your hands to God's promises, and find hope for yourself, your neighbor, and your world. In prayer, you encounter God not only in the small voice and the soft breeze, but also in the midst of the turmoil of the world, in the distress and joy of

your neighbor, and in the loneliness of your own heart.
—*With Open Hands* by Henri J. M. Nouwen

Cast aside everything that might extinguish this small flame which is beginning to burn within you, and surround yourself with everything which can feed and fan it into a strong flame. — *The Art of Prayer*

When at last I cling to you with all my being, for me there will be no more sorrow, no more toil. Then at last I shall be alive with true life, for my life will be wholly filled by you. — *Confessions* by St Augustine

No one had taught me that if a branch detaches itself from the vine and tries to be a vine itself, it will wither and die. No one had pointed out that if a shepherd is not fed as well as the sheep, that shepherd will begin to starve and may end up *devouring* the sheep. In our hunger, we feed on others in many covert as well as overt ways! Or perhaps a shepherd determined to "die to self" may allow the sheep to devour him or her! That too can happen in many grim ways. We have all seen (and sometimes experienced) ministries that have become a hemorrhage, a dying, rather than a fulfilling and fulfilled life. — *Feed My Shepherds* by Flora Slosson Wuellner

We befriend the world whenever we demand that others be what only God has promised to be: faithful and sure. All human relationships, even our most intimate alliances, are temporary and incomplete. When we demand that another person provide safety, certainty, and fulfillment of our deepest desires, we turn from God to an idol for the fulfillment of our needs.

When we turn from God, we inevitably demand of others the very things we miss in our relationship with God. If we don't know his deep care and protection, then we will insist another human being provide what we lack. — *The Healing Path* by Dan Allender

Prayer is the outgrowth of both silence and solitude. In silence we let go of our manipulative control. In solitude we face up to what we are in the depths of our being. Prayer then becomes the offering of who we are to God: the giving of that broken, unclean, grasping, manipulative self to God for the work of God's grace in our lives. — *Invitation to a Journey* by M. Robert Mulholland Jr.

Our urge to be set free from this isolation can become so strong that it bursts forth in violence. Then our need for an intimate relationship — for a friend, a lover, or an appreciative community — turns into a desperate grabbing for anyone who offers some immediate satisfaction, some release of tension, or some temporary feeling of at-oneness. Then our need for each other degenerates into a dangerous aggression that causes much harm and only intensifies our feelings of loneliness. — *Making All Things New* by Henri J. M. Nouwen

Letting Go

I. Opening Prayer

Take, Lord, and receive all that I am and have.
You've given it all to me; I give it all back to you. Do
with me as you want. Just give me your love and your
grace and that's enough.

—St. Ignatius

II. Psalm 130

III. Daily Scripture Readings

Monday	Colossians 3:1-17
Tuesday	Hebrews 12:1-3
Wednesday	Mark 8:31-38
Thursday	Romans 12:1-3
Friday	Philippians 3:1-14
Saturday	1 John 2:15-17
Sunday	Genesis 22:1-19

IV. Readings for Reflection

V. Reflection and Listening: silent and written

VI. Prayer: for the church, for others, for myself

VII. Song   *I Lift My Hands*

VIII. Closing Prayer

Lord God, be the delight of our hearts, even as we are
the delight of yours. And help us to leave behind all
thoughts, actions, and attitudes that do not reflect the
beauty of that delight. May everything else pale in
comparison with the passion we have to be truly yours.
In the name of Jesus. Amen.

Readings for Reflection-

In the end, there are only two ways to live. We can live with either clenched fists or with open hands. You can't have them both. Clenched fists are a refusal: a refusal to let go, a refusal to trust, a refusal to give up control. And unfortunately, in the spiritual life, clenched fists also keep you from being able to receive anything from God. Only empty hands can receive. Therefore, we must let go of whatever our hands are full of before we can ever expect to receive any of the fullness, or the life, that God wants to give us.

—Jim Branch, March, 2016

Seeking to live a spiritual life while staying in close contact with the world is no easy matter. If you think so, you are dangerously mistaken.

We live in a world, and we have to do business with the world. Because of their work, or position, some must even live as worldly men do, taking part in the luxuries of the world. Yet inwardly we are strangers to the world and enemies of its way of thinking and its false system of honor. For at this present time, we are living in exile from our true home — and so we must abide in two worlds, living like men and women, but thinking and acting like angels! If we would lead others, with spiritual wisdom and insight, we must live inwardly as men and women who see ourselves protected as in a mighty fortress.

Our first rampart is this: to understand that nothing this world offers is eternal or lasting, and nothing earthly can offer the hope or security of knowing life eternal. In fact, earthly things can transfix us, trap us, keep us from forsaking all in order to know God. If you come to see things this way, you will keep this world and all of its alluring offers from having any power over your spirit.

This is the manner by which we become *detached* from the things of this earth — whether people, or possessions, or honored positions. And this detachment is a great good, because all these things, great or lovely as they may seem, will come to an end. We need to let them go, and become *attached* to things eternal... namely Jesus.
— *The Way of Perfection* by Teresa of Avila

As long as I am plagued by doubts about my self-worth, I keep looking for gratification from people around me and yield quickly to any type of pain, mental or physical. But when I can slowly detach myself from this need for human affirmation and discover that it is in relationship with the Lord that I find my true self, an unconditional surrender to him becomes not only possible but even the only desire, and pain inflicted by people will not touch me in the center. When my "self" is anchored not in people but in God, I will have a much greater resistance against pain. — *The Genesee Diary* by Henri J. M. Nouwen

I worry too much. Autumn trees ask me not to worry. They, like Jesus, suggest trust rather than worry. So often in autumn I want to go lean my head against a tree and ask what it feels like to lose so much, to be so empty, so detached, to take off one's shoes that well, and then simply to stand and wait for God's refilling. It sounds so simple, so easy. It isn't easy. But it is possible.

I think I've met one person in my lifetime who was truly empty. I didn't ask her what it felt like, but I remember a quiet joy that seemed to permeate her spirit, and she looked free.

We autumn strugglers must try hard not to wear discouragement as a cloak if we can't wear enough emptiness to make us free. It takes a long time to get as far as even wanting to be empty.

Our hearts are hungering for the *Sacrament of Letting Go*. Once we discover that we already possess enough grace to let go, trust begins to form in the center of who we are. Then we can take off our shoes and stand empty and vulnerable, eager to receive God's next gift.

— *Seasons of Your Heart* by Macrina Wiederkehr

Moods are worth my attention. I am discovering during these first weeks in Genesee that I am subject to very different moods, often changing very quickly. Feelings of depressive fatigue, of low self-esteem, of boredom, feelings also of anger, irritation, and direct hostility, and feelings of gratitude, joy, and excitement — they can all be there, sometimes even during one day.

I have the feeling that these quickly changing moods show how attached I really am to the things given me: a friendly gesture, pleasant work, a word of praise, a good book, etc. Little things can quickly change sadness into joy, disgust into contentment, and anger into understanding or compassion.

Somewhere during these weeks I read that sadness is the result of attachment. Detached people are not the easy victims of good or bad events in their surroundings and can experience a certain sense of equilibrium. I have the feeling that this is an important realization for me. When my manual work does not interest me, I become bored, then quickly irritated and sometimes even angry, telling myself that I am wasting my time. When I read a book that fascinates me, I become so involved that time runs fast, people seem friendly, my stay here worthwhile, and everything one big happy event.

Of course both "moods" are manifestations of false attachments and show how far I am from a healthy form of "indifference."

Thinking about all of this, I guess my main problem still is that I have not really made prayer my priority. Still the only reason that I am here — I mean the only reason I should be here — is to learn to pray. But, in fact, much of what I am doing is motivated by many other concerns: getting back in shape, learning some skills, knowing more about birds and trees, getting to know interesting people — such as John Eudes — and picking up many ideas and experiences for future teaching. But if prayer were my only concern, all these other things could be received as free gifts. Now, however, I am obsessed by these desires which are false, not in themselves, but by their being in the wrong place in the hierarchy of values. That, I guess, is the cause of my moodiness. For the time being it seems so important to be at least aware of it. — *The Genesee Diary* by Henri J. M. Nouwen

Only prayer allows us to hear another voice, to respond to the larger possibilities, to find a way out of our need to order and control. Then the questions that seem to shape our identity will not matter so much: Who says good things about me? Who doesn't? Who is my friend? My enemy? How many like me? As we make God the center of our lives, our sense of who we are will depend less on what others think of or say about us. We will cease being prisoners of the interpersonal. — *Turn My Mourning Into Dancing* by Henri J.M. Nouwen

We have to keep letting go, and slowly and surely the great full life of God will invade us in every part, and men will take knowledge of us that we have been with Jesus. — *My Utmost for His Highest* by Oswald Chambers

Between

I. Opening Prayer
O Lord, our God, so much of this life is lived *in between*;
between the now and the not yet, between arriving and
departing, between birth and death and rebirth, between
growing up and growing old, between questions and
answers. Help us not to live only for some distant day
when the *in between* will be no more, but help us to step
into the mystery of that sacred space here and now —
knowing that it will be a place of genuine change and
true transformation.

II. Psalm 46

III. Daily Scripture Readings
Monday	Matthew 14:22-33
Tuesday	Psalm 73:1-28
Wednesday	Psalm 71:1-24
Thursday	Lamentations 3:19-33
Friday	2 Timothy 4:1-8
Saturday	Psalm 84:1-12
Sunday	Jeremiah 6:16

IV. Readings for Reflection

V. Reflection and Listening: silent and written

VI. Prayer: for the church, for others, for myself

VII. Song *Cleft of the Mountain*

VIII. Closing Prayer
Lord Jesus, Help me to trust you fully in the midst of
this life that seems so chaotic and unsure at times. Give
me, this day, a firm place to set my feet as I walk toward
you through this ever-changing world. Amen.

Reading for Reflection-

Recently I have found myself captured by a gospel passage that has come to life for me...once again. It is the coming of Jesus to the disciples on the sea (Matthew 14:22-33). It is a truly incredible story, one that has spoken to me often through the years in a multitude of ways. But there has been one particular aspect of this story that has been a wonderful source of reflection for me lately. It involves that sacred space that Jesus invites Simon Peter to step out into. It is the space *between*: between the boat and Jesus, between letting go and being taken hold of, between the old and familiar and the new and unknown, between control and agenda and dependence and detachment. It is a space that is both completely terrifying and unbelievably exciting. It is the space before your answer has come, or your problem has been solved. It is the space where you must trust the heart of God alone for your life. It is the space of genuine transformation.

—Jim Branch, October, 2005

Paul Tournier, in *A Place for You*, describes the experience of being in between—between the time we leave home and arrive at our destination; between the time we leave adolescence and arrive at adulthood; between the time we leave doubt and arrive at faith. It is like the time when a trapeze artist lets go of the bars and hangs in midair, ready to catch another support: it is a time of danger, of expectation, of uncertainty, of excitement, of extraordinary aliveness. —*A Long Obedience in the Same Direction* by Eugene H. Peterson

We keep praying that our illusions will fall away. God erodes them from many sides, hoping they will fall. But we often remain trapped in what we call normalcy, "the way things are." Life becomes problem-solving, fixing, explaining, and taking sides with winners and losers. It can be a pretty circular and even nonsensical existence.

Instead, we have to allow ourselves to be drawn into sacred space, into liminality. All transformation takes place there. We have to move out of "business as usual" and remain on the "threshold" (*limen*, in Latin) where we are betwixt and between. There, the old world is left behind, but we're not sure of the new one yet. That's a good space. Get there often and stay there as long as you can by whatever means possible. It's the realm where God can best get at us because we are out of the way. In sacred space the old world is able to fall apart, and the new world is able to be revealed. If we don't find liminal space in our lives, we start idolizing normalcy. We end up believing it's the only reality, and our lives shrivel. — *Everything Belongs* by Richard Rohr

Why didn't God just keep us, instead of sending us here to wander through all of this stuff we call our lives? Would God really run the risk of some of us not making it home again? What is the object of the exercise here, and what are our lives about? Selfish creature that I am, what am I supposed to be about while I am here?

"I don't know even now what it was that I was waiting to see," says a character in one of Eudora Welty's stories, "but in those days I was convinced that I saw it at almost every turn." I too have been looking, waiting all my life to see something I am not sure I will recognize, but know for certain is there. "You are traveling a new road with which you are very familiar," a friend once said to me at a critical juncture in my life.

I need to see why it is that we are here to see anything at all. I have caught only fleeting glimpses of it from time to time—as through a glass darkly, one might say— no matter how fiercely I watch. I hear a rustling behind me or a whisper on the wind, detect a smile or a gesture between friends or lovers or strangers, touch a stone or a blossom or the hand of my children — and it is there. I watch and listen with a fierceness reserved only for this search.

When I was younger, I worried a good deal about whether or not I was going to make it home to God. I was never quite convinced that those who interpreted the Story in the way that the trap-the-teacher man did were right, but I met enough of them to be more than a little afraid.

What I fear now is that I will somehow miss what it is that I am supposed to learn here, something important enough that the Dreamer dispatched me, and the rest of us, here to learn. What I fear now is that I will somehow miss the point of living here at all, living here between the dreaming and the coming true. — *Between the Dreaming and the Coming True* by Robert Benson

So here I stand, looking at the ground, smelling the faint fragrance of God. Never once did it occur to me that when I found God's trail again, it would ruin my life forever – for once you feel the breath of God on your skin, you can never turn back, you can never settle for what was, you can only move on recklessly, with abandon, your heart filled with fear, your ears ringing with the constant whisper, "Fear not."

Once you find where the trail is, you are faced with a sobering truth – in order to go on, you must let go of what brought you here. You cannot go on without turning your back on what brought you to this place. It is like swinging on a trapeze. Once you have gained the courage to swing, you never want to let go...and then, without warning (around age 50, for me), you look up and see another trapeze swinging towards you, perfectly timed to meet you, and you realize you are being asked to let go and grab onto the other trapeze.

You have to release your grip. You have to reach out. You have to experience the glorious terror of inbetween-ness as you disconnect from one and reach for the other.

This past year has been a time of letting go, one finger at a time, and these last few weeks have been a terrifying weightlessness, a wait-less-ness, a paralyzing stretch for the unknown. I haven't reached the other bar yet. I am somewhere in between, but I can tell you this: my heart is filled with an exhilaration, an anxious anticipation that just as I get to the other bar, I will not grasp it, but I will instead be grasped by the hand of Jesus.

I can hardly wait.

—Mike Yaconelli

Waiting is not a very popular attitude. Waiting is not something that people think about with great sympathy. In fact, most people consider waiting a waste of time. Perhaps this is because the culture in which we live is basically saying, "Get going! Do something! Show you are able to make a difference! Don't just sit there and wait!" For many people, waiting is an awful desert between where they are and where they want to go. And people do not like such a place. They want to get out of it by doing something. —*A Spirituality of Waiting* by Henri J. M. Nouwen

Waiting as we see it in people on the first pages of the Gospel, is waiting with a sense of promise. "Zechariah, your wife Elizabeth is to bear you a son." "Mary, Listen! You are to conceive and bear a son" (Luke 1:13, 31). People who wait have received a promise that allows them to wait. They have received something that is at work in them, like a seed that has started to grow. This is very important. We can only really wait if what we are waiting for has already begun for us. So waiting is never a movement from nothing to something. It is always a movement from something to something more.

Zechariah, Mary, and Elizabeth were living with a promise that nurtured them, that fed them, and that made them able to stay where they were. And in this way, the promise itself could grow in them and for them. — *A Spirituality of Waiting* by Henri J. M. Nouwen

This life, therefore, is not righteousness, but growth in righteousness, not health but healing, not being but becoming, not rest but exercise. We are not yet what we shall be, but we are growing toward it; the process is not finished but it is going on. This is not the end but it is the road; all does not yet gleam in glory but all is being purified.

— Martin Luther

Becoming

I. Opening Prayer

God of our creation and re-creation, you who are constantly at work to shape me in the wholeness of Christ, you know the hardness of the structures of my being that resist your shaping touch. You know the deep inner rigidities of my being that reject your changing grace. By your grace soften my hardness and rigidity; help me to become pliable in your hands. Even as I pray this, may there be a melting of my innate resistance to your transforming love. Amen. — *Invitation to a Journey* by M. Robert Mulholland Jr.

II. Psalm 37

III. Daily Scripture Readings

Monday	Romans 12:1-21
Tuesday	Galatians 5:16-26
Wednesday	2 Corinthians 3:1-18
Thursday	Isaiah 29:13-16
Friday	Jeremiah 18:1-6
Saturday	Matthew 5:1-16
Sunday	Ephesians 4:17-5:2

IV. Readings for Reflection

V. Reflection and Listening: silent and written

VI. Prayer: for the church, for others, for myself

VII. Song   *May the Mind of Christ, My Savior*

VIII. Closing Prayer

Father, forgive us when we think that life is more about what we are doing than about who we are becoming. Help us to remember that more than anything else you want our hearts. Allow us to give them to you fully, that we might receive yours in return; changing us more into the likeness your Son Jesus. In His name we pray. Amen.

Readings for Reflection-

becoming by Jim Branch

there is something
beginning to poke its head
through the soil
that has been becoming
all through the long cold winter
but is just now
finally ready to show itself
to burst into the fullness
of all that it was meant to be
now free from the comfort
and confines of the rich dark soil
the struggle to become has ended
it stretches out its arms
to touch the life-giving sunlight
dancing in the fullness
of the intent of its maker
finally free to be
all it was dreamt to be

The desire for transformation lies deep in every human heart. This is why people enter therapy, join health clubs, get into recovery groups, read self-help books, attend motivational seminars, and make New Year's resolutions. The possibility of transformation is the essence of hope. Psychologist Aaron Beck says that the single belief most toxic to a relationship is the belief that the other person cannot change.

This little word *morph* has a long history. It actually comes from one of the richest Greek words in the New Testament, and in a sense this little word is the foundation of this whole book. *Morphoo* means "the inward and real formation of the essential nature of a person." It was a term used to describe the formation and growth of an embryo in a mother's body.

Paul used this word in his letter to the Galatians: "...until Christ is formed in you." He agonized until Christ should be born in those people, until they should express his character and goodness in their whole being. Paul said they — like us — are in a kind of spiritual gestation process. We are pregnant with possibilities of spiritual growth and moral beauty so great that they cannot be adequately described as anything less than the formation of Christ in our very lives.

Paul used another form of this word when he told the Christians in Rome that God had predestined them to be "conformed to the image of his Son." This word, *summorphizo*, means to have the same form as another, to shape a thing into a durable likeness. Spiritual growth is a molding process: We are to be to Christ as an image is to the original.

Still another form of the word appears in Romans when Paul says we are not to be conformed to the world around us but "*transformed* by the renewing of your minds." This word is *metamorphoo*, from which comes the English word *metamorphosis*. A creeping caterpillar is transformed into a soaring butterfly — yet as the children of God we are to undergo a change that makes that one barely noticeable.

When morphing happens, I don't just *do* the things Jesus would have done; I find myself *wanting* to do them. They appeal to me. They make sense. I don't just go around trying to do right things; I *become* the right sort of person. — *The Life You've Always Wanted* by John Ortberg

Now is the time to strain — to pull at yourself until you assume the shape you are to become. God knows what that is.

—Philip LeVine

Dear Potter,
The lump of clay that I am
keeps crying for some form
day by day
I yearn for you to mold me.

This is a trust-song, Lord
I am in your hands like clay
I am ready to be transformed:

I expect
    to be molded
I expect
    to be beautiful
I expect
    to be loved.

And if by chance
someone should drop me
as your apprentices sometimes do,

I expect
    to be hurt.

I'm just trying to say
I have surrendered
    to your dream for me
I am in your hands
    like clay.
— *Seasons of Your Heart* by Macrina Wiederkehr

The journey between the dreaming and the coming true is a journey made on holy ground. It is a journey made through silence and longing where, if we will listen, we can hear the whisper of the Dreamer echoing deep within us, calling us to become what the Dreamer sees when our names were first whispered: saints who believe in and pay attention for and recognize the Voice; saints who live our lives in joy and confidence and hope rather than judgment and anxiety and desperation; saints whose hours and days and lives are spent carrying people to the Christ, lending each other a hand when one has fallen, slipping along the river that brings joy to the heart of God, carrying God's peace and love and presence and life to those we meet along the way.

That is what we have been sent here to do. And we will. The Dreamer's dream will always come true.
— *Between the Dreaming and the Coming True* by Robert Benson

Eustace was silent for so long that Edmund thought he was fainting; but at last he said' "It's all right now. Could we go and talk somewhere? I don't want to meet the others just yet."

"Yes, rather, anywhere you like," said Edmund. "We can go and sit on the rocks over there. I say, I am glad to see you — er — looking yourself again. You must have had a pretty beastly time."

They went to the rocks and sat down looking out across the bay while the sky got paler and paler and the stars disappeared except for one bright one low down and near the horizon.

"I won't tell you how I became a — a dragon till I can tell the others and get it all over," said Eustace. "By the way, I didn't even know it was a dragon till I heard you all using the word when I turned up here the other morning. I want to tell you how I stopped being one."

"Fire ahead," said Edmund.

"Well, last night I was more miserable than ever. And that beastly arm-ring was hurting like anything —"

"Is that all right now?"

Eustace laughed — a different laugh from any Edmund had heard him give before — and slipped the bracelet easily off his arm. "There it is," he said, "and anyone who likes can have it as far as I'm concerned. Well, as I say, I was lying awake and wondering what on earth would become of me. And then — but, mind you, it may have been all a dream. I don't know."

"Go on," said Edmund, with considerable patience.

"Well, anyway, I looked up and saw the very last thing I expected: a huge lion coming slowly toward me. And one queer thing was that there was no moon last night, but there was moonlight where the lion was. So it came nearer and nearer. I was terribly afraid of it. You may think that, being a dragon, I could have knocked any lion out easily enough. But it wasn't that kind of fear. I wasn't afraid of it eating me, I was just afraid of it — if you can understand. Well, it came close up to me and looked straight into my eyes. And I shut my eyes tight. But that wasn't any good because it told me to follow it."

"You mean it spoke?"

"I don't know. Now that you mention it, I don't think it did. But it told me all the same. And I knew I'd have to do what it told me, so I got up and followed it. And it led me a long way into the mountains. And there was always this moonlight over and round the lion wherever we went. So at last we came to the top of a mountain I'd never seen before and on top of this mountain there was a garden — trees and fruit and everything. In the middle of it there was a well.

"I knew it was a well because you could see the water bubbling up from the bottom of it: but it was bigger than most wells — like a very big, round bath with marble steps going down into it. The water was as clear as anything and I thought if I could get in there and bathe it would ease the pain in my leg. But the lion told me I must undress first. Mind you, I don't know if he said any words out loud or not.

"I was going to say that I couldn't undress because I hadn't any clothes on when I suddenly thought that dragons are snaky sort of things and snakes can cast their skins. Oh, of course, thought I, that's what the lion means. So I started scratching myself and scales began coming off all over the place. And then I scratched a little deeper and, instead of just scales coming off here and there, my whole skin started peeling off beautifully, like it does after an illness, or as if I was a banana. In a minute or two I just stepped out of it. I could see it lying there beside me, looking rather nasty. It was a most lovely feeling. So I started to go down into the well for my bathe.

"But just as I was going to put my feet into the water I looked down and saw that they were all hard and rough and wrinkled and scaly just as they had been before. Oh, that's all right, said I, it only means I had another smaller suit on underneath the first one, and I'll have to get out of it too. So I scratched and tore again and this underskin peeled off beautifully and out I stepped and left it lying beside the other one and went down to the well for my bathe.

"Well exactly the same thing happened again. And I thought to myself, oh dear, how ever many skins have I got to take off? For I was longing to bathe my leg. So I scratched away for the third time and got off a third skin, just like the two others, and stepped out of it. But as soon as I looked at myself in the water I knew it had been no good.

"Then the lion said — but I don't know if it spoke — 'You will have to let me undress you.' I was afraid of his claws, I can tell you, but I was pretty near desperate now. So I just lay flat down on my back to let him do it.

"The very first tear he made was so deep that I thought it had gone right into my heart. And when he began pulling the skin off, it hurt worse than anything I've ever felt. The only thing that made me able to bear it was just the pleasure of feeling the stuff peel off. You know — if you've ever picked a scab of a sore place. It hurts like billy-oh but it is such fun to see it coming away."

"I know exactly what you mean," said Edmund.

"Well, he peeled the beastly stuff right off — just as I thought I'd done it myself the other three times, only they hadn't hurt — and there it was lying on the grass: only ever so much thicker, and darker, and more knobbly-looking than the others had been. Then he caught hold of me — I didn't like that much for I was very tender underneath now that I'd no skin on — and threw me into the water. It smarted like anything but only for a moment. After that it became perfectly delicious and as soon as I started swimming and splashing I found that all the pain had gone from my arm. And then I saw why. I'd turned into a boy again. You'd think me simply phony if I told you how I felt about my own arms. I know they've no muscle and are pretty mouldy compared with Caspian's, but I was so glad to see them.

"After a bit the lion took me out and dressed me — "

"Dressed you. With his paws?"

"Well I don't exactly remember that bit. But he did somehow or other: in new clothes — the same I've got on now, as a matter of fact. And then suddenly I was back here. Which is what makes me think it must have been a dream."

"No, it wasn't a dream," said Edmund.

"Why not?"

"Well, there are the clothes, for one thing. And you have been — well, un-dragoned, for another."

"What do you think it was then?" asked Eustace.

"I think you've seen Aslan," said Edmund.
— *The Voyage of the Dawn Treader* by C. S. Lewis

Souls are like wax waiting for a seal. By themselves they have no special identity. Their destiny is to be softened and prepared in this life, by God's will, to receive, at their death, the seal of their own degree of likeness to God in Christ.

And this is what it means, among other things, to be judged by Christ.

The wax that has melted in God's will can easily receive the stamp of its identity, the truth of what it was meant to be. But the wax that is hard and dry and brittle and without love will not take the seal: for the hard seal, descending upon it, grinds it to powder.

Therefore if you spend your life trying to escape from the heat of the fire that is meant to soften and prepare you to become your true self, and if you try to keep your substance from melting in the fire — as if your true identity were to be hard wax — the seal will fall upon you at last and crush you. You will not be able to take your own true name and countenance, and you will be destroyed by the event that was meant to be your fulfillment. — *New Seeds of Contemplation* by Thomas Merton

The man who has struggled to purify himself and has had nothing but repeated failures will experience real relief when he stops tinkering with his soul and looks away to the perfect One. While he looks at Christ, the very things he has so long been trying to do will be getting done within him. It will be God working in him to will and to do. — *The Pursuit of God* by A. W. Tozer

Love changes us in ways that the law cannot. Spiritual formation, a term used to describe the process of being changed into the image of Christ, doesn't happen by following disciplines. It happens by falling in love. When we fall in love with Jesus, all the other loves in our life fall into place. And those that once competed with Christ now subordinate themselves to him. Everything in our life finds its proper value once we have properly valued him. — *The Divine Embrace* by Ken Gire

We die; indeed we have to die in order to be resurrected, restored and renewed. We die and we die and we die in this life, not only physically — within seven years every cell in your body is renewed — but emotionally and spiritually as change seizes us by the scruff of the neck and drags us forward into another life. We are not here simply to exist. We are here in order to become.
— *Absolute Truths* by Susan Howatch

Above all, trust in the slow work of God.
We are, quite naturally, impatient in everything to reach the end without delay.
We should like to skip the intermediate stages.
We are impatient of being on the way to something unknown, something new,
and yet it is the law of all progress that it is made by passing through some stages of instability —
and that it may take a very long time...
Only God could say what this new spirit gradually forming within you will be.
Give our Lord the benefit of believing that His hand is leading you,
and accept the anxiety of feeling yourself in suspense and incomplete.

— Teilhard de Chardin

Awake

I. Opening Prayer

Lord, awaken me, you whose love burns beyond the stars; light the flame of my lantern that I may always burn with love. — *A Traveler Toward the Dawn* by John Eagan

II. Psalm 28

III. Daily Scripture Readings

Monday	Romans 13:11-14
Tuesday	Mark 5:21-43
Wednesday	1 Samuel 3:1-21
Thursday	2 Kings 6:8-23
Friday	Luke 24:13-35
Saturday	Genesis 28:10-22
Sunday	Ephesians 5:1-21

IV. Readings for Reflection

V. Reflection and Listening: silent and written

VI. Prayer: for the church, for others, for myself

VII. Song   *Crown Him with Many Crowns*

VIII. Closing Prayer

O God and Father, I repent of my sinful preoccupation with visible things. The world has been too much with me. You have been here and I knew it not. I have been blind to Your presence. Open my eyes that I may behold You in and around me. For Christ's sake, Amen. — *The Pursuit of God* by A. W. Tozer

Readings for Reflection-

But make sure that you don't get so absorbed and exhausted in taking care of all your day-by-day obligations that you lose track of the time and doze off, oblivious to God. The night is about over, dawn is about to break. Be up and awake to what God is doing! God is putting the finishing touches on the salvation work he began when we first believed. We can't afford to waste a minute, must not squander these precious daylight hours in frivolity and indulgence, in sleeping around and dissipation, in bickering and grabbing everything in sight. Get out of bed and get dressed! Don't loiter and linger, waiting until the very last minute. Dress yourselves in Christ, and be up and about! (Romans 13:11-14, The Message)

It is amazing how easily we can get lulled to sleep at times. I guess that's why so often the Scriptures encourage us to stay awake and to wait in eager expectation, anticipating Christ's return at any moment. It is an actively passive waiting that's called for, if that's even possible. We cannot control the *how* or the *when* or the *where* of his coming, so, in that sense, it must be passive. We can, however, control *how* we will wait for that coming. Therefore, it must also be active. We must stay on our toes, or on our tiptoes, one might say. We must be on the edge of our seats and not settled back into the comfort and ease of our La-Z-Boy. We must stay ready, both watching and waiting. That is the kind of wakefulness that is called for. We must keep our spiritual wits about us. We must be careful to do the things that keep our souls most awake and alert, whatever those things may be. Because, ultimately, Christ will come. And when he does, will he find us ready?

Most Holy God, wake me up from my soul's deep slumber and bring my life under your complete control. By your grace, awaken me daily to the reality of your presence within and around me. And, by the power of

your Spirit, make me responsive to your will and your
direction. Amen.

—Jim Branch, May, 2014

> We may ignore, but we can nowhere evade
> the presence of God.
> The world is crowded with Him.
> He walks everywhere incognito.
> And the incognito is not always hard to
> penetrate.
> The real labour is to attend.
> In fact, to come awake.
> Still more, to remain awake.
> —*Letters to Malcom* by C. S. Lewis

Spiritual awakening is a two-sided experience. It is an
encounter with the living God; it is also an encounter
with our true self. It is coming to see something of
ourselves as we are and coming to see something of God
as God is.

This experience can be gradual or radical. It can take
place through everyday events or in an extraordinary
experience. It can be one focal experience or a whole
sequence that finally falls together for us. On some
occasions, moments of awakening begin with an
experience of who God is, such as Isaiah's—"I saw the
Lord sitting upon a throne, high and lifted up" (Isaiah
6:1). Then, in the light of that experience, we awake to
who we are—"Woe is me!...I am a man of unclean lips"
(Isaiah 6:5). On other occasions, like Jacob, we may be
very much aware of who we are as we seek to escape
from the mess we have made of our life (Genesis 27:41-
44). Then we encounter God in the midst of our
turmoil—"Surely the Lord is in this place, and I did not

know it" (Genesis 28:16). Awakening can come in a variety of ways.

Two basic emotions go with awakening: it is both a *comfort* and a *threat*. It is a comfort because there is a sense of awakening to deeper realities of who we are and who God is. But at the same time there is threat: in that awakening, we recognize that we are not what we ought to be and that God is something far more than we thought. And so there is an ambivalence in genuine awakening. Something in us hungers for this, yet something in us also resists.

Genuine awakening is the awareness of a door being opened to a whole new dynamic of being. We realize we have come to a threshold of some sort, and there is need of a response. Our response may be immediate, or it may come after much wrestling and recurrence. Some people are aroused into early stages of wakefulness and then quickly subside into sleep. They don't like what is out there. It is not time to get up yet. They will be roused up again and lie back down again, and that pattern can continue until finally they come to the point of awakening: they step across the threshold of the open door into a new relationship with God.

Awakening is seen in the classical Christian tradition as the beginning of the process: the first step of our journey, our pilgrimage, toward wholeness. — *Invitation to a Journey* by M. Robert Mulholland Jr.

contemplation by Jim Branch

what is this that stirs within?
willing to guide if I will listen
a faint whisper   yet not

an almost imperceptible knowing
awakened from a sleep

in which One was calling softly
knowing — but not sure how
hearing — but not sure when
dreaming?

as a soft voice in a sleeping child's ear
knowing to the depths what was whispered
and the delight of the Whisperer

Those who have shaken off sleep eventually become
all awake within.
— Clement of Alexandria

He now knew the way to Anvard but of course he
could not go there: that would only mean running into
the arms of Rabadash's troopers. "What on earth am I to
do?" said Shasta to himself. But he remounted his horse
and continued along the road he had chosen, in the faint
hope of finding some cottage where he might ask for
shelter and a meal. He had thought, of course, of going
back to Aravis and Bree and Hwin at the hermitage, but
he couldn't because by now he had not the least idea of
the direction.

"After all," said Shasta, "this road is bound to get
somewhere."

But that all depends on what you mean by
somewhere. The road kept on getting to somewhere in
the sense that it got to more and more trees, all dark and
dripping, and to colder and colder air. And strange, icy
winds kept blowing the mist past him though he never
blew it away. If he had been used to mountain country
he would have realized that this meant he was now very
high up — perhaps right at the top of the pass. But
Shasta knew nothing about mountains.

"I do think, said Shasta, "that I must be the most unfortunate boy that ever lived in the whole world. Everything goes right for everyone except me. Those Narnian lords and ladies got safe away from Tashbaan; I was left behind. Aravis and Bree and Hwin are all as snug as anything with that old Hermit: of course I was the one who was sent on. King Lune and his people must have got safely into the castle and shut the gates long before Rabadash arrived, but I get left out."

And being very tired and having nothing inside him, he felt so sorry for himself that the tears rolled down his cheeks.

What put a stop to all this was a sudden fright. Shasta discovered that someone or somebody was walking beside him. It was pitch dark and he could see nothing. And the Thing (or Person) was going so quietly that he could hardly hear any footfalls. What he could hear was breathing. His invisible companion seemed to breathe on a very large scale, and Shasta got the impression that it was a very large creature. And he had come to notice this breathing so gradually that he had really no idea how long it had been there. It was a horrible shock.

It darted into his mind that he had heard long ago that there were giants in these Northern countries. He bit his lip in terror. But now that he really had something to cry about, he stopped crying.

The Thing (unless it was a Person) went on beside him so very quietly that Shasta began to hope he had only imagined it. But just as he was becoming quite sure of it, there suddenly came a deep, rich sigh out of the darkness beside him. That couldn't be imagination! Anyway, he had felt the hot breath of that sigh on his chilly left hand.

If the horse had been any good — or if he had known how to get any good out of the horse — he would have risked everything on a breakaway and a wild gallop.

But he knew he couldn't make that horse gallop. So he went on at a walking pace and the unseen companion walked and breathed beside him. At last he could bear it no longer.

"Who are you?" he said, scarcely above a whisper.

"One who has waited long for you to speak," said the Thing. It's voice was not loud, but very large and deep.

"Are you—are you a giant?" asked Shasta.

"You might call me a giant," said the Large Voice. "But I am not like the creatures you call giants."

"I can't see you at all," said Shasta, after staring very hard. Then (for an even more terrible had come into his head) he said, almost in a scream, "You're not—not something dead are you? Oh please—please do go away. What harm have I ever done to you? Oh, I am the unluckiest person in the whole world!"

Once more he felt the warm breath of the Thing on his hand and face. "There," it said, "that is not the breath of a ghost. Tell me your sorrows."

Shasta was a little reassured by the breath: so he told how he had never known his real father or mother and had been brought up sternly by the fisherman. And then he told the story of his escape and how they were chased by the lions and forced to swim for their lives; and of all their dangers in Tashbaan and about his night among the tombs and how the beasts howled at him out of the desert. And he told about the heat and thirst of their desert journey and how they were almost at their goal when another lion chased them and wounded Aravis. And also, how very long it was since he had had anything to eat.

"I do not call you unfortunate," said the Large Voice.

"Don't you think it was bad luck to meet so many lions?" said Shasta.

"There was only one lion," said the Voice.

"What on earth do you mean? I've just told you there were at least two the first night, and—"

"There was only one: but he was swift of foot."

"How do you know?"

"I was the lion." And as Shasta gaped with open mouth and said nothing, the Voice continued. "I was the lion who forced you to join with Aravis. I was the cat who comforted you among the houses of the dead. I was the lion who drove the jackals from you while you slept. I was the lion who gave the Horses the new strength of fear for the last mile so that you should reach King Lune in time. And I was the lion you do not remember who pushed the boat in which you lay, a child near death, so that it came to shore where a man sat, wakeful at midnight, to receive you."

"Then it was you who wounded Aravis?"

"It was I."

"But what for?"

"Child," said the Voice, "I am telling you your story, not hers. I tell no one any story but his own."

"Who are you?" asked Shasta.

"Myself," said the Voice, very deep and low so that the earth shook: and again "Myself," loud and clear and gay: and then the third time "Myself," whispered so softly you could hardly hear it, and yet it seemed to come from all around you as if the leaves rustled with it.

Shasta was no longer afraid that the Voice belonged to something that would eat him, nor that it was the voice of a ghost. But a new and different sort of trembling came over him. Yet he felt glad too.

The mist was turning from black to gray and from gray to white. This must have begun to happen some time ago, but while he had been talking to the Thing he had not been noticing anything else. Now, the whiteness around him became a shining whiteness; his eyes began to blink. Somewhere ahead he could hear birds singing. He knew the night was over at last. He could see the mane and ears and head of his horse quite

easily now. A golden light fell on them from the left.
He thought it was the sun.

He turned and saw, pacing beside him, taller than the
horse, a Lion. The horse did not seem to be afraid of it
or else could not see it. It was from the Lion that the
light came. No one ever saw anything more terrible or
beautiful. —*A Horse and His Boy* by C. S. Lewis

My starting point is that we're already there. We
cannot attain the presence of God because we're already
totally in the presence of God. What's absent is
awareness. Little do we realize that God is maintaining
us in existence with every breath we take. As we take
another it means that God is choosing us now and now
and now. We have nothing to attain or even earn.
—*Everything Belongs* by Richard Rohr

Spirituality means waking up. Most people, even though
they don't know it, are asleep. They're born asleep, they
live asleep, they marry in their sleep, they breed children
in their sleep, they die in their sleep without ever
waking up. They never understand the loveliness and
the beauty of this thing we call human existence.
—*Awareness* by Anthony De Mello

Silence

I. Opening Prayer

> Uncrowd my heart, O God,
> until silence speaks
> in your still small voice;
> turn me from the hearing of words,
> and the making of words,
> and the confusion of much speaking,
> to listening,
> waiting,
> stillness,
> silence.
>
> — Thomas Merton

II. Psalm 23

III. Daily Scripture Readings

Monday	Ecclesiastes 5:1-7
Tuesday	Mark 1:29-39
Wednesday	Habakkuk 2:18-20
Thursday	Psalm 131:1-3
Friday	Lamentations 3:19-28
Saturday	1 Thessalonians 4:11-12
Sunday	Isaiah 30:15-18

IV. Readings for Reflection

V. Reflection and Listening: silent and written

VI. Prayer: for the church, for others, for myself

VII. Song   *Be Still, My Soul*

VIII. Closing Prayer

O God of peace, *who hast* taught us that in returning and

rest we shall be saved, in quietness and in confidence shall be our strength: By the might of *thy* Spirit lift us, we pray *thee*, to *thy* presence, where we may be still and know that *thou art* God; through Jesus Christ our Lord. *Amen.*

— The Book of Common Prayer

Readings for Reflection-

"You don't have to sit outside in the dark," wrote Annie Dillard. "If however, you want to look at the stars, you will find that darkness is necessary. But the stars neither require nor demand it." Thus, "You don't have to sit in silence," a dear friend once told me, "but if you want to hear from God, you will find that silence is necessary." And I believe it. Furthermore, I have found it to be true time after time. If I am serious about living a life at attention, if I have a deep longing to consistently hear the voice of God in my life, if I have any hope of ever living a life where *recognizing* him is a possibility, I must begin to practice silence and solitude in some kind of meaningful way. There is simply no way around it. Silence and solitude deepen the quality of our life with God. *— Becoming* by Jim Branch

What deadens us most to God's presence within us, I think, is the inner dialogue that we are continuously engaged in with ourselves, the endless chatter of human thought. I suspect that there is nothing more crucial to true spiritual comfort, as the huge monk in cloth of gold put it, than being able from time to time to stop that chatter including the chatter of spoken prayer. If we choose to seek the silence of the holy place, or to open ourselves to its seeking, I think there is no surer way than by keeping silent.

God knows I am no good at it, but I keep trying, and once or twice I have been lucky, graced. I have been conscious but not conscious of anything, not even of myself. I have been surrounded by the whiteness of snow. I have heard the stillness that encloses all sounds stilled the way whiteness encloses all colors stilled, the way wordlessness encloses all words stilled. I have sensed the presence of a presence. I have felt a promise promised.

I like to believe that once or twice, at times like those, I have bumbled my way into at least the outermost suburbs of the Truth that can never be told but only come upon, that can never be proved but only lived for and loved. — *Telling Secrets* by Frederick Buechner

Somewhere we know that without a lonely place our lives are in danger. Somewhere we know that without silence words lose their meaning, that without listening speaking no longer heals, without distance closeness cannot cure. Somewhere we know that without a lonely place our actions quickly become empty gestures. The careful balance between silence and words, withdrawal and involvement, distance and closeness, solitude and community forms the basis of the Christian life and should therefore be the subjects of our most personal attention. Let us therefore look somewhat closer, first at our life in action, and at our life in solitude. — *Out of Solitude* by Henri J. M. Nouwen

Retire from the world each day to some private spot, even if it be only the bedroom (for a while I retreated to the furnace room for want of a better place). Stay in the secret place till the surrounding noises begin to fade out of your heart and a sense of God's presence envelopes you...Listen for the inward Voice till you learn to recognize it. Stop trying to compete with others. Give yourself to God and then be what and who you are without regard to what others think...Learn to pray inwardly every moment. After a while you can do this even while you work....Read less, but more of what is important to your inner life. Never let your mind remain scattered for very long. Call home your roving thoughts. Gaze on Christ with the eyes of your soul. Practice spiritual concentration. All of the above is contingent upon a right relation to God through Christ and daily meditation on the Scriptures. Lacking these, nothing will help us; granted these, the discipline recommended will go far to neutralize the evil effects of externalism and to make us acquainted with God and our own souls. — *The Pursuit of God* by A. W. Tozer

To be calm and quiet all by yourself is hardly the same as sleeping, but means being fully awake and following with close attention every move going on inside you. Silence requires the discipline to recognize the urge to get up and go again as a temptation to look elsewhere for what is close at hand. It offers the freedom to stroll in your own inner yard, and to rake the leaves there and clear the paths so you can easily find the way to your heart. Perhaps there will be much fear and uncertainty when you first come upon this "unfamiliar terrain," but slowly you will discover an order and a familiarity which deepens your longing to stay home. — *With Open Hands* by Henri J. M. Nouwen

Settle yourself in solitude and you will come upon Him in yourself.
— Teresa of Avila

The fruit of solitude is increased sensitivity and compassion for others. There comes a new freedom to be with people. There is new attentiveness to their needs, new responsiveness to their hurts. — *Celebration of Discipline* by Richard Foster

Without solitude it is virtually impossible to live a spiritual life. Solitude begins with a time and place for God, and Him alone. If we really believe not only that God exists but also that He is actively present in our lives — healing, teaching, and guiding — we need to set aside time and space to give Him our undivided attention. — *Making All Things New* by Henri J.M. Nouwen

Hasten unto Him who calls you in the silences of your heart. — *A Testament of Devotion* by Thomas R. Kelly

A second, more positive, meaning of silence is that it protects the inner fire. Silence guards the inner heat of religious emotions. This inner heat is the life of the Holy Spirit within us. Thus, silence is the discipline by which the inner fire of God is tended and kept alive.

Diadochus of Photiki offers us a very concrete image: "When the door to a steambath is continually left open, the heat inside rapidly escapes through it; likewise the soul, in its desire to say many things, dissipates its remembrance of God through the door of speech, even though everything it says may be good. Thereafter the intellect, though lacking appropriate ideas, pours out a welter of confused thoughts to anyone it meets, as it no longer has the Holy Spirit to keep its understanding free from fantasy. Ideas of value always shun verbosity, being foreign to confusion and fantasy. Timely silence, then, is precious, for it is nothing less than the mother of the wisest thoughts. — *The Way of the Heart* by Henri J.M. Nouwen

. . . We are none of us very good at silence. It says too much. — *Telling the Truth* by Frederick Buechner

For it is only in solitude that we discover the sufficiency of a God who also yearns for us — so much so that in

Jesus Christ he came looking for us. — *Sacred Thirst* by
M. Craig Barnes

Silence is nothing else but waiting for God's Word
and coming from God's Word with a blessing. But
everybody knows that this is something that needs to be
practiced and learned, in these days when talkativeness
prevails. Real silence, real stillness, really holding one's
tongue come only as the sober consequence of spiritual
stillness.

But this stillness before the Word will exert its
influence upon the whole day. If we have learned to be
silent before the Word, we shall also learn to manage our
silence and our speech during the day.

The silence of the Christian is listening silence,
humble stillness that may be interrupted at any time for
the sake of humility. — *Life Together* by Dietrich
Bonhoeffer

> In the quietness of life,
> When the flowers have shut their eye,
> And a stainless breadth of sky
> Bends above the hill of strife,
> Then, my God, my chiefest Good,
> Breathe upon my lonelihood:
> Let the shining silence be
> Filled with Thee, my God, with Thee.
— "Petition and Communion," by Percy C. Ainsworth

Intimacy

I. Opening Prayer

O God, who existed before all things, draw near to my heart today as I draw near to yours. Grant that as we are together during this time—as well as this day—I will know of your presence to the very core of my being. Let me experience the intimacy with you that I was created for. In the name of Jesus, the Word made flesh. Amen.

II. Psalm 131

III. Daily Scripture Readings

Monday	Isaiah 62:1-12
Tuesday	Song of Songs 7:10-13
Wednesday	Psalm 139
Thursday	Revelation 21:1-7
Friday	Song of Songs 4:9-16
Saturday	Hosea 2:14-23
Sunday	John 17:20-26

IV. Readings for Reflection

V. Reflection and Listening: silent and written

VI. Prayer: for the church, for others, for myself

VII. Song   *Draw Me Close to You*

VIII. Closing Prayer

Lord you are my Lover, it is you whom I desire. You flow through my body like a stream, you shine on my face like the sun. Let me be your reflection.

—St. Mechthild of Magdeburg

Readings for Reflection-

I've been thinking a lot about the idea of intimacy lately; particularly about what it really is and how it is created, nurtured, and sustained. That has also led me to consider what the main obstacles and hindrances are to intimacy and its cultivation in relationships. I have a suspicion that, like most things, if we consider how intimacy is developed between people it will help us to know more about the dynamics and design of intimacy with God.

The word intimacy comes from the Latin word *intimus,* referring to what is *interior* or *inside.* Thus intimacy only has a possibility of happening when we choose to reveal and expose our insides to one another in a loving way. It therefore requires mutual disclosure. By its very nature intimacy can never be a one way street. This is also true when we consider our intimacy with God. For the truth is that God seeks and desires intimacy with the human soul. And once we experience that kind of intimacy, only the language of lovers can describe what is going within us. That is what the saints and the poets have been trying to teach us for centuries.

God longs for intimacy with us, therefore, he discloses or reveals himself to us. He does not merely reveal ideas or theological concepts about himself, but he actually shows us who he is. He opens his infinite heart and allows us to see inside. His desire in doing so is that it might completely capture our hearts in return and give us the desire and the courage to disclose ourselves to him — not that he needs us to do that, for he obviously knows us better than we know ourselves. This disclosure is more about what happens in us as we open ourselves to him; it grows this Divine intimacy within us. Therefore we must stay attentive to both movements: to how God is revealing and disclosing himself to us, as well as how we are intentionally and

courageously revealing and exposing ourselves to him.
It is two steps in an incredibly beautiful dance.

—Jim Branch, May, 2013

one

full of myself
may it never be
but only you
my dear jesus

as rain falling into a pond
becomes one
no longer any rain
only the pond
as a stream flowing into the sea
becomes one
no longer any stream
only the sea
as light coming into a room
from two windows
becomes one
no longer windows
only light

may i melt into you
so that there is
no more me
but only you
my beloved jesus
—*Pieces II*, Jim Branch
Inspired by the writings of Teresa of Avila

God created us for a purpose more astonishing and sublime than we can imagine. Every great Christian theologian and saint has borne witness to this high purpose. The human being is created in the divine image and likeness in order to have continual and intimate communion with the One who made us. We are created to love and be loved by God, born to serve and be served by Christ, destined to enjoy the vitality of the Holy Spirit and in turn receive God's delight in us forever! Such is God's good pleasure and our highest bliss. — *The Way of Forgiveness: Participants Book* by Marjorie Thompson

My meditations on the story of the woman who poured her perfume all over Jesus has elevated the affections of my heart toward Jesus. Just like the woman in the story, I long to be passionately indifferent to the reactions of those around me, lost in the extravagant expression of my affection for Jesus. I want my love for God to become as wild, reckless, and free as his for me.
— *Running on Empty* by Fil Anderson

smile by Jim Branch

a sweet sweet song
filled with love and affection
sung with a tender caress
my song to you
the love of my heart
whispered softly in your ear
to bring a smile to your lips

but then a change
a turn of the tables
you spin it around
and let me know the song is yours

sung constantly over me

you pull me close
take me to yourself
sing tenderly in my ear
the song of songs
now the smile belongs to me

God dwells within you. You are yourself the tabernacle,
his secret hiding place. Rejoice, exult, for all you could
possibly desire, all your heart's longing is so close, so
intimate as to be within you; you cannot *be* without him.

— John of the Cross

giggle   by Jim Branch

i can't stifle the giggle
when your mouth draws close to my ear
whispers of affection
light up my heart
and then my face
they make me beam
others see and think it odd
but they don't hear
they don't feel your breath upon them
if they did, they'd giggle too

Intimacy is, in both love and faith, full of tensions.
When fulfillment is delayed, desire is bitter. Between
falling in love and consummating love, between the
promise and the fulfillment, between the boundaries,
that is, that are defined by covenant, it is the task of

224

persevering and patient prayer to keep love ardent and faith zealous.

Which is why prayer is the chief pastoral work in relation to a person's desires for and difficulties with intimacy. Anything less or other than prayer fails to deal with either the ultimacy of the desires or the complexity of the difficulties. Prayer with and for persons centers the desire in God and puts the difficulties in perspective under God. Prayer is thus the language, *par excellence,* of the covenant: it is quintessential pastoral conversation that takes seriously the relationships that matter most, both human and divine. In prayer the desires are not talked about, they are expressed to God. In prayer the difficulties are not analyzed and studied, they are worked through with God. If the goal is intimacy, it will not be arrived at by teaching or counsel or therapy (although any of these ministries may provide assistance) but by dealing personally with those who count, with Creator and creature. — *Five Smooth Stones for Pastoral Work* by Eugene H. Peterson

O living flame of love
That tenderly wounds my soul
In its deepest center! Since
Now you are not oppressive,
Now Consummate! If it be your will:
Tear through the veil of this sweet encounter!

O sweet cautery,
O delightful wound!
O gentle hand! O delicate touch
That tastes of eternal life
And pays every debt!
In killing you changed death into life.
O lamps of fire!
In whose splendors

The deep caverns of feeling,
Once obscure and blind,
Now give forth, so rarely, so exquisitely,
Both warmth and light to their beloved.

How gently and lovingly
You wake in my heart,
Where in secret you dwell alone;
And in your sweet breathing,
Filled with good and glory,
How tenderly you swell my heart with love.

—John of the Cross

As I sit and hold my ten month old son, his eyes totally fixed on mine, indiscernible sounds of love streaming from his lips, I am amazed (once again) at such love, such connection, such relationship, such intimacy—with no words required. This is what I was made for (I feel it in the very core of my soul) by a God who shows himself to be a God of intimate relationship.

What a wonderfully terrifying thing to realize, that the very nature of the Creator is one of total intimacy. The first part of John tells us that the Word was *with* God—toward God, facing God. The very essence of the relationship between God and the Word was (and is) one of connection, intimacy, relationship—face-to-face communication. What a joy it is to know that he is wonderfully able to meet the needs of his children for connection and deep relationship.

It is wonderful because only one that has experienced total intimacy can give us hope for a similar state of existence for ourselves. And it is terrifying because of the notion of being face-to-face with one who can see into my very soul—no protection, no hiding, no masks, just the real me—completely vulnerable. It strikes fear in my heart, fear of being seen by God — inadequate, ugly, real, afraid I won't measure up. I don't, however, have to measure up, for God's eyes are not like mine. He looks lovingly and longingly at his children more deeply even than I look at my own, as I stand over their beds at night with a heart bursting so with love that I can't keep my hands from their hair or my lips from their cheeks. He looks at me and sees his son, his beloved, and desires that I sit facing him all of the days of my life; uttering whatever indiscernible sounds of love and affection that are at my disposal.

As I can readily see in my children, I was created for intimacy. I can't, however, expect to be truly connected with anyone until I am able to be truly connected with Jesus. My capacity for intimacy (with spouse, child, or friend) comes directly from him and his desire that I experience the joys of true connectedness (John 15:7). And oh what a gift are those few seconds or minutes or hours when *True Intimacy* breaks through the isolation of our ordinary lives to grace (and I know it's grace) us with its presence. Those are moments to savor, to sit and marvel over.

—Jim Branch, December, 1995

The Song

I. Opening Prayer
O Lord, as we spend time with you and your Word this day, let us hear the words of your Ancient Song; and let us listen closely for the Song of God that rises in our hearts. In Christ. Amen.

II. Psalm 100

III. Daily Scripture Readings
Monday	Song of Songs 2:10-13
Tuesday	Isaiah 12:1-6
Wednesday	Zephaniah 3:14-20
Thursday	Isaiah 26:1-9
Friday	Exodus 15:1-21
Saturday	Psalm 95
Sunday	Psalm 98

IV. Readings for Reflection

V. Reflection and Listening: silent and written

VI. Prayer for the Church, for others, for myself

VII. Song   *Thy Mercy, My God*

VIII. Closing Prayer
Everything in all of creation, O Lord, is a unique song of yours. And when we sing our song — that song that is buried deeply within each of us — we are indeed being who we were made to be. We are in harmony (*shalom*) with the voice of our Maker. Help us to sing our song (Your song) clearly and fully this day. In the name of Jesus. Amen.

Readings for Reflection-

harmony by Jim Branch

when i come to that quiet place,
back into the harmony
from which and for which i was made,
i am able to breathe again
with the divine breath.
i am able to become one again with all that is,
to join the true voice of my soul
with that of the heavenly chorus.
i join the breeze in the trees
and the rippling waters
and the rolling hills
in being what we were all made to be.
o the beauty. o the freedom. o the delight.
and it is not until i rejoin this eternal harmony
that i am able to recognize how disharmonious
my life has been in the past days and weeks.
i have not even resembled the me
i was made to be,
but have been some distorted
and desperate version of my true self.
but now, as i return to this silent space,
return to this tranquility and this peace,
i can become myself once again.
i can find my divinely given voice
and sing.

In the darkness something was happening at last. A voice had begun to sing. It was very far away and Digory found it hard to decide from what direction it was coming. Sometimes it seemed to come from all directions at once. Sometimes he almost thought it was coming out of the earth beneath them. Its lower notes were deep enough to be the voice of the earth herself.

There were no words. There was hardly even a tune. But it was, beyond comparison, the most beautiful noise he had ever heard. It was so beautiful he could hardly bear it. The horse seemed to like it too; he gave the sort of whinny a horse would give if, after years of being a cab-horse, it found itself back in the old field where it had played as a foal, and saw someone whom it remembered and loved coming across the field to bring it a lump of sugar.

"Gawd!" said Cabby. "Ain't it lovely?"

Then two wonders happened at the same moment. One was that the voice was suddenly joined by other voices; more voices than you could possibly count. They were in harmony with it, but far higher up the scale: cold, tingling, silvery voices. The second wonder was that the blackness overhead, all at once, was blazing with stars. They didn't come out gently one by one, as they do on a summer evening. One moment there had been nothing but darkness; next moment a thousand, thousand points of light leaped out—single stars, constellations, and planets, brighter and bigger than any in our world. There were no clouds. The new stars and new voices began at exactly the same time. If you had seen and heard it, as Digory did, you would have felt quite certain that it was the stars themselves who were singing, and that it was the First Voice, the deep one, which had made them appear and made them sing.

"Glory be!" said Cabby. "I'd ha' been a better man all my life if I'd known there were things like this."

The Voice on the earth was now louder and more triumphant; but the voices in the sky, after singing loudly with it for a time, began to get fainter. And now something else was happening.

Far away, and down near the horizon, the sky began to turn grey. A light wind, very fresh, began to stir. The sky, in that one place, grew slowly and steadily paler.

230

You could see shapes of hills standing up dark against it. All the time the Voice went on singing.

There was soon enough light for them to see one another's faces. The Cabby and the two children had open mouths and shining eyes; they were drinking in the sound, and they looked as if it reminded them of something. Uncle Andrew's mouth was open too, but not open with joy. He looked more as if his chin had simply dropped away from the rest of his face. His shoulders were stooped and his knees shook. He was not liking the Voice. If he could have got away from it by creeping into a rat's hole, he would have done so. But the Witch looked as if, in a way, she understood the music better than any of them. Her mouth was shut, her lips were pressed together, and her fists were clenched. Ever since the song began she had felt that this whole world was filled with Magic different from hers and stronger. She hated it. She would have smashed that whole world, or all worlds, to pieces, if it would only stop the singing. The horse stood with its ears well forward, and twitching. Every now and then it snorted and stamped the ground. It no longer looked like a tired old cabhorse; you could now well believe that its father had been in battles.

The eastern sky changed from white to pink and from pink to gold. The Voice rose and rose, till all the air was shaking with it. And just as it swelled to the mightiest and most glorious sound it had yet produced, the sun arose.

Digory had never seen such a sun. The sun above the ruins of Charn had looked older than ours; this looked younger. You could imagine that it laughed for joy as it came up. And as its beams shot across the land the travelers could see for the first time what sort of place they were in. It was a valley through which a broad, swift river wound its way, flowing eastward towards the sun. Southward there were mountains, northward there were lower hills. But it was a valley of mere earth, rock and water; there was not a tree, not a bush, not a blade of grass to be seen. The earth was of many colours: they were fresh, hot and vivid. They made you feel excited; until you saw the Singer himself, and then you forgot everything else.

It was a Lion. Huge, shaggy, and bright it stood facing the risen sun. Its mouth was wide open in song and it was about three hundred yards away.
— *The Magician's Nephew* by C. S. Lewis

If enough of us were to ungarble our words, perhaps God's story might be more clearly heard and understood. Perhaps the song that God sings into the wind that whispers all around us in the trees would be on more lips and taught to more children. My friend Russell Montfort once remarked that he suspects that "we die with half our music left in us." Maybe we do not know the words to our own song.

And it is not just our own little melody that suffers; the whole chorus is not as good. If you leave out enough of the words, even the Song of the whole universe will sound funny.

The Song needs my word. It is not the same song without it. And I am the only one who has ever heard it, the only one who can ever listen to its echo deep inside and know whether or not the life that I am living — what I am doing with my hours and days and work and other selves to love — rhymes with it, and sings it clearly at all.
— *Between the Dreaming and the Coming True* by Robert Benson

I have been greatly instructed by the story of Ulysses, when he was sailing past the islands of the Sirens. These Sirens had the power of charming by their songs all who listened to them, and of inducing them to leap into the sea. To avert this danger, Ulysses filled the ears of his crew with wax, that they might not hear the fatal music, and bound himself to the mast with knotted cords; and thus they passed the isle in safety. But when Orpheus was obliged to sail by the same island, he gained a better victory, for he himself made sweeter music than that of the Sirens, and enchanted his crew with more alluring songs; so that they passed the dangerous charmers not only with safety, but with disdain. Wax and knotted cords kept Ulysses and his crew from making the fatal leap; but inward delights enabled Orpheus and his crew to reign triumphant over the very source of temptation itself. And just so is it with the Kingdom of which we speak. It needs no outward law to bind it, but reigns by right of its inward life. — *The Christian's Secret of a Happy Life* by Hannah Whitall Smith)

One day a friend of mine was walking through a shopping mall with his two-year-old son. The child was in a particularly cantankerous mood, fussing and fuming. The frustrated father tried everything to quiet his son, but nothing seemed to help. The child simply would not obey. Then, under some special inspiration, the father scooped up his son and, holding him close to his chest, began signing an impromptu love song. None of the words rhymed. He sang off key. And yet, as best he could, this father began sharing his heart. "I love you," he sang. "I'm so glad you're my boy. You make me happy. I like the way you laugh." On they went from one store to the next. Quietly the father continued singing off key and making up words that did not rhyme. The child relaxed and became still, listening to this strange and wonderful song. Finally, they finished shopping and went to the car. As the father opened the door and prepared to buckle his son into his carseat, the child lifted his head and said simply, "Sing it to me again, Daddy! Sing it to me again!"

Prayer is a little like that. With simplicity of heart we allow ourselves to be gathered up into the arms of the Father and let him sing his love song over us. — *Prayer: Finding the Heart's True Home* by Richard J. Foster

When he awoke, the song was there. Its melody beckoned and begged him to sing it. It hung upon the wind and settled in the meadows where he walked. He knew its lovely words and could have sung it all, but feared to sing a song whose harmony was far too perfect for human ear to understand. And still at midnight it stirred him to awareness, and with its haunting melody it drew him with a curious mystery to stand before an open window. In rhapsody it played among the stars. It rippled through Andromeda and deepened Vega's hues. It swirled in heavy strains from galaxy to galaxy and gave him back his very fingerprint. "Sing the Song!" the heavens seemed to cry. "We never could have been without the melody that you alone can sing." — *The Singer* by Calvin Miller

When you feel invited to remain in silence at Our Lord's feet like Magdalen just looking at Him with your heart without saying anything, don't cast about for any thoughts or reasonings, but just remain in loving adoration. Follow the whisperings of the Holy Ghost. If He invites you to beg, beg; if to be silent, remain silent; if to show your misery to God, just do so. Let Him play on the fibers of your heart like a harpist, and draw forth the melody He wishes for the Divine Spouse. — *Union with God* by Columba Marmion

Union with God is a song that does not die in the hearing, a flavor which does not abate in the eating, and embrace which gives delight without end.

—St. Augustine

The Dance

I. Opening Prayer
My God and Father, Lord of the dance, allow me to see this day and this moment for what it really is — an invitation to dance the dance of life and faith with the One who made me. May I dance this day with joy and passion, knowing that there will never be another one just like it. In the name of Jesus I Pray. Amen.

II. Psalm 149

III. Daily Scripture Readings
Monday	Psalm 149:1-5
Tuesday	Luke 7:24-35
Wednesday	Psalm 19:1-6
Thursday	Matthew 22:1-14
Friday	Isaiah 55:9-12
Saturday	2 Samuel 6:1-23
Sunday	Jeremiah 31:1-14

IV. Readings for Reflection

V. Reflection and Listening: silent and written

VI. Prayer: for the church, for others, for myself

VII. Song   *Canticle of the Sun*

VIII. Closing Prayer
Lord God, draw me out on the dance floor of life this day and fill my ears and heart with the beautiful music of Your great affection. Give me such an awareness of your presence that my feet just can't be still. Dance with me as I dance with you. Amen.

Readings for Reflection-

O God, Lord of all, with all of creation my heart rejoices in you this day. Your Spirit and your word are like music that leads my soul to dance! And what a wonder-filled dance it is! Let me always be a good dance partner, willing and able to move to the leading of your Holy Spirit. Thank you that you *take pleasure in your people.* Thank you that *you adorn us with salvation.* May we be glad and rejoice, may we leap for joy and spin around. May we dance the dance of life and joy with you this day. Amen.

—Jim Branch, April, 2015

The cosmic dance of the universe is perhaps best articulated in the last three paragraphs of *New Seeds of Contemplation*, Merton's most popular and best-loved book. The basic image is a favorite of the mystics, the image of God as bridegroom dancing with his bride, that is, all of creation, at a wedding feast. How often we've seen at a wedding reception the bridegroom with an enormous smile and tender love sweep his bride into his arms and out onto the dance floor; then the other couples follow. So also our cosmic God of creation. He is so deeply in love with his whole creation, especially us his rational creation, that he is engaged in a joyous dance daily with us, the work of his hands. This dance is going on all the time around us and *in* us, in every breath we draw and in every heartbeat. To live fully then is to tap into this reality that lies below the surface of things and to touch this rich river of joy and love that is being poured out into this world. —*A Traveler Toward the Dawn* by John Eagan

What is serious to men is often very trivial in the sight of God. What in God might appear to us as "play" is

236

perhaps what He Himself takes most seriously. At any rate the Lord plays and diverts Himself in the garden of His creation, and if we could let go of our own obsession with what we think is the meaning of it all, we might be able to hear His call and follow Him in His mysterious, cosmic dance. We do not have go very far to catch echoes of that game, and of that dancing. When we are alone on a starlit night; when by chance we see the migrating birds in autumn descending on a grove of junipers to rest and eat; when we see children in a moment where they are really children; when we know love in our own hearts; or when, like the Japanese poet Basho we hear an old frog land in a quiet pond with a solitary splash — at such times the awakening, the turning inside out of all values, the "newness," the emptiness and the purity of vision that make themselves evident, provide a glimpse of the cosmic dance.

For the world and time are the dance of the Lord in emptiness. The silence of the spheres is the music of a wedding feast. The more we persist in misunderstanding the phenomena of life, the more we analyze them out into strange finalities and complex purposes of our own, the more we involve ourselves in sadness, absurdity and despair. But it does not matter much, because no despair of ours can alter the reality of things, or stain the joy of the cosmic dance which is always there. Indeed, we are in the midst of it, and it is in the midst of us, for it beats in our very blood, whether we want it to or not.

Yet the fact remains that we are invited to forget ourselves on purpose, cast our awful solemnity to the winds and join in the general dance. —*New Seeds of Contemplation* by Thomas Merton

I did not mean for all of this to happen to me. Or any of it, for that matter. I am still astonished by it all, and still a little afraid of it actually.

I only started out to put a little formal devotion into my life, a kind of crash course in organized prayer. At best, I had this vague notion of wanting to be a person whose first words in the morning were a prayer, a prayer that rose up in me as I rose up in bed. I am not even very certain where that notion came from. But since the day that it entered my head, nothing in my life is the same. Everything has changed—utterly, completely, irrevocably.

It started out harmlessly enough: my father had given me a copy of a book that he had been talking about for some months. There was a note inside: "Your brother and sister and Mom and I have been sort of going along through this book together. Next week we will be on week #17—Dad." Unbeknownst to him, I already had a copy of the book, he and I had been talking about it, and I confess that I did not even open the copy that he gave me until years later. The note was inside the front cover and I did not see it until he had been dead for two years. There were a lot of things to which I was not paying much attention in those days.

It is a small book, bound in blue leather, with a gold cross stamped on the front and three silk ribbons inside. Its pages are made of Bible paper. The book is divided into fifty-two weeks, laid out against the liturgical calendar, with a pattern to follow for prayer and scripture and reading and meditation each day and each week.

I cannot say exactly what motivated me to open the book on the particular March day that I finally did, how much of it was a deep sense of wanting to begin a disciplined routine of prayer and devotion, or how much of it had to do with marking my father's passing and wanting to be near him again in some way. It is clear now that I was being drawn slowly but steadily to a life that was more quiet, more contemplative, as I have come to know it to be called.

The morning I came across the book, I was working in a loft studio that my father helped me to carve out of the attic space above my living room. I sat at my writing table and looked over the rail and down into the living room at the patterns the morning sun was making on the floor below. I looked out the window through the fields of the farm across the way to see if the neighbors' horses were stirring yet. Beyond the farm I could see the steeple on a small church some friends of mine attend. I opened the book and something must have opened deep within me as well, though imperceptibly at first, even to myself. Certainly it was with no grand plan on my part.

"Painting cannot be taught," said Picasso once, "it can only be found." I think that in many ways that is true of prayer as well.

I do not write about prayer as one who knows the mysteries of prayer but as one, among many, who is drawn by the mystery of prayer. I never think of myself as a theologian or a teacher. On the days that I lead retreats, I think of myself only as the head cheerleader, and I am honored to be even that. On the very best of my other days, I consider myself a poet.

Sometimes I wish that I could sing or dance or paint or compose symphonies or build cathedrals to express somehow what all of this means to me. I wish I were a priest or a robin or a child or a sunset.

"I rage at my inability to express it all better," wrote Monet to a friend. "You'd have to use both hands and cover hundreds of canvases." A fountain pen and a blank page seem inadequate to me almost all of the time. Yet they are the tools that have chosen me.

Freelance copywriting and editing projects were what I did at the time to make a living. For me, it was the writer's equivalent of taking in laundry. My studio was pretty much covered up with piles of paper, mountains of stuff. I had been given a chance to ghostwrite a book, and I discovered that it was pretty hard to write a book in the same room where all the other work I was trying to do was calling out to me all the time about the deadlines to come and the money to collect.

Frederick Buechner tells of how he wrote for years in a Sunday school classroom at a church near where his little girl went to school. He would get up in the morning, put on a jacket and tie as though he were just like other fathers, and go off to work, dropping his daughter at school on his way. Then he would take morning prayers with the pastor of the church and go upstairs to write until it was time for him to pick his daughter up from school and head for home.

I looked across the field that morning and decided to give the pastor of the little church a call to see if they would let me work there. It was astounding to me but they said yes, I would be welcome to come and write there. It turned out that the pastor had known my father and he was kind to me because my father had been kind to him. It was not the first time that such a thing happened to me and I do not for a moment expect that it will be the last.

And so began the stretch of some months of rising early and doing the things that it took to help get young children to day care and preschool and so forth, and then over to the church to spend time in the sanctuary alone with the little blue book: reading from the saints and the scriptures, reciting the psalms, whispering the prayers, and scribbling in my journal. After a while, I would go upstairs to write until it was time to go and pick up the children and head off home.

Somewhere in that spring an ancient rhythm began to resonate within me, calling me, drawing me, compelling me to join in the general Dance.

I seemed then, and still seem, to have no control over my heart's response to that rhythm. Like the way one's feet start tapping when someone plays a country tune, one simply cannot stop even if one tries. My advice is that if you do not want to tap your feet, stay away from the jukebox. If you do not want to pray, then do not go near prayer books. Once your heart has heard the music, it is happy only when it is dancing. —*Living Prayer* by Robert Benson

In the little blue book, on page 115, in the readings for week 17, where I would have started in with my father had I started in when he gave me the book and the note, there is this sentence written by Nikos Kazantzakis: "Only he who obeys a rhythm superior to his own is free."

More than a decade has now passed since I first read that sentence. I did not even highlight it then, the way I did so many sentences in the book. I was not seeking anything like that at the time and could not have had any idea what such a sentence might mean to me or anyone else.

Nothing in my life is the same now. I do not live in the same house or even with the same people. Most of the material possessions that I had then are long gone, not by some great devout sacrifice on my part, but torn from my grasping hands by bankruptcy or divorce or other crisis. I fight a constant battle against depression, and I live a life that pretty much keeps me out of the mainstream most of the time. I am not complaining, nor am I bragging. I am simply trying to make the point that since the day I said yes to the tune that called me to the Dance, nothing has ever been the same. That is not to say, as some would have you believe, that everything has gone along swimmingly after my grand experience of the Transcendent. Much of it, most of it, has been really hard.

But from this vantage point, I can look back across those days and see that the rhythm of the Dance had begun to call me. It was so new to me then that I did not recognize it for what it was, and for what it is.

A life of prayer — or the spiritual life or the interior life, whatever term one uses for this journey that we have undertaken — is not completely linear, any more than one's intellectual or emotional life is linear. It is cyclical; it turns and turns again, and carries us along with it.

It is that turning that caught my attention then. It is that turning, that Dance, if you will, and its rhythms and steps and habits and joys and sorrows that draws me now.

If we are to live lives that enable us to hear more clearly who we really are, then we will have to learn to move to a rhythm that is superior to the ones we have fashioned for ourselves, or the ones a consumer society has foisted upon us. We will have to discover the rhythms of prayer and life that can be found in the steps of the Ancient of Dance of the Ancient of Days: the liturgy, the Eucharist, the calendar and the mass, the prayers of confession and intercession and recollection and contemplation, the habits of reading and retreat and working with our hands, the practices of hospitality and forgiveness and being with the poor.

Our lives must be shaped by the same rhythms that shaped the ancients, those who have gone before us. Only then will we be able to take up our places and join the general Dance. — *Living Prayer* by Robert Benson

Keep risking that your heart's desire is trustworthy. There is always another, deeper step you can take toward more complete trust, a more all-encompassing possibility of love. It will be this way until consecration becomes as ordinary and natural as breathing, until every act of every day is simply sacred, until there is no more separation of life from prayer, until each precious moment, awake and asleep, is consciously, knowingly infused with love, until compassion reigns and justice pervades all things, and until life becomes what it was

meant to be: sheer enjoyment and pure dancing in the
spaciousness of love. — *The Awakened Heart* by Gerald G.
May

Before meeting the disciples on the boat, Jesus is alone
on the mountain. He walks down slowly— grinning
after listening to affectionate words from his father and
soaking up the stillness after a day crowded with people
and noise. His eyes sparkle as God stirs the wind and
sprinkles refreshing drops of rain onto his face through
the evergreen boughs. Jesus probably loves walking on
the water the way I love walking on the beach in a
storm. The fury of the wind and water career
ecstatically about, but he doesn't feel scared, just
exhilarated by nature swirling through the air and at his
feet. He is dancing in the waves while the disciples
cower in fear. Peter senses this wild peace as Jesus
approaches:

"Don't be afraid," Jesus laughs
as he sees the stricken faces
and hears a barely audible
whisper, "It's a ghost—"
from the quaking boat.
"It's only me."

Peter, scared as the rest
but intrigued by the peace
in the Voice
stutters through fear,
"Jesus, if it's really you,
ask me to come dance on the water."

"Come,
dance with me," answers Jesus.

So Peter steps off the boat

onto the whirling, raging dance floor.
He looks into Jesus' eyes,
letting him lead the first steps
on the water,
and, for a few miraculous moments,

they dance.

Amazed at the wildness of the dance,
Peter looks away just as the
sea and sky and fish
dance more fiercely to welcome
him to the revelry.

Fear grips him as
he begins to sink,
realizing his feet
are anchored on nothing
but mystery,
moving to a rhythm
he doesn't yet understand —
though nature seems to know
the same song
that coursed through him
in the beginning,

which frightens and excites
him all the more.

"Lord, save me!" he cries
and looks up to find the playful eyes
of the One he has come to love
but not understand.

"Why did you doubt?" Jesus smiles
as he reaches down for Peter's frigid hand
and pulls him gently into the boat.

"We could have danced all night."

The storm slows its dance to the
rhythm of waves lapping a lullaby
against the small boat.
Disciples look in awe
on the peaceful, smiling One
and their friend
who is beginning to never recover
from a taste of the dance.

"Truly you are the Son of God," they mutter.
"No one else could dance like that . . ."
— *Storm Dance* by Caroline McKinney Karnes

The universe is dancing. And the smallest bit of
matter knows, unerringly and interiorly, the dance. Let
there be no more talk of flashing signal lights. No more
solitary figures sending out messages in quantum
bottles to be picked up light years later on some distant
star. No more cumbersome cosmic intelligence network
dependent on the measurable flight of photons. The
timing of this dance must take into account something
more than the speed of light. It must take in to account a
"knowing" universe. — *And the Trees Clap Their Hands* by
Virginia Stem Owens

Once I applied my personal rhythm of response to
my prayer life, I felt a profound sense of release and
relief. Not only did I naturally respond to God's love
from the rhythm of my own way of relating, *but now I
had found the way that would last a lifetime!* My own
natural "discipline" was deeply planted in my own
inner uniqueness. I had just never bothered to look at
my uniqueness and respect it. I did not have to "take
on" or "enter into" anything. I had only to observe the

way my most fulfilling relationships worked and respond in that way in my relationship to God.

For me, this new approach meant that I could pray sitting down and meditating in depth, or I could talk to God spontaneously through the day. I could pray for five or ten minutes instead of an hour. It was all right if I prayed after lunch or late in the evening instead of before breakfast. I could walk in silence with God, listen to music with God, or exercise or dance in my living room with God. — *Feed My Shepherds* by Flora Slosson Wuellner

The Soil of Your Soul

I. Opening Prayer

Father,

Allow the soil of my soul to be a place that is fertile and receptive to all that you desire to plant in my heart. Tend it carefully and nurture all that has sprung up in me that is of you; that I may be a garden of your delight. Through Jesus. Amen.

II. Psalm 65

III. Daily Scripture Readings

Monday	Mark 4:1-20
Tuesday	Mark 4:26-29
Wednesday	Mark 4:30-32
Thursday	Matthew 13:24-30
Friday	John 12:20-28
Saturday	Isaiah 5:1-7
Sunday	1 Corinthians 3:1-9

IV. Readings for Reflection

V. Reflection and Listening: silent and written

VI. Prayer: for the church, for others, for myself

VII. Song   *You Have Redeemed My Soul*

VIII. Closing Prayer

Grow yourself in me O God. Make me receptive to the ways that you water and tend this garden of my heart. Prune me where I need pruning, nurture me where I need nurturing, weed me where I need weeding, and care for me tenderly where I need your tender care. Help me to trust in you, O Gardner of my soul. In the name of Jesus. Amen.

Readings for Reflection-

unnamed by Jim Branch

watering the seed
       and watching
       and believing
       and hoping
       and waiting
       for it to grow and emerge from the soil
       so it can be seen
what sort of thing is this that grows within?
       in the deep rich darkness that is not dark to you
       knowing that there is growth within
       but not knowing quite what it is
       knowing and not knowing
trusting the seed to do its job
       it knows what it is to become
       and when
and so I water
       and watch
       and believe
       and hope
       and wait
       and know
       and not know

When you meditate or abide in your quiet times of communion, you do not charge in and do something, like saying, "I will now be good and move mountains by my act of faith." No, you water your garden, knowing that these ideas are growing into a heavenly garden; the indwelling spirit doeth the work, not you. You merely water it. Do you not see the comfort there is in that? I can tell you in primer language that a very gentle, calm, unemotional, selfless, and patient attitude toward your spiritual growth is essential—such as all old gardeners

know. They know that patience, hoeing, watering, and certain order, a quiet rhythm, bring a heavenly beauty.
— *Letters of the Scattered Brotherhood* by Mary Strong

Living things need an appropriate climate in order to grow and bear fruit. If they are to develop to completion, they require an environment that allows their potential to be realized. The seed will not grow unless there is soil that can feed it, light to draw it forth, warmth to nurture and moisture that unlocks its vitality. Time is also required for its growth to unfold.

Meditation is the attempt to provide the soul with the proper environment in which to grow and become. In the lives of people like St. Francis or St. Catherine of Genoa one gets a glimpse of what the soul is able to become. Often this is seen as the result of heroic action lying beyond the possibility of ordinary people. The flowering of the human soul, however, is more a matter of the proper spiritual environment than of particular gifts or disposition or heroism. How seldom we wonder at the growth of the great redwood from a tiny seed dropped at random on the littered floor of the forest. From one seed is grown enough wood to frame several hundred houses. The human soul has seed potential like this if it has the right environment. Remember that only in a few mountain valleys were the conditions right for the Sequoia gigantean, the mighty redwood, to grow.

For both the seed and the soul, these things all take time. In both cases there is need for patience. Most of us know enough not to poke at the seed to see if it is sprouting, or to try to hurry it along with too much water or fertilizer or cultivation. The same respect must be shown for the soul as its growth starts to take place. Growth can seldom be forced in nature. Whether it is producing a tree or a human personality, nature unfolds its growth slowly, silently. — *The Other Side of Silence* by Morton T. Kelsey

I find you there in all these things
I care for like a brother.
A seed, you nestle in the smallest of them,
and in the huge ones spread yourself hugely.

Such is the amazing play of powers:
they give themselves so willingly,
swelling in the roots, thinning as the trunks rise,
and in the high leaves, resurrection.
— *The Book of Hours* by Rainer Maria Rilke

Every moment and every event of every man's life on earth plants something in his soul. For just as the winds carries thousands of invisible and visible winged seeds, so the stream of time brings with it germs of spiritual vitality that come to rest imperceptibly in the minds and wills of men. Most of these unnumbered seeds perish and are lost, because men are not prepared to receive them: for such seeds as these cannot spring up anywhere except in the good soil of liberty and desire.

The mind that is the prisoner of its own pleasure and the will that is the captive of its own desire cannot accept the seeds of a higher pleasure and a supernatural desire.

For how can I receive the seeds of freedom if I am in love with slavery and how can I cherish the desire of God if I am filled with another and opposite desire? God will not plant His liberty in me because I am a prisoner and I do not even desire to be free. I love my captivity and I lock myself in the desire for things that I hate, and I have hardened my heart against true love. (*Seeds of Contemplation* by Thomas Merton)

Once again, give up all concerns about success and failure. What you are doing in these times of formal meditation is planting the prayer within yourself so that it will be there through the rest of the day. It is indeed very much like planting a seed in the ground. You just put it there and let it take its natural course. Don't keep digging it up to see how it is growing. Don't try to manipulate or control it; just notice it, appreciate it. Entrust its care to God. — *The Awakened Heart* by Gerald G. May

Spiritual disciplines are like garden tools. The best spade and hoe in the world cannot guarantee a good crop. They can only make it more likely the growth will be unobstructed. The mystery of maturation lies in the heart of the seed, the outcome of planting depends largely on the vagaries of weather. Still, tools are important in helping to ensure that planted seeds will bear fruit. Tools can remove stones and roots, aerate the soil, weed and water the garden.

Disciplines like prayer, scriptural reflection, and hospitality have the character of garden tools. They keep the soil of our love clear of obstruction. They keep us open to the mysterious work of grace in our heart and our world. They enable us not only to receive but to respond to God's love, which in turn yields the fruits of the Spirit in our lives. — *Soul Feast* by Marjorie J. Thompson

A seed only flourishes by staying in the ground in which it is sown. When you keep digging the seed up to check whether it is growing, it will never bear fruit. Think about yourself as a little seed planted in rich soil. All you have to do is stay there and trust that the soil contains everything you need to grow. This growth takes place even when you do not feel it. Be quiet, acknowledge your powerlessness, and have faith that one day you will know how much you have received. — *The Inner Voice of* Love by Henri J. M. Nouwen

I love the plough that opens up the earth, lays bare the soil where seed can fall. It matters little that the widening wound of earth still hesitates, uncertain of the nutrients it has to offer falling seed. The seed is sown, the wound of earth closed up again. The broken soil becomes a womb, a sheltering tomb of life protecting what must die to live. We wait then for signs of life: the stem, the leaf, the bud, the fruit or vegetable to wend its way from dark to light. The image of the plough opening the soil to welcome seed offers us a metaphor for the human heart. The heart too must be prepared, readied to receive its daily seed. No more looking back!

I love the Word of God that pierces the human heart, lays bare the soul where seed can fall. The sower's passion invites the heart to receptivity. The sower looks not back to see if the heart is worthy. Sower and plough become one. With contemplative awareness they trust the widening wound of the opening heart. This laying bare the heart's good soil is a moment of readiness. She or he who receives the seed of the Word of God receives also the silence of the Word and waits to be transformed. No more looking back!

I love the disciple who allows the heart to be pierced. Obedient to the piercing Word and broken heart, the disciple learns to wait, trusting the Word to die and live within the heart's good soil. The disciple's heart becomes a sheltering womb and tomb for what must die to live. I love the one who is transformed into a disciple by surrendering to the Word of God. Rooted in obedience to the Word, there is no more looking back!
— *Abide* by Macrina Wiederkehr

Ordinary

I. Opening Prayer

Lord Jesus, help me to be attentive to your presence and your voice this day. Help me to not get so caught up in the comings and goings of it that I miss you completely. Thank you that you desire my company and my attention. Help me to give you both. Amen. —*Pieces* II by Jim Branch

II. Psalm 98

III. Daily Scripture Reading

Monday	John 2:1-11
Tuesday	Luke 2:41-52
Wednesday	Isaiah 53:1-6
Thursday	Acts 4:1-13
Friday	Exodus 3:1-14
Saturday	2 Corinthians 4:7-18
Sunday	Genesis 28:10-22

IV. Readings for Reflection

V. Reflection and Listening: silent and written

VI. Prayer: for the church, for others, for myself

VII. Song *How Great is Our God*

VIII. Closing Prayer

Our Father, help us to see you today in all that we come into contact with, knowing that you use ordinary things to give us an extraordinary sense of your presence in our lives. In the name of Jesus. Amen.

Readings for Reflection-

How do you feel about the word *ordinary*? What does it do within you? *Ordinary* is not the most popular word in the English language. As a matter of fact, it is far from it, though it need not be. Because the word *ordinary* comes from the word *ordinalis* which refers to numbers in a series, and ultimately comes from the Latin root *ordo*, from which we get the word *order*. So if the word *ordinary* does not conjure up good images for us, maybe we should look at its origin and see how we feel about the word *order*. I, for one, was never really drawn to the word *ordinary*, particularly in my younger days. Although I'll have to admit that the older I get, the more the word has grown on me in a very good way, especially considering its roots. I am, however, really drawn to the word *order*. There's just something about it that I like

When it comes to the church calendar, Ordinary Time is often viewed in very much the same way. All of the other seasons have a particular aim, focus, or feast attached to them it seems, making them feel especially significant. Therefore, when we come to Ordinary Time it is easy to view it as something lesser or inferior in quality because of its lack of those elements. But nothing could be further from the truth. In fact, Ordinary Time is not inferior at all, it is actually quite the opposite. Ordinary Time is the space in which we live most of our lives, which if for no other reason makes it incredibly significant. It is the season in which we learn the art of loving and following Jesus in the context of our everyday lives, walking with and living for him on a day to day basis. In the words of Philip Reinders: *"With all the big holidays and celebrations over, Ordinary Time offers us the space to find our place in God's story. We've celebrated and taken in the momentous life of Jesus; now we need a long stretch of days to absorb and assimilate it.*

In Ordinary Time, we fully take in the gospel, allowing it to take shape in our daily living, making connections between Jesus' story and our lives"

Therefore, Ordinary Time is of incredible significance. For not only is it the largest segment of the liturgical year, but it is also, by its very nature, the season where we learn the significance of taking care to order our lives in certain ways. For if, in our heart of hearts, what we most deeply desire in our lives is a living union with God, it will not *just fall on our heads.* We will have to desire it and intentionally seek it out. Ordinary Time is the time and the season where we must do just that; where we prayerfully order our lives in ways that create fruitful space for God to move and to work and to act. And there's nothing ordinary about that!

—Jim Branch, July, 2015

"Jesus has so diligently searched for the lowest place that it would be very difficult for anyone to tear it from him."

Nazareth was the lowest place: the place of the poor, the unknown, of those who didn't count, of the mass of workers, of people subjected to work's grim demands just for a scrap of bread.

But there is more. Jesus is the "Holy One of God." But the Holy One of God realized his sanctity not in an extraordinary life, but one impregnated with ordinary things: work, family and social life, obscure human activities, simple things shared by all people.

The perfection of God is cast in a material which people almost despise, which they don't consider worth searching for because of its simplicity, its lack of interest, because it is common to all of us. —*Letters from the Desert* by Carlo Carreto

It is a serious thing to live in a society of possible gods and goddesses, to remember that the dullest and most uninteresting person you talk to may one day be a creature which, if you saw it now, you would be strongly tempted to worship...There are no ordinary people. You have never talked to a mere mortal.
— *The Weight of Glory* by C. S. Lewis

You enter the extraordinary by way of the ordinary. Something you have seen a thousand times you suddenly see as if for the first time like the looking glass over the mantle or the curtains of the bed.
— *Telling the Truth* by Frederick Buechner

Pastoral work, I learned later, is the aspect of Christian ministry that specializes in the ordinary. It is the nature of pastoral life to be attentive to, immersed in, and appreciative of the everyday texture of people's lives — the buying and selling, the visiting and meeting, the going and coming. — *The Contemplative Pastor* by Eugene Peterson

God sent the Spirit of truth, he dwells in your heart. You have only to listen, to follow, and he will lead you to the complete truth. He leads through all the events and circumstances of your life. Nothing in your life is so insignificant, so small (so ordinary), that God cannot be found at its center. We think of God in the dramatic things, the tempestuous seas; but he is the little things too, in a smile of a passer-by or the gnarled hands of an old man, in a daisy, a tiny insect, falling leaves. God is in music, in laughter, and in sorrow too. And the grey times, when monotony stretches out ahead, these can be the times of steady, solid growth into God. — *Prayer* by Mother Frances Dominic

Our mundane experiences contain all the stuff of
holiness and of human growth in grace. Our world is
rife with messages and signatures of the Spirit. Our
encounters with one another are potential sites of
awakening and energizing that characterize the Spirit.
But so much goes unnoticed. We fail to recognize the
light that shines through all the chinks and the dusty
panes of our daily lives. We are too busy to name the
event that is blessed in its ordinariness, holy in its
uniqueness, and grace-filled in its underlying challenge.
— *Every Bush Is Burning* by Joan Puls

Barefoot
by Rachel G. Hackenberg

May I walk in this day
as though with bare feet:

more attuned to the hard earth and to
the extravagance of my daily comforts,

more inclined to splash playfully
in puddles than to avoid them,

more sensitive to the toe-stubbing-stones
that we so casually toss into one others' paths,

slowed down by necessity of caution
to be more mindful of spirit and direction,

deliberately risking the softening of calluses
to sense more fully the mystery of holy ground.

The man who knows God hears his step in the tramp of daily events, discerns him near at hand to help, and hears his answer to the appeal of prayer in a hundred happenings outwardly small and insignificant, where another man can talk only of remarkable coincidence, amazing accident, or peculiar turns of events. That is why periods when the life of faith is strong, and men have enthusiastically surrendered themselves to God, have also been times rich in miracles.

— Walter Eichrodt

Earth's crammed with heaven,
And every common bush afire with God:
But only [those] who see, take off [their] shoes;
The rest sit round it, and pluck blackberries.
— *Aurora Leigh* by Elizabeth Barrett Browning

Time

I. Opening Prayer
Lord,

Help me walk slowly and deeply with you through the hours and minutes of this day — that I might find all of you that is to be found within it. Allow me not to miss you because of hurry or busyness, but let me sense the fullness of your presence in each moment. Slow down both my feet and my heart that I might be more present to you as I go about my normal activities. In the Name of Jesus I pray. Amen.

II. Psalm 90

III. Daily Scripture Readings
Monday	Ecclesiastes 3:1-11
Tuesday	Psalm 103:13-19
Wednesday	2 Corinthians 5:11-6:2
Thursday	Isaiah 58:11-14
Friday	Mark 13:32-37
Saturday	Luke 12:35-48, 54-56
Sunday	Hebrews 3:7-19

IV. Readings for Reflection

V. Reflection and Listening: silent and written

VI. Prayer: for the church, for others, for myself

VII. Song   *Come, Now is the Time to Worship*

VIII. Closing Prayer
O Christ, when I look at you I see that you were never in a hurry, never ran, but always had time for the pressing necessities of the day. Give me that disciplined,

poised life with time always for the thing that matters.
For then I would be a disciplined person. Amen.
— *The Way* by E. Stanley Jones

Readings for Reflection-

"How we spend our days is, of course, how we spend our lives," wrote Annie Dillard, knowing full well how easy it is for each of us to *miss it* in this life. One day after another can simply slip past, almost without our even noticing it.

Whether it be busyness, or chaos, or mundane routine, somehow days can have the tendency to lull us to sleep if we are not careful, if we are not attentive to the fact that each day, and each moment of each day, is itself a holy invitation. After all, it is no accident that the first thing in Scripture that God called holy was a day (Genesis 2:3). It is almost as if God himself, from the very beginning, had to remind us that days are both sacred and significant. In fact, they are the time and the space where we meet him, and know him.

Days are themselves invitations, opportunities, and doorways into holiness. Therefore, let us not allow one more of them slip by unnoticed, but let us engage each little day, and each little moment of that day, with all the life and zeal and attention and expectation we can muster. Because before we know it, one day will have turned into another, and another, and a lifetime will have passed us by.

— Jim Branch, July, 2012

The Greek word *chronos* means "time" in a quantitative sense, chronological time, time that you can divide into minutes and years, time as duration. It is the sense that we mean when we say, "What time is it?" or "How much time do I have?" or ""Time like an ever-flowing stream," in one of the hymns we sing. But in Greek there is also the word *kairos*, which means "time" in the qualitative sense — not the kind that a clock measures but time that cannot be measured at all, time that is characterized by what happens in it. *Kairos* time is the kind that you mean when you say that "the time is ripe" to do something, "It's time to tell the truth," a truth-telling kind of time. Or "I had a good time" — the time had something about it that made me glad. The ancient poet who wrote the Book of Ecclesiastes was using time in a *kairos* sense when he wrote of a time to weep and a time to laugh, a time to keep silence and a time to speak. — *The Hungering Dark* by Frederick Buechner

In each moment of chronological time, the divine value of each moment is available to us in proportion to our sensitivity to the Spirit of Christ. The Spirit suggests what is to be done at each moment in our relationship to God, ourselves, other people, and the cosmos. When we listen to the movements of the Spirit rather than to our own bright ideas and self-centered programs for happiness, the internal commentary that normally sustains our emotional upsets comes to an end, enabling us to accept difficult situations and people.
— *Awakenings* by Thomas Keating

"My hour has not yet come" (John 2:4). Jesus lived with a keen sense of the opportune time. He recognized the deep rhythms of God's purpose flowing through his days, and sensed when they would coalesce into the weighty hour. There would be the hour of the final table fellowship (Luke 22:14), abandonment (John 16:32), glorification (John 17:1), departure (John 13:1), and unexpected return (Luke 12:40). There would be episodes of healing (John 4:52), seasons of true worship (John 4:23), and moments of remembrance (John 16:4).

So conscious was Jesus of the steadfast love of God enduring throughout the meandering course of human history that he could give himself freely and fully to the current events surrounding him. Far from being swept along by time's rush and tumble, Jesus lived life purposefully and therefore patiently.

—John Mogabgab

slow by Jim Branch

the pace of this amazing journey
    seems to be lessening as each year goes by
    not from need but from desire
    desire to see, desire to notice, desire to pay attention
but life continues on
    frenetically around
    passing by on the right and the left
    people on their way to who knows where
    zipping here and darting there
    rushing to this and racing to that
    a frenzy of activity
    afraid to miss anything
    and yet so much is missed.
the landscape of the journey goes unnoticed
    the incredible detail of life is overlooked
    invitations to transcendence are passed by
i want to travel at a very slow pace
    looking and longing for depth
    seeing the intricacies of life
    accepting the invitation to sit and watch
    yearning for others to join me
yet few seem willing to walk slowly enough to keep up

Perhaps our most hidden sin is that we have so little time for one another. We need so much more than television has to offer. We need to relearn how to relate eye to eye, hand to hand, heart to heart. We have to encourage one another to keep walking toward Jesus, toward joy, toward truth. — *Free to Be Nothing* by Edward Farrell

Men nowadays take time far more seriously than eternity. — *A Testament of Devotion* by Thomas Kelly

Hope that grows out of trust puts us in a different relationship to the hours and days of our lives. We are constantly tempted to look at time as chronology, as *chronos*, as a series of disconnected incidents and accidents. This one way we think we can manage time or subdue tasks. Or a way that we feel the victims of our schedules. For this approach also means that time becomes burdensome. We divide our time into minutes and hours and weeks and let its compartments dominate us.

As still not completely converted people we immerse ourselves in clock time. Time becomes a means to an end, not moments in which to enjoy God or pay attention to others. And we end up believing that the real thing is always still to come. Time for celebrating or praying or dreaming gets squeezed out. No wonder we get fatigued and deflated! No wonder we sometimes feel helpless or impoverished in our experience of time.

But the gospel speaks of "full" time. What we are seeking is already here. The contemplative Thomas Merton once wrote, "The Bible is concerned with time's fullness, the time for an event to happen, the time for an emotion to be felt, the time for a harvest or for the celebration of a harvest" (*The Literary Essays of Thomas Merton*). We begin to see history not as a collection of events interrupting what we "must" get done. We see time in light of faith in the God of history. We see how the events of this year are not just a series of incidents and accidents, happy or unhappy, but the molding hands of God, who wants us to grow and mature.

Time has to be converted, then, from *chronos*, mere chronological time, to *kairos*, a New Testament Greek word that has to do with opportunity, with moments that seems ripe for their intended purpose. Then, even while life continues to seem harried, while it continues to have hard moments, we say, "Something good is happening amid all this." We get glimpses of how God might be working out his purposes in our days. Time becomes not just something to get through or manipulate or manage, but the arena of God's work with us. Whatever happens — good things or bad, pleasant or problematic — we look and ask, "What might God be doing here?" We see the events of the day as continuing occasions to change the heart. Time points to Another and begins to speak to us of God. — *Turn My Mourning Into Dancing* by Henri J. M. Nouwen

I will never forget the afternoon that I was called to the emergency room where Duane Barney was just rushed after a heart attack. Duane was the chair of the search committee that brought me to the church, and was my frequent advisor. I depended greatly on his mature spiritual counsel, and I depended even more on his gracious friendship.

When I arrived at the hospital, I found Virginia, his wife, sitting with another member of our church staff. After talking about his condition with the physician, we prayed, talked to each other, read some Scripture, and then we prayed some more. We made a few phone calls to family members who lived out of town. Then we got to that point where you just sit quietly and wait for some news. We waited for a long time. In life, the waiting is so important because it prepares us for the news that comes not from a doctor, but from the Savior.

After about a half hour, Virginia absentmindedly picked up Duane's DayTimer, which had been given to her by the ambulance driver. As she began to thumb through the pages, a gentle smile emerged on her tear-streaked face. On every page, at the bottom of a full day of appointments, Duane had made a list of things for which he was particularly thankful that day. And at the top of every list was the name Virginia.

Duane did not survive that heart attack, but Virginia did. Knowing that she was so dearly loved made all the difference at the end of Duane's life.

Since that day in the waiting room, I have often wondered what people would learn about me if they picked up my DayTimer. Would they discover that I, like Duane, used each day as an expression of gratitude? Or would they simply see a life that had been crammed into the half-hour slots on each page? — *Hustling God* by M. Craig Barnes

I have squandered more money and time on toys and diversions than I would like to tell. We are allotted only a few years to labor in this vineyard. Are we squandering or investing the precious resources of time, talent, and treasure which have been entrusted us by our heavenly Master? — *That I May Know God* by Kenneth Boa

There is never enough time to do everything, but there is always enough time to do the important. — *Awake My Soul* by Timothy Jones

Not long after moving to Chicago, I called a wise friend to ask for some spiritual direction. I described the pace at which things tend to move in my current setting. I told him about the rhythms of our family life and about the present condition of my heart, as best I could discern it. What did I need to do, I asked him, to be spiritually healthy?

Long pause.

"You must ruthlessly eliminate hurry from your life," he said at last. Another long pause.

"Okay, I've written that one down," I told him, a little impatiently. "That's a good one. Now what else is there?" I had many things to do, and this was a long-distance conversation, so I was anxious to cram as many units of spiritual wisdom into the least amount of time possible.

Another long pause.

"There is nothing else," he said.

He was the wisest spiritual mentor I have known. And while he doesn't know every detail about every grain of sin in my life, he knows quite a bit. And from an immense quiver of spiritual sagacity, he drew only one arrow. "There is nothing else," he said, "You must ruthlessly eliminate hurry from your life."

Imagine for a moment that someone gave you this prescription, with the warning that your life depends on it. Consider the possibility that perhaps your life *does* depend on it. Hurry is the great enemy of spiritual life in our day. Hurry can destroy our souls. Hurry can keep us from living well. As Carl Jung wrote, "Hurry is not *of* the devil; hurry *is* the devil."

Again and again, as we pursue spiritual life, we must do battle with hurry. For many of us the great danger is not that we will renounce our faith. It is that we will become so distracted and rushed and preoccupied that we will settle for a mediocre version of it. We will just skim our lives instead of actually living them. — *The Life You've Always Wanted* by John Ortberg

When I imagine my own life simple and uncomplicated, I picture my room and desk tidy, everything in its place.

I myself am moving gracefully and graciously from one task to the next with precision, on schedule but with no strain or pressure. The schedule and the tasks are perfectly synchronized. It could all be so simple, I say to myself, if everything were only in its place.

But it isn't. It's complicated. It's complicated because people don't stay in place. They aren't predictable, they foul up my schedule, they interfere with my agenda, they make demands I hadn't programmed. It's complicated because there is too much to do, too many tasks, too many needs, too much going on. I can't keep up with it all; I'm always at least a step or two behind. I can't do everything that needs to be done; I feel burdened, sometimes even guilty, for being so limited. And I think maybe I'm doing it wrong, and if I could just figure out how to do it right I'd be able to meet everyone's needs. It's complicated because there's never enough time. In my anxiety to conquer time by controlling its dispensation, I feel myself victimized by it. I am unable to find time, take time, get time: all control words.

Mostly what I find is frustration. My life is out of control. I feel a need to be in control of my life and all the factors, situations, and people that complicate it. I set myself over-against them and need to dominate them, to subject them to my agenda, fit them into my program. I do have an agenda, and I don't want it interrupted. I set up my day and I offer it to God.

But there's something wrong in the picture. When I imagine — or when I experience — the simple way, everything moves in a rhythm. There is an Agenda, and I'm in tune with it, but it's not my creation. I don't need to worry about controlling; I don't need to be anxious that it won't all work out. I'm not in command and don't need to be.... The interruptions are as integral to the scene as anything I had planned. I only receive the

day and the program that comes to me during the day
from God. And that's what makes the difference.
—*Reflections on Simplicity* by Elaine M. Prevallet

i'm trying to catch up with myself,
but the faster i run, the
more of myself i leave behind,
—*A Heart* Exposed by Steven James

Balance

I. Opening Prayer

Dear Jesus,

During this day help me quiet all the thoughts that fill my head—where I must go, whom I must see, and what I must do. In their place, give me a sense of your order, your peace, and your time.

Help me to understand that you are in control, and I can trust you with my day. Help me to realize that nothing on my to-do list is important if it is not what you want me to do.

I give all my tasks to you and trust you to bring order to them. In these moments, dear Jesus, come to me, be with me, and free me from the tyranny of "to do."

—*Quiet Spaces* by Patricia F. Wilson

II. Psalm 127

III. Daily Scripture Readings

Monday	Psalm 62:1-12
Tuesday	Matthew 11:28-30
Wednesday	Isaiah 30:15
Thursday	Matthew 6:25-34
Friday	Isaiah 55:1-13
Saturday	Luke 10:38-42
Sunday	Hebrews 10:19-26

IV. Readings for Reflection

V. Reflection and Listening: silent and written

VI. Prayer: for the church, for others, for myself

VII. Song   *Be the Center*

VIII. Closing Prayer

You have taught us that in returning and rest we shall be saved, in quietness and confidence we shall be strengthened. By Your Spirit lift us to Your Presence where we may be still and know that You are God.

—*Living Prayer* by Robert Benson

Readings for Reflection-

When most of us think of the word *balance,* we think of a life with the proper amounts of everything, a life in which our work and play and family and friendships and faith all receive comparable amounts of attention and energy. In the spiritual life, however, the word balance must be defined differently. As a matter of fact, the word balance might not be the most appropriate word to use at all. The word *centered* might be more accurate. Because in the life of faith, balance means having Christ as the center around which everything else revolves. Thus, life is only balanced when everything is centered on Christ. He is the hub of the wheel; the focal point of our lives that allows them to function the way they were created to function. So that means the question is not *"Do we have enough of God in our lives?"* but *"Is Christ the center of our lives? What do our lives revolve around?"* The answer to these questions will tell us a lot about whether or not our lives are truly balanced.

—Jim Branch, August, 2004

Most of our conflicts and difficulties come from trying to deal with the spiritual and practical aspects of our life separately instead of realizing them as parts of a one whole. If our practical life is centered on our own interests, cluttered up by possessions, distracted by ambitions, passions, wants and worries, beset by a sense of our own rights and importance, or anxieties for our own future, or longings for our own success, we need not expect that our spiritual life will be a contrast to all this. The soul's house is not built on such a convenient plan: there are few soundproof partitions in it. Only when the conviction — not merely the idea — that the demand of the Spirit, however inconvenient, comes first and IS first, rules the whole of it, will those objectionable noises die down which have a way of penetrating into the nicely furnished oratory, and drowning all the quieter voices by their din. — *The Spiritual Life* by Evelyn Underhill

Here the deeper meaning of any rule in the spiritual life becomes visible. Instead of giving us methods to control and direct and determine our own life, a spiritual rule wants to offer an open and free space within and among us where God can touch us with God's loving presence. It wants to make it possible for us not so much to find God as to be found by God, not so much to direct our life towards God, as to be directed by God, not so much to love God, as to be loved by God.

This might sound quite passive. But the contrary is true. It requires active spiritual work to keep space for God. Why? Our ever-present fears keep trying to fill up every bit of free space with countless thoughts, words and actions that can give us the illusion that after all we are in control. Even though we have learned the hard way how little in control we really are, and even though we continue to suffer from the consequences of a life built on illusion, it remains very difficult to let God be the director and guide of our lives. — Henri J. M. Nouwen, from the Foreword to *Rule for a New Brother*

I had come to wonder sometimes at the lack of depth in my prayer. I began to worry, too, at the sense of imbalance in my life and at the lack of centeredness as well. I began to wonder if those things had a connection to my prayer. I began to realize that the longing that I had, and have, for the presence of God could no longer be filled by a few stolen moments of extemporaneous prayer. I began to have a sneaking suspicion that prayer was a larger and deeper and richer and more astonishing thing than I had known before. I began to desire a way of life that was more like the lively and reasonable sacrifice that is called for by the words of the Eucharist.

Although my life had been spent largely in the church and around people of faith, I had had a growing sense that I could go no deeper in my journey without some manner of instruction and experience in some ways of prayer other than the one I already knew. "We fool ourselves if we think that such a sacramental way of living is automatic," wrote Richard Foster once, in a book about prayer and discipline. "This kind of living communion does not just fall on our heads. We must desire it and seek it out. We must order our lives in particular ways." — *A Good Life* by Robert Benson

The action of those whose lives are given to the Spirit has in it something of the leisure of Eternity; and because of this, they achieve far more than those whose lives are enslaved by the rush and hurry, the unceasing tick-tick of the world. In the spiritual life it is very important to get our timing right. Otherwise we tend to forget that God, Who is greater than our heart, is greater than our job too. It is only when we have learnt all that this means that we possess the key to the Kingdom of Heaven. — *The Spiritual Life* by Evelyn Underhill

More recently I'm beginning to understand that, in my life with God, the word *discipline* means the endeavor to create space in my life in which *God* can act. Discipline means being intentional about preventing everything in my life from being filled up. The diligent watchfulness guards my soul from intrusions that crowd out God.

Marking off space for God to be at work is a challenge because God likes doing things with me that I hadn't counted on. He likes to decide the agenda rather than docilely going along with my carefully scripted list of activities. If I leave God too little space, the desires God has for me and for our time together simply don't happen. This is the why of solitude with God. I simply make room for God to do what only God is able to do. Yet the excuses I make (to myself and to others) for not making this space are endless. Why would I want to cheat myself out of God's deepest longing for me? Is it because I don't trust God? Is it because I'm addicted to being in charge? Is it because I'm simply afraid to let go and rest in the silence of God's presence?

If I am ever to enjoy a rhythm of solitude and silence, I will always need to exert some effort. However, the effort is not to be building outwardly but to protect that little cell of my heart, the part of me where God and I get to be together — to protect it and then to find the solitude where God will enter and spend time with me.
— *Running on Empty* by Fil Anderson

Only by taking our life apart from time to time and examining it carefully, and then putting it back together thoughtfully and prayerfully, only then can we have some measure of confidence that we are living the life that we were meant to lead.

"Only he who obeys a rhythm that is superior to his own," wrote Kazantzakis, "is free."

The superior rhythm is the one that was made by God and whispered into us at the time that we were whispered into being. It is a rhythm that is based on the light and darkness of the day itself. It is a rhythm that supports all of our lives — prayer, rest, community and work. — *A Good Life* by Robert Benson

What I am looking for is some sort of balance in my life—a balance "so delicate, so risky, so creative", as Maria Boulding puts it, that she likens it to a bird in flight, a dancer in motion. One of the favorite words in the Rule of St. Benedict is "run", St. Benedict tells me to run to Christ. If I stop for a moment and consider what is being asked of me here, and what is involved in the act of running, I think of how when I run I place first one foot and then the other on the ground, that I let go of my balance for a second and then immediately recover it again. It is risky, this matter of running. By daring to lose my balance I keep it. —*Living with Contradiction* by Esther de Waal

Perhaps the answer for all of us fainthearted ones is to do less and not more. To walk slower rather than faster. To be more present to this day than we are to tomorrow. To just stand there sometimes rather than just do something.

Perhaps we need to remember that the work we do is not actually the center of the universe. The work that we do—whatever it is, whatever hat we are wearing, however great or small it may seem to us or to anyone else at the time—is to be done in the service of the Center of the Universe. —*A Good Life* by Robert Benson

For the spiritual life is simply a life in which all that we do comes from the centre, where we are anchored in God: a life soaked through and through by a sense of reality and calm, and self-given to the great movement of His will. —*The Spiritual Life* by Evelyn Underhill

Space

I. Opening Prayer
Teach me, God to make room for you in all the events and affairs of my days. Then I shall find rest. Then I will be at peace with myself and with you. —*A Guide to Prayer for All Who Seek God* by Rueben P. Job and Norman Shawchuck

II. Psalm 18

III. Daily Scripture Readings

Monday	Psalm 31:1-8
Tuesday	Deuteronomy 8:1-20
Wednesday	Genesis 26:12-22
Thursday	Deuteronomy 11:8-32
Friday	John 8:31-38
Saturday	Matthew 6:5-6
Sunday	Psalm 37:1-11

IV. Readings for Reflection

V. Reflection and Listening: silent and written

VI. Prayer: for the church, for others, for myself

VII. Song   *How Deep the Father's Love*

VIII. Closing Prayer
O Lord, the house of my soul is too small for you to enter: make it more spacious by your coming.

—St. Augustine

Readings for Reflection-

We throw open our doors to God and discover at the same moment that he has already thrown open his door to us. We find ourselves standing where we always hoped we might stand – out in the wide open spaces of God's grace and glory, standing tall and shouting our praise. (Romans 5:2 - The Message)

I read these words the other day and just can't get away from them. They have continued to echo and reverberate deeply within me ever since. I guess that's because the idea of *spaciousness* has been one that I have always been drawn to. Maybe it's because of the freedom and life and grace that is inherent in a spacious place. A spacious place offers room: room to roam, room to grow, room to flourish, room to be, and room to become.

I like room. I don't like to be crowded or constricted. And I don't just like room, I *need* room, the life of God within me requires it. It seems to me that the very life of the Spirit is one of spaciousness, ever expanding us within. The more deeply we journey into God, the more room there is, and the more spacious and free life becomes. I like that. I like it a lot. It is so inviting. It makes me want to throw my doors completely open to him; knowing that when I do I will find his doors already wide open to me, with the wide open spaces of his grace and love going on and on and on. What could be more inviting than that?

—Jim Branch, October, 2011

Most of us, most of the time, just fill our spaces up or dull our awareness of them. We grab a book, run to the television, work on a project, socialize, have a drink. I used to think women were more comfortable with space than men; nowadays I am not so sure. Women perhaps feel more guilty about taking time in freedom for themselves, while men feel more anxious. But it is a tiny difference. Either way, real space can be very unpleasant.

We somehow must realign our attitudes toward spaciousness. We must begin to see it as presence rather than absence, friend instead of enemy. — *The Awakened Heart* by Gerald G. May

Spaciousness is always a beginning, a possibility, a potential, a capacity for birth. Space exists not in order to be filled but to create. In space, to the extent we can bear the truth of the way things are, we find the ever-beginning presence of love. Take the time, then; make the space. Seek it wherever you can find it, do it however you can. The manner does not matter, and the experience you have there is of secondary importance. Seek the Truth, not what is comfortable. Seek the real, not the easy. — *The Awakened Heart* by Gerald G. May

All forms of spiritual discipline help us to make more space for God in our lives. Fasting and prayer, the traditional disciplines of Lent, seem to be two of the most effective tools in clearing away our self-preoccupation so we can be more responsive to God's life in and through and around us. — *Soul Feast* by Marjorie J. Thompson

It is an addiction of the first order that we feel we must always be filling up our spaces. It goes along with our addictions to work, to productivity, to efficiency. Sometimes, though, we do not like spaciousness because of what appears to us within it. — *The Awakened Heart* by Gerald G. May

Certain kinds of plants need support in order to grow properly. Tomatoes need stakes, beans must attach themselves to suspended strings. Creeping vines like clematis and wisteria will grow on any structure they can find. Rambling roses take kindly to garden walls, archways, and trellises. Without support, these plants would collapse in a heap on the ground. Their blossoms would not have the space and the sun they need to flourish, and their fruits would rot in contact with the soil. We would be unable to enjoy their beauty and their sustenance.

When it comes to spiritual growth, human beings are much like these plants. We need structure and support. Otherwise our spirituality grows only in a confused and disorderly way. The fruit of the Spirit in us gets tangled and is susceptible to corruption, and the beauty of our lives is diminished. We need structure in order to have enough space, air, and light to flourish. Structure gives us the freedom to grow as we are meant to. — *Soul Feast* by Marjorie J. Thompson

In biblical Hebrew, the letters *yodh* and *shin* combine to form a root that connotes "space and the freedom and security which is gained by the removal of constriction." From this *YS* root come words like *yesha* and *yeshuah*, referring to salvation. When you think about it, it makes sense that space would be intimately associated with salvation. Space is freedom: freedom from confinement, from preoccupation, from oppression, from drivenness, and from all the other interior and exterior forces that bind and restrict our spirits. We need space in the first place simply to recognize how compelled and bound we are. Then we need space to allow the compulsions to ease and the bonds to loosen. In the Hebrew sense, our passion needs elbowroom. To the extent that space is permitted by grace and our own willingness, we discover expanding emptiness in which consecration can happen, room for love to make its home in us. — *The Awakened Heart* by Gerald G. May

As our lives and faith progress, the heart expands and with the sweetness of love we move down the paths of God's commandments. Never departing from His guidance...we patiently share in Christ's passion, so we may eventually enter into the Kingdom of God.
— *The Rule of St. Benedict*

Our "dwelling place" may be physical—a room, apartment, or house. It may also be a metaphor for mental and emotional [and spiritual] "space." We can invite others into our inner world of thoughts and feelings, sharing gifts of heart and mind. Gracious inner space gives others room to play, question, and converse; room to be heard and understood; room to reveal themselves as they choose. — *Soul Feast* by Marjorie J. Thompson

Our journey toward abundant living is like walking a spiritual labyrinth repeatedly, from and ever deepening inner space. We walk toward the center to be transformed by God's love; then we walk outward to transform our small space in the world by reflecting God's love. There is no intention to trick us or get us lost along the journey. But there is mystery. Always mystery. And awe. And amazing grace. — *Abundance* by Marilyn Brown Oden

Simplicity and regularity are the best guides in finding our way. They allow us to make the discipline of solitude as much a part of our daily lives as eating and sleeping. When that happens, our noisy worries will slowly lose their power over us and the renewing activity of God's Spirit will slowly make its presence known.

Although the discipline of solitude asks us to set aside time and space, what finally matters is that our hearts become like quiet cells where God can dwell, wherever we go and whatever we do. — *Making All Things New* by Henri J. M. Nouwen

"The further up and further in you go, the bigger everything gets. The inside is larger than the outside."

Lucy looked hard at the garden and saw that it was not really a garden at all but a whole world, with its own rivers and woods and sea and mountains. But they were not strange: she knew them all.

"I see," she said, "this is still Narnia, and more real and more beautiful than Narnia down below....I see...world within world, Narnia within Narnia."

"Yes," said Mr. Tumnus, "like an onion: except that as you continue to go in and in, each circle is larger than the last." — *The Last Battle* by C. S. Lewis

"Think glorious thoughts of God — and serve Him with a quiet mind!" And it is surely a fact that the more glorious and more spacious our thoughts of Him are, the greater the quietude and confidence with which we do our detailed work will be. Not controversial thoughts, or narrow conventional thoughts, or dry academic thoughts, or anxious worried thoughts. All these bring contraction instead of expansion to our souls; and we all know that this inner sense of contraction or expansion is the unfailing test of our spiritual state. — *The House of the Soul and Concerning the Inner Life* by Evelyn Underhill

Moving Through Suffering

I. Opening Prayer
Father, I know my wounded and broken places oh so well. At times they can consume me and keep me from being able to hear your voice. Help me to see my pain as an invitation to know you more intimately rather than a reason to doubt the goodness of your heart. Help me to know that through my pain you desire to accomplish something very good in me. In the name of Jesus, the author of our salvation, who was "made perfect through suffering." Amen.

II. Psalm 121

III. Daily Scripture Reading
Monday	Psalm 66:8-12
Tuesday	Hebrews 2:10-18
Wednesday	1 Peter 4:12-19
Thursday	Romans 8:18-38
Friday	Psalm 109:21-26
Saturday	Hebrews 4:14-16
Sunday	Psalm 42:1-11

IV. Readings for Reflection

V. Reflection and Listening: silent and written

VI. Prayer: for the church, for others, for myself

VII. Song   *It is Well*

VIII. Closing Prayer
Father, heal my wounds and make them a source of life for others; as you did with your Son Jesus. In whose name we pray. Amen.

Readings for Reflection-

You *let* it happen, this *riding over our heads*, whoever or whatever that may have been. You didn't cause it, but you could have stopped it. I know it doesn't happen every day, but I have seen you spring into action and miraculously come to someone's aid or defense. I have seen you come to protect or deliver. And yet, for some reason, in this case, you didn't. You allowed *it*. Does that mean you sat idly by and watched? Or does it mean that—although the brokenness of this world was its cause—you are big enough to bring beauty out of the tragedy? You saw *it* coming, and *let* it stand, because of what you knew *it* would do within us. You knew that the groaning it would produce would have an effect on us like nothing else could or would.

So where exactly were you when we were going through the fire, being consumed by the agonizing flames of grief or sadness or mourning or pain? What were you doing while the mighty waters rushed over us and swept us away, as we struggled and fought to survive and keep our heads above water? Were you with us in some mysteriously hidden way that we were not able to completely comprehend at the time? Were you in the midst of the fire with us, shielding us from the fury of the flames? Were you in the middle of the raging currents beside us, holding and sustaining us— keeping us afloat? After all, you know what the groaning is like; in fact, you know it like no other. Did it break your heart to have to watch this *riding over us* unfold; to know the depths of the pain we were going through, and not intervene? How hard that must have been for you.

When we are in the midst of *the groan* it is hellish. It is hard to believe, or even consent to the fact, that something good might possibly result from the chaos and brokenness. Much less to think that it could be some strange path to a place called *abundance*. That is almost unthinkable. Yet all of us, on the backside of this *riding over*, usually have to admit that something took place within us — or among us — that could have happened no other way. We would never have chosen the path in a million years — not then, and most likely not again — but we can't deny the beauty of the new place where we eventually arrived. How in the world did we get there? Who would've imagined that the groans and cries and tears and struggle would have brought us to that place; that place where our hearts were both broken and expanded, where our souls were both crushed and deepened beyond measure. Who could've dreamt that the effect of the fire and the water would have been to make us more like Jesus — he who *suffers with* and delivers, he who *weeps over* and heals?

There has been a lot of groaning going around lately. It seems to be coming from every direction. I guess it is true that "each one of us sits beside a pool of tears." And it is so hard to watch the groaners groan and the mourners mourn and the strugglers struggle and not be able to do anything but pray. It is so tempting to try and come to the rescue, but rescue is not really possible, or even preferable. Because something much deeper is going on. In the words of Gerald May, "There is no way out, only through." Something deep and wonderful happens in the *going through*. So we must resist the urge to provide an escape — if that were even possible — because the struggle, or the groaning, or the grief, or the pain is the very thing that is able to do a beautiful work within us. All there is for us to do is trust. Trust that God really is in control. Trust that God really is up to something, in spite of all appearances. Trust that God really is big enough to sustain, to comfort, to deliver, to heal, and ultimately to transform. Trust that through the fire and through the water lies *a place of abundance*.
— *Watch and Wait* by Jim Branch

In praying about my wounds I have come to believe that the reason these wounds take so long to heal is that I spend more time attacking them than trying to understand them. I keep trying to clog up the hole made by the wound. The reality is that I keep stuffing my wound with other addictions, always hoping for some miraculous cure. The healing needs to happen right there in that broken place because it is there that I am vulnerable. It is there in that crack in my spirit that the light of Christ can slip through and help me understand the wound. When Jesus rose, his wounds were still visible. The scars could be seen right in the midst of the glory. Is my life, patterned after Christ, to be any different?

The scars in my life have become my badges of victory and glory. Some healing has taken place, yet as I pray with these scars I am able to see that I will probably have to live with some of the pain I've inherited from my cluttered life. I am learning to befriend my scars and find the gifts hidden underneath. — *Seasons of Your Heart* by Macrina Wiederkehr

The heart is stretched through suffering, and enlarged. But O the agony of this enlarging of the heart, that one may be prepared to enter into the anguish of others! Yet the way of holy obedience leads out from the heart of God and extends through the Valley of the Shadow.

But there is also removable suffering, yet such as yields only to years of toil and fatigue and uncon-querable faith and perchance only to death itself. The Cross as dogma is painless speculation; the Cross as lived suffering is anguish and glory. Yet God, out of the pattern of His own heart, has planted the Cross along the road of holy obedience. And he enacts in the hearts of those He loves the miracle of willingness to welcome suffering and to know it for what it is — the final seal of

His gracious love. I dare not urge you to your Cross. But He, more powerfully, speaks within you and me, to our truest selves, in our truest moments, and disquiets us with the world's needs. By inner persuasions He draws us to a few very definite tasks, *our* tasks, God's burdened heart particularizing His burdens in us. And He gives us the royal blindness of faith, and the seeing eye of the sensitized soul, and the grace of unflinching obedience. Then we see that nothing matters, and that everything matters, and that this my task matters for me and for my fellow men and for Eternity. And if we be utterly humble we may be given strength to be obedient even unto death, yea the death of the Cross.

In my deepest heart I know that some of us have to face our comfortable, self-oriented lives all over again. The times are too tragic, God's sorrow is too great, man's night too dark, the Cross is too glorious for us to live as we have lived, in anything short of holy obedience.

—*A Testament of Devotion* by Thomas Kelly

Suffering-
Pain, humiliation, sickness, and failure-
Is but a kiss of Jesus.

Once I met a lady who had a terrible cancer. She was suffering so much.
I told her,
"Now you come so close to Jesus on the cross that he is kissing you."
Then she joined hands and said,
"Mother Teresa, please tell Jesus to not stop kissing me."
It was so beautiful. She understood.

Suffering is a gift of God
A gift that makes us most Christlike.
People must not accept suffering as a punishment.

—*No Greater Love* by Mother Teresa

The heart of Christianity is a cross, the sign of a love unto death, and beyond into resurrection. I am beginning to understand that there is no way of following Jesus except by undergoing what he underwent. Unless I die, I can never bear fruit.

No one in this world can escape suffering, but not all suffering is the cross. Suffering cannot be avoided, but one can escape the cross. The cross must be a choice, a free decision, or it is not the sign of Jesus' love. The cross is an invitation; each person must say yes to Jesus taking us, blessing us, breaking us, and passing us around. — *Gathering the Fragments* by Edward J. Farrell

Many of us are tempted to think that if we suffer, the only important thing is to be relieved of our pain. We want to flee it at all costs. But when we learn to move through suffering, rather than avoid it, then we greet it differently. We become willing to let it teach us. We even begin to see how God can use it for some larger end. Suffering becomes something other than a nuisance or curse to be evaded at all costs, but a way into deeper fulfillment. Ultimately mourning means facing what wounds us in the presence of One who can heal. — *Turn My Mourning Into Dancing* by Henri J. M. Nouwen

I think there is an important lesson for us to learn here about how to help others in the grieving process: it is always futile and unproductive to try and explain tragedy in some comprehensive way. Saying piously that a loss is "the will of God" does not solve anything and may even create a sense of anger in the person who has been hurt. The calamities of life are all deeply mysterious and the more we try to "explain" them to each other and fix the blame and responsibility here or there, the farther we get from the truth. Job's friends, because of their misguided intellectualizing, actually stimulated in him a seething resentment against God and the whole universe. Admittedly, he might have come to this position on his own, but there is no doubt he was driven forward by his friends.

The basic issue in grief is never a rational explanation anyway. What matters is the nature of life itself and the One who gives it. Not until Job got to that level — to having it out with the Ultimate One — did healing begin to flow from him. This climactic stage finally came when Job, the one who was made, stood face to face with the One who did the making. — *Tracks of a Fellow Struggler* by John R, Claypool

Don't vex your minds by trying to explain the suffering you have to endure in this life...

Even in the midst of your suffering you are in his kingdom. You are always his children, and he has his protecting arm around you...Don't ask why; don't try to understand. Does a child understand everything his father does? Can he comprehend parental wisdom? No — but he can confidently nestle in his father's arms and feel perfect happiness, even while the tears glisten in his eyes, because he is his father's child — *Reverence for Life* by Albert Schweitzer

But there can finally be no outlet, no anesthesia, no self-inflicted way of ending the pain. The beams of love must be borne. No human love affair can substitute for the divine one; no drug or food will really fill the emptiness; no overwork or preoccupation can finally overshadow the yearning; no ascetical extremes can stop the pain. There is no way out — only through. As the poetry of the John of the Cross so vividly attests, the wound of love must remain open until God heals it. It is God's way of drawing every hidden "no," "maybe," or "yes but," into one completely joyous, unreserved

"Yes!" It is love's way of becoming everything. — *The Awakened Heart* by Gerald G. May

Were it possible for us to see further than our knowledge reaches, and yet a little way beyond the outworks of our divining, perhaps we would endure our sadnesses with greater confidence than our joys. For they are moments when something new has entered into us, something unknown; our feelings grow mute in shy perplexity, everything in us withdraws, a stillness comes, and a new, which no one knows, stands in the midst of it and is silent.

I believe that almost all our sadnesses are the moments of tension that we find paralyzing because we no longer hear our surprised feelings living. Because we are alone with the alien thing that has entered into our self; because everything intimate and accustomed is for an instant taken away; because we stand in the middle of a transition where we cannot remain standing. For this reason the sadness too passes: the new thing in us, the added thing, has entered into our heart, has gone into its inmost chamber and is not even there any more, — is already in our blood. And we do not learn what it was. We could easily be made to believe that nothing has happened, and yet we have changed, as a house changes into which a guest has entered. We cannot say who has come, perhaps we shall never know, but many signs indicate that the future enters into us in this way in order to transform itself in us long before it happens. And this is why it is so important to be lonely and attentive when one is sad: because the apparently uneventful and stark moment at which our future sets foot in us is so much closer to life than that other noisy fortuitous point of time at which it happens to us as if from outside. The more still, more patient and more open we are when we are sad, so much the deeper and so much the more unswervingly does the new go into

us, so much the better do we make it ours, so much the more will it be our destiny, and when on some later day it "happens" (that is, steps forth out of us to others), we shall feel in our inmost selves akin and near to it.
— *Letters to a Young Poet* by Rainer Maria Rilke

In times of upheaval, a voice from heaven says, "Be still and know that I am God."

It doesn't say, "Be still and know why."

In a distant day the gradual sacrament of understanding may be offered to us.

Today what is offered us is the body and blood of Christ, who suffered, as George McDonald once said, not that we might not suffer, but that our suffering might be like his.

His greatest suffering was the Cross.

Part of that suffering was an unanswered question.
— *The Weathering Grace of God* by Ken Gire

But if we are willing, the experience of grief can deepen and widen our ability to participate in life. We can become more grateful for the gifts we have been given, more open-handed in our handling of the events of life, more sensitive to the whole mysterious process of life, and more trusting in our adventure with God
— *Tracks of a Fellow Struggler* by John R. Claypool

No one can escape it; everyone must somehow either make friends with suffering or be broken by it. No one can come close to another, let alone love him, without coming close to his suffering. Christ did far more, he wed himself to our suffering, he made death his bride, and in the consummation of his love, he gave her his life.
— *The Risen Christ: Forty Days after the Resurrection* by Caryll Houselander

"I walked a mile with Pleasure;
She chatted all the way;
But left me none the wiser
For all she had to say.

I walked a mile with Sorrow;
And ne'er a word said she;
But, oh! The things I learned from her,
When Sorrow walked with me."

—Robert Browning Hamilton

Broken

I. Opening Prayer
O persistent God,
deliver me from assuming your mercy is gentle.
Pressure me that I may grow more human,
not through the lessening of my struggles,
but through the expansion of them…
Deepen my hurt
until I learn to share it and myself openly,
and my needs honestly.
Sharpen my fears until I name them
and release the power I have locked in them
and they in me.
Accentuate my confusion
until I shed those grandiose expectations
that divert me from the small, glad gifts
of the now and the here and the me.
Expose my shame where it shivers,
crouched behind the curtains of propriety,
until I can laugh at last
through my common frailties and failures,
laugh my way toward becoming whole.
— *Guerrillas of Grace* by Ted Loder

II. Psalm 31

III. Daily Scripture Readings
Monday	Psalm 51:1-19
Tuesday	Luke 22:24-34
Wednesday	Genesis 32:22-32
Thursday	Isaiah 53:1-12
Friday	Luke 22:54-62
Saturday	Psalm 147:1-11
Sunday	2 Corinthians 4:7-12

IV. Readings for Reflection

V. Reflection and Listening: silent and written

VI. Prayer: for the church, for others, for myself

VII. Song   *Come Ye Sinners*

VIII. Closing Prayer
Now,
O Lord,
calm me into a quietness
that heals
and listens,
and molds my longings
and passions,
my wounds
and wonderings
into a more holy
and human
shape.
— *Guerrillas of Grace* by Ted Loder

Readings for Reflection-

that left a mark by Jim Branch

it was not invited
and at the time not welcomed
but nonetheless it came calling
bursting through the door
barging into my settled life
turning everything upside down
wounding me to the bone
leaving a deep mark
both upon and within
one that has taken up residence inside

entering my very bloodstream
it will never leave
it is a part of me now
a companion and a guide
willing to teach if i am willing to listen
willing to lead if i am willing to follow
life as it was before
has ceased to exist
nothing will ever be the same
it is not bitterness
it is reality
i am forever different
in an incredibly painful
but very good way
thanks be to God
for loving me enough
to wound me

Jesus was broken on the cross. He lived his suffering and death not as an evil to avoid at all costs but as a mission to embrace. We too are broken. We live with broken bodies, broken hearts, broken minds, or broken spirits. We suffer from broken relationships.

How can we live our brokenness? Jesus invites us to embrace our brokenness as he embraced the cross and live it as part of our mission. He asks us not to reject our brokenness as a curse from God that reminds us of our sinfulness but to accept it and put it under God's blessing for our purification and sanctification. Thus, our brokenness can become a gateway to new life.
— *Bread for the Journey* by Henri Nouwen

I am sure God wants us to be whole and healthy in every way possible, but love neither depends upon these things nor ends with them. In fact, blessings sometimes come through brokenness that could never come in any other way. In reflecting on my own life, I have to conclude that grace has come through me more powerfully sometimes when I have been very dysfunctional and maladjusted. Love transcends all possible adjustments and continually invites us through and beyond them. — *The Awakened Heart* by Gerald G. May

the limp by Jim Branch

i walk with a limp
a true thing of beauty
that came about
when you took me to the ground
wrestling and struggling
when you tore me to pieces
that you might make me whole

thank you
for loving me
too much to allow me
to continue to live falsely
to continue to be someone
other than the one
you created me to be

that you would care enough
to wound me
your beloved
that i might live truly
and become my truest self
makes this limp
a true thing of beauty

a living reminder
of your great affection

Frederick Buechner once said, "To be a writer, one must be a good steward of their pain." I think that is true as well for those who would pray. To be such a steward creates the possibility that others might be healed by your witness to such a thing, that others might see mercies granted to you in your suffering as evidence of the compassion of God for those who are broken. This gift of our brokenness is often the only real gift that we can give or receive with any real honesty and with any real hope and with any real power. We do not demonstrate our faith when we live in the light, we show our faith when we live in the dark.

To embrace one's brokenness, whatever it looks like, whatever has caused it, carries with it the possibility that one might come to embrace one's healing, and then that one might come to the next step: to embrace another and their brokenness and their possibility for being healed. To avoid one's brokenness is to turn one's back on the possibility that the Healer might be at work here, perhaps for you, perhaps for another. It is to turn one's back on another, one for whom you just might be the Christ, one for whom you might, even if just for a moment, become the Body and Blood. —*Living Prayer* by Robert Benson

The first response, then, to our brokenness is to face it squarely and befriend it. This may seem quite unnatural. Our first, most spontaneous response to pain and suffering is to avoid it, to keep it at arm's length; to avoid, circumvent or deny it. Suffering—be it physical, mental or emotional—is almost always experienced as an unwelcome intrusion into our lives, something that should not be there. It is difficult, if not impossible, to see anything positive in suffering; it must be avoided away at all costs.

When this is, indeed, our spontaneous attitude toward brokenness, it is no surprise that befriending it seems, at first, masochistic. Still, my own pain in life has taught me that the first step to healing is not a step away from the pain, but a step toward it. When brokenness is, in fact, just as intimate a part of our being as our chosenness and our blessedness, we have to dare to overcome our fear and become familiar with it. Yes, we have to find the courage to embrace our own brokenness, to make our most feared enemy into a friend and to claim it as an intimate companion. I am convinced that healing is often so difficult because we don't want to know the pain. Although this is true of all pain, it is especially true of the pain that comes from a broken heart. The anguish and agony that result from rejection, separation, neglect, abuse and emotional manipulation serve only to paralyze us when we can't face them and keep running away from them. When we need guidance in our suffering, it is first of all guidance that leads us closer to our pain and makes us aware that we do not have to avoid it, but can befriend it. — *Life of the Beloved* by Henri J. M. Nouwen

When loneliness is among the chief wounds of the minister, hospitality can convert that wound into a source of healing. Concentration [meditation and prayer] prevents the minister from burdening others with his pain and allows him to accept his wounds as helpful teachers of his own and his neighbor's condition. Community arises where the sharing of pain takes place, not as a stifling form of self-complaint, but as a recognition of God's saving promises. — *The Wounded Healer* by Henri J. M. Nouwen

You cannot be multiplied enough to be shared. You can only be broken enough to be shared. — *Living Prayer* by Robert Benson

The great spiritual call of the Beloved Children of God is to pull their brokenness away from the shadow of curse and put it under the light of the blessing. This is not as easy as it sounds. The powers of darkness around us are strong, and our world finds it easier to manipulate self-rejecting people than self-accepting people. But when we keep listening attentively to the voice calling us the Beloved, it becomes possible to live our brokenness, not as confirmation of our fear that we are worthless, but as an opportunity to purify and deepen the blessing that rests upon us. Physical, mental or emotional pain lived under the blessing is experienced in ways radically different from physical, mental or emotional pain lived under the curse. Even a small burden, perceived as a sign of our worthlessness, can lead us to deep depression—even suicide. However, great and heavy burdens become light and easy when they are lived in the light of the blessing. What seemed intolerable becomes a challenge. What seemed a reason for depression becomes a source of purification. What seemed punishment becomes a gentle pruning. What seemed rejection becomes a way to a deeper communion. —*Life of the Beloved* by Henri J. M. Nouwen

To be broken is not a choice; it is a gift. —*Leading With a Limp* by Dan B. Allender

Gathering

I. Opening Prayer

O Lord our God, help us to be faithful to gather what you have provided for our hearts and souls this day — that we may feed on you and live. In the name of Jesus, the bread of life. Amen.

II. Psalm 147

III. Daily Scripture Readings

Monday	John 6:1-14
Tuesday	Exodus 16
Wednesday	Zephaniah 3:14-20
Thursday	Jeremiah 31:1-14
Friday	Deuteronomy 30:1-10
Saturday	Isaiah 40:6-11
Sunday	Ezekiel 34:11-16

IV. Readings for Reflection

V. Reflection and Listening: silent and written

VI. Prayer: for the church, for others, for myself

VII. Song   *I'll Find You There*

VIII. Closing Prayer

Lord Jesus, thank you that you are present in the midst of the broken pieces of this day. May we find you there as we gather them up and may it help us to trust both your provision for us, as well as the goodness of your heart. Amen.

Readings for Reflection-

gathering by Jim Branch

scattered pieces littering the hillside
scraps from what once fed multitudes
casualties of the train wreck of provision and need
leftovers, unwanted, discarded, useless
or so it seems

a death; a loss; a heartbreak
a wound; a brokenness; a darkness
loneliness; despair; isolation
the scattered pieces of this life
littering the ground of my being
unwanted; unwelcome; uninvited
fit only to be mourned and thrown away
or so it seems

until touched by the hand of one
who brings beauty from ashes
who utters the words of life and hope
"gather all the broken pieces"
weaving the fragments of my brokenness
into the me that was planned from the beginning
"let nothing be wasted"
and suddenly that which seemed to have no value
becomes meaningful and beautiful in your care
these parts make a whole
they serve a divine purpose

"I will rescue the lame and gather what has been
scattered"
and make it into a vital part of you;
the object of my great delight and affection

so sing and shout

brighten up and spin around
for I am gathering your pieces
and restoring you
into a fearful and wonderful creation
and nothing will be wasted

Gather the pieces that are left over. Let nothing be wasted.
(John 6:12)

The call came at about 9:30 pm on a typical Thursday
evening in early December. I had just returned home
from somewhere or another and was talking with my
wife in the living room about the events of the day when
our oldest son called on his cell phone to ask if he could
go to the church coffee shop with some friends. As she
spoke to him there was an abrupt halt in the
conversation. A significant amount of panic and anxiety
filled her usually calm face. Our oldest son, as his
mother was listening, had just been involved in an
automobile accident. I quickly got news of his location
and headed for the door, not being able to get there fast
enough. Fears and prayers consumed the drive until I
reached the scene. As I arrived I saw him in one piece,
unhurt, and standing with a few friends in the midst of
the broken glass and police lights and passersby. My
only desire at that moment was wrap my arms around
him, which I did as he began to express his sorrow and
sadness. "I'm so sorry. I'm so sorry," was all he could
say, which was met only by my relief and gratitude that
he was unhurt.

"I'm just so glad you are okay."

So we stood there in the middle of the road and
waited as reports were written and information was
exchanged and wrecker services were called. Looking
down at my feet all I could see was broken pieces…
glass, plastic, metal, etc. The pieces were littering the
street, such an appropriate description of the scene in

general—broken. Broken glass. Broken pieces. Broken hearts. Broken world. Broken.

That's when the words came. Words that I had been captured by months before that were returning at just the right time. *"Gather the pieces that are left over. Let nothing be wasted."* Words that offered such comfort and hope. Words that spoke of God's heart and God's presence even in the midst of the broken pieces of this life. It was as if Jesus was saying to me, "I am here. I am with you even in the brokenness. Gather the pieces and you will find me. You are not alone in this. With me nothing is wasted. I will use even the most broken situations to mold and make you into the amazing creation that I have always longed for you to be."

What a crazy world this is that we live in, a world where brokenness is unfortunately a part of life. Death and suffering, war and violence, conflict and strife; everything from anger, hatred, and racism to hurricanes, tornados, and tsunamis. We can't avoid it or deny it, no matter how hard we may try. But the beautiful thing is that brokenness does not have the last word…wholeness does. For no matter how broken the heart, or the life, or the circumstance; we have this amazing God who says, "With me nothing is wasted. Gather the pieces, I am in the midst of them."

—Jim Branch, December, 2004

This book is about seeing and harvesting. Seeing the holy in the ordinary! Harvesting angels out of what appears to be the crumbs of daily existence! Spending your days in the fast lane of life impairs the quality of your seeing. If you want to see to the depths, you will need to slow down. You live in a world of theophanies. Holiness comes wrapped in the ordinary. There are burning bushes all around you. Every tree is full of angels. Hidden beauty is waiting in every crumb. Life wants to lead you from crumbs to angels, but this can

happen only if you are willing to unwrap the ordinary
by staying with it long enough to harvest its treasure.
— *A Tree Full of Angels* by Macrina Wiederkehr

We need to see clearly how important it is to use well
all the gifts our Father has given us for the good of us all.
Then we will take care to gather up the fragments, even
if it does take a little extra time and energy. — *Breaking
Bread* by M. Basil Pennington

The Eucharist is a gathering of Jesus' disciples to be at
his table, to sit at his feet like Mary in Bethany, to rest
their heads on his heart like John, to climb the mountain
of transfiguration like Peter, James and John, to be with
him in prayer during his agony in the Garden of
Gethsemane, to breakfast with him on a Galilean beach,
to listen to his voice inviting us to come and rest, to
listen, to eat, drink and be holy. — *Gathering Fragments*
by Edward J. Farrell

> And yet, though we strain
> against the deadening grip
> of daily necessity,
> I sense there is mystery:
>
> All life is being lived.
>
> Who is living it, then?
> Is it the things themselves,
> or something waiting inside them,
> like an unplayed melody in a flute?
>
> Is it the winds blowing over the waters?
> Is it the branches that signal to each other?
>
> Is it the flowers

interweaving their fragrances,
or streets, as they wind through time?

Is it the animals, warmly moving,
or the birds, that suddenly rise up?

Who lives it, then? God, are you the one
who is living life?
— *The Book of Hours* by Rainer Maria Rilke

Not every meal is a banquet or a special celebration. True, there are high moments, times for delicacies and treats. But still, we need our daily bread. We need to nourish ourselves with the staples of life even if they do not always tickle our palates. Each day we need to sit at the table with Jesus and eat the Bread of his Word to nourish the life he has given us. On days we do not let him break for us the Bread of the Word, our spirits languish. If our lives are not filled with joy and all the other fruits of the Spirit, it is because we do not ask, do not seek. His table is always spread. We want always to keep our Bible spread out before us in our homes, in our offices, in our places of ministry, to remind ourselves of this. Let it be there as a tempting dish filled with enticing morsels, inviting us to nibble constantly and to sit down regularly and eat heartily. There is never a moment when we cannot enjoy, be nourished, and be refreshed by the table talk of Jesus. *Taste and see how good the Lord is!* — *Breaking Bread* by M. Basil Pennington

Questions

I. Opening Prayer

O God, our Father, Creator of all that is, give us the courage to wrestle with the questions you ask us rather than jumping to some immediate answer — thereby cutting off any possibility of real growth or struggle. Help us stay in the question long enough to hear what it is you have for us there. In the name of Jesus. Amen.

II. Psalm 13

III. Daily Scripture Readings

Monday	John 1:35-42
Tuesday	John 5:1-9
Wednesday	John 11:17-44
Thursday	John 13:1-15
Friday	John 21:1-19
Saturday	Mark 8:1-30
Sunday	Mark 10:46-52

IV. Readings for Reflection

V. Reflection and Listening: silent and written

VI. Prayer: for the church, for others, for myself

VII. Song   *How Firm a Foundation*

VIII. Closing Prayer

It seems to me Lord
that we search
much too desperately
for answers
when a good question
holds as much grace

as an answer. — *Seasons of Your Heart* by Macrina Wiederkehr

Readings for Reflection-

Jesus was masterful in the art of asking great questions. Time after time in the gospels we run into amazingly simple, yet deeply profound questions that Jesus asks various people. I think he did this because he knew the great value of questions. A good question creates dialogue and interaction and life. It promotes thought and reflection and discovery. A good question invites us to go inward, to the very core of our being, and seek something deep within ourselves. Therefore, we would be wise, it would seem, to pay careful attention to the questions that Jesus asks. Because it just might be that those very questions are not only meant for the ones he meets in the pages of Scripture, but for us as well.

—Jim Branch, March, 2016

Jesus is too much for us. The Church is a kind of collective teenager. Perhaps we're gradually getting ready to let the Gospel talk straight to us. We have always wanted answers, because in an early stage of human life the first thing we need is certainty. But Jesus doesn't offer us any certainties; he offers us a journey of faith. Jesus doesn't give us many answers; he tells us what the right questions are, what questions the human soul has to wrestle with to stumble onto Christ and the truth.

Our formulations determine what we're really looking for. Our questions determine what we ultimately find and discover. Answers acquire power too quickly; they often turn our words into ammunition to be used against others. And answers make trust unnecessary, they make listening dispensable, they make relations with others superfluous. Having my answers, I don't need you in order to take my journey. I need only my head, my certainties, and my conclusions. It's all private. But Jesus said we have to live in this world so as to be dependent on one another. The real meaning of a poor life is a life of radical dependency, so I can't arrange my life in such a way that I don't need you. We can't do it alone. — *Simplicity* by Richard Rohr

You are so young, so before all beginning, and I want to beg you, as much as I can, dear sir, to be patient with all that is unsolved in your heart and try to love the questions themselves like locked rooms and like books that are written in a very foreign tongue. Do not now seek the answers, which cannot be given you because you would not be able to live them. And the point is, to live everything. Live the questions now. Perhaps you will gradually, without noticing it, live along some distant day into the answer. — *Letters to a Young Poet* by Rainer Maria Rilke

"Why do you cry when you pray?" he asked, as though he knew me well.

"I don't know," I answered, troubled.

I had never asked myself that question. I cried because...because something inside me felt the need to cry. That was all I knew.

"Why do you pray?" he asked after a moment.

Why did I pray? Strange question. Why did I live? Why did I breathe?

"I don't know, "I told him, even more troubled and ill at ease.

"I don't know."

From that day on, I saw him often. He explained to me, with great emphasis, that every question possessed a power that was lost in the answer...

"Man comes closer to God through the questions he asks Him," he liked to say. "Therein lies true dialogue. Man asks and God replies. But we don't understand His replies. We cannot understand them. Because they dwell in the depths of our souls and remain there until we die. The real answers, Eliezer, you will find only within yourself."

"And why do you pray, Moishe?" I asked him.

"I pray to the God within me for the strength to ask Him the real questions." — *Night* by Elie Wiesel

Each one who is born comes into the world as a question for which old answers are not sufficient.

— Thomas Merton

There are questions, lots of questions. And it is good to live in the question. A pat answer is closed, it is finished; that's it. It goes nowhere and leaves little room for hope. A question, the mystery, opens the space for us. It is full of possibility. It gives hope of life and even more abundant life. Our faith, solid as it might be is full of questions. And therefore full of life and hope.
— *Living in the Question* by M. Basil Pennington

A possibility I would like to suggest is this: live with the questions the Lord asks. Take up a Bible and open to the Gospels. Look for the questions Jesus asks of us: Who do you say that I am? What do you want? Are you not worth more than many sparrows? Why do you not believe? Living with these, one after the other — and there are many in the Gospels — can bring us to wholly other, much richer perspective on our lives, maybe to seeing our lives the way God sees them, shot through with light, the joy, the fullness of the risen life of Christ.
— *Living in the Question* by M. Basil Pennington

As a culture, we have to be taught the language of descent. That is the great language of religion. It teaches us to enter willingly, trustingly into the dark periods of life. These dark periods are good teachers. Religious energy is in the dark questions, seldom in the answers. Answers are the way out, but not what we are here for. But when we look at the questions, we look for the opening to transformation. Fixing something doesn't usually transform us. We try to change events in order to avoid changing ourselves. We must learn to stay with the pain of life, without answers, without conclusions, and some days without meaning. That is the path, the perilous dark path of true prayer.
— *Everything Belongs* by Richard Rohr

The real question is "What does this have to say to me?" Those who are totally converted come to every experience and ask not whether or not they liked it, but what does it have to teach them. "What's the message in this for me? What's the gift in this for me? How is God in this event? Where is God in this suffering?"
— *Everything Belongs* by Richard Rohr

Sometimes…we have to do a thing in order to find out the reason for it. Sometimes our actions are questions, not answers.

— John Le Carre

Fear

I. Opening Prayer

O Lord our God, help us to live our lives with the faith and courage necessary to live by love and not by fear. Forgive me when my seeing and my thinking get so distorted that I allow fear to control me and make me its slave—even when I don't fully realize it. Seize my heart and soul with your perfect love in such a way that it drives out all fear and gives me the freedom to truly love, rather than manipulate, those in my life and world. In the name of Jesus. Amen.

II. Psalm 27

III. Daily Scripture Readings

Monday	Mark 6:45-52
Tuesday	1 John 4:16-21
Wednesday	Genesis 3:6-10
Thursday	Isaiah 43:1-7
Friday	2 Timothy 1:6-12
Saturday	Isaiah 41:8-10
Sunday	Romans 8:12-17

IV. Readings for Reflection

V. Reflection and Listening: silent and written

VI. Prayer: for the church, for others, for myself

VII. Song   *Isaiah 43*

VIII. Closing Prayer

Lord Jesus,

Help me to hear your words, "Take courage! It is I. Don't be afraid." and to believe them in the deepest places of my heart. Help me to live my life by those words this day. For your sake and by your Spirit and in your name. Amen.

Readings for Reflection-

The older I get, the more I realize that quite possibly the biggest single enemy of our spiritual lives (other than Satan himself) is fear. Fear seems to be at the very core of all the things that battle against my heart and soul. At the core of my busyness is fear. At the core of my insecurity is fear. At the core of my anxiety is fear. At the core of my competitiveness…you guessed it — fear. Fear of not having what it takes. Fear of not having any value. Fear of not being lovable. The list goes on and on.

And maybe the main reason this enemy is so strong and dangerous is that by and large it is a hidden enemy. We never really look beneath the surface of our more familiar enemies to spot it. We rarely follow any of these foes down far enough to see what is at their root. And when we don't know what we are really fighting, how can we possibly be victorious? We just keep getting defeated over and over again. This fear robs us of the intimacy we were created for. It robs us of the freedom that God longs for us to enjoy. It robs us of genuinely loving relationships. It simply controls the way we live our lives.

What are we to do? How can we possibly fight against this? A first step would seem to be identifying and *naming* our fears. Somehow naming our fears takes some of their power away to control us. Ann Lamott once said, "When you make friends with fear, it can't rule you." Once our enemy is identified it makes it much easier to wage war.

Secondly, we need to remember that our real enemy (Satan) is the "father of lies." He will use his lies to manipulate us into believing whatever he can. Because of this, it seems that we need to ask ourselves, "What lies are we believing that are simply not true? How is our seeing or thinking distorted?" When the disciples were on the sea battling against the storm (Mark 6:45-52) they screamed out in terror because they thought Jesus was a ghost. Now it wasn't really a ghost upon the water, they just thought it was. It was their distorted thinking and seeing that gave power to their fears. Once they saw things clearly and therefore thought about things more accurately — they were able to put everything in perspective.

Which brings us to the biggest weapon we have been given to wage war against fear, and that is what John calls "perfect love" (1 John 4:18). It is perfect love that puts everything in perspective for us. Once the voice of perfect love calls out to us, "Take courage. It is I. Don't be afraid." Then we are reminded that the love of the one who made us, and called us into being, and cares for us more than we can even care for ourselves is in control of all things. And his heart for us is good. He can be trusted even when circumstances look dire, because he loves us so immensely and completely. When he speaks his words of affection and peace, and we hear and truly believe them, then we know that if he is with us all will be well. Whatever it is, whatever the seas look like, all will be well.

—Jim Branch, November, 2004

We are fearful people. The more people I come to know and the more I come to know people, the more I am overwhelmed by the negative power of fear. It often seems that fear has invaded every part of our being to such a degree that we no longer know what a life without fear would feel like. There always seems to be something to fear: something within us or around us, something close or far away, something visible or invisible, something in ourselves, in others, or in God.

There never seems to be a totally fear-free moment. When we think, talk, act or react, fear always seems to be there: an omnipresent force that we cannot shake off. Often fear has penetrated our inner selves so deeply that it controls, whether we are aware of it or not, most of our choices and decisions. —*Lifesigns* by Henri J.M. Nouwen

Before He sinned, Adam enjoyed unclouded fellowship with God. There were no walls, no distance, no tension. But sin immediately brought terrible consequences. Among them was the presence of a new emotion: fear.

In response to this new emotion, Adam fled from God and went into hiding. Obviously an all-seeing God knew that Adam was fearfully crouching behind the tree. But He called out to Adam and asked a question — the first question asked of sinful man by a Holy God: "Adam, where are you?" Perhaps God wanted to create in Adam a realization of his plight and to provoke a confession of sin (i.e. God knew where Adam was, but wanted Adam to realize where Adam was). Only exposed problems motivate people to ask for help. Note Adam's response: "I was afraid because I was naked; so I hid myself" (Gen. 3:10). His answer separates naturally into three distinct parts:

    1. *I was afraid...Adam's core emotion*
    2. *Because I was naked (exposed)...his core motivation*
    3. *So I hid myself...his core strategy*

...Adam hid in an effort to avoid dealing with what he feared — rejection. —*Encouragement: The Key to Caring* by Dr. Lawrence J. Crabb Jr.

Fear is the great enemy of intimacy. Fear makes us run away from each other or cling to each other but does not create true intimacy. When Jesus was arrested in the garden of Gethsemane, the disciples were overcome by fear and they all "deserted him and ran away" (Mt. 26:56). And after Jesus was crucified they huddled together in a closed room "for fear of the Jews" (John. 20:19). Fear makes us move away from each other to a "safe" distance, or move toward each other to a "safe" closeness, but fear does not create the space where true intimacy can exist. Fear does not create a home. It forces us to live alone or in a protective shelter but does not allow us to build an intimate home. —*Lifesigns* by Henri J.M. Nouwen

We live in a time in which we are constantly tempted to let our fears rule our lives. More than ever our world gives us reasons to fear. We are afraid for our own inner impulses which we are not able fully to understand or control, we are afraid of the many strangers surrounding us and threatening to invade our lives, we are afraid of the increasing capability of humanity to destroy itself and we are afraid of a God who can punish us with eternal damnation. The greater our fears the less our freedom. In order to alleviate our fears we often become very active, busy and full of worries about our future, always on guard for possible dangers. Our fears also make us very self-centered since they make us live our lives as an ongoing battle for survival.

Jesus came to cast out our fears. He announced a God of perfect love in whom no fear can exist. He himself and all his messengers, whether angels or apostles, say constantly; "Do not be afraid." But it is far from easy not to let the many real fears make us deaf and blind to the God of perfect love. The news of every day, the concrete emergencies of our own daily life and our own inner self-doubt make us often fearful before we are fully aware of it ourselves.

What we truly need is a safe space to dwell, to take off our heavy armour and let the perfect love of God touch us, heal us and guide us from the land of fear to

the land of God. — Henri J. M. Nouwen, from the
Foreword of *Rule for a New Brother,*

True religion is never about fear. It is always about
moving beyond fear. Yet many of us were religiously
trained to be comfortable with fear. Most of you reading
this were given the quote, "The fear of the Lord is the
beginning of wisdom" (Psalm 111:10 and Proverbs 1:7).
We were taught "fear of God" as a virtue when we were
small children. In fact, the word "fear" in both Psalms
and Proverbs means the awe that small children have for
someone they honor and respect. It is not the fear of
being harmed, but the awe of reverence and honor for
someone we look up to and are devoted to. That's a
very different concept, and the English word "fear"
doesn't do it justice. To live in awe before God's wonder
is a virtue. "Anxiety about many things" is what Jesus
says we needn't have (Luke 12:22-32). Anxiety and faith
seem to be opposites for Jesus. — *Everything Belongs* by
Richard Rohr

"There is nothing like it on earth when the spirit of God
comes pouring through, and he has poured through me
in fair weather and foul, for sixty-four years."

"Have there been dry spells?" asked the rector.

The preacher pushed his plate away and Lottie rose
to clear the table. Father Tim smelled the kind of coffee
he remembered from Mississippi — strong and black and
brewed on the stove.

"My brother, dry is not the word. There was a time I
went down like a stone in a pond and sank clear to the
bottom. I lay on the bottom of that pond for two
miserable years, and thought I'd never see the light of
day in my soul again."

"I can't say my current tribulation is anything like
that. But in an odd way, it's something almost worse."

"What's that?" Absalom Greer asked kindly.

314

"When it comes to feeding his sheep, I'm afraid my sermons are about as nourishing as cardboard."

"Are you resting?"

"Resting?"

"Resting. Sometimes we get so worn out with being useful that we get useless. I'll ask you what another preacher once asked: Are you too exhausted to run and too scared to rest?"

Too scared to rest! He'd never thought of it that way. "When in God's name are you going to take a vacation?" Hoppy had asked again, only the other day. He hadn't known the truth then, but he felt he knew it now — yes, he was too scared to rest.

The old preacher's eyes were as clear as gemstones. "My brother, I would urge you to search the heart of God on this matter, for it was this very thing that sank me to the bottom of the pond."

They looked at one another with grave understanding. "I'll covet your prayers," said Father Tim. — *At Home in Mitford* by Jan Karon

And there is another important point about love, something we have heard often, maybe even know in our heads, but forget so easily once we close the Bible. God's love is so powerful and expansive that it leaves no place for its hurtful, destroying opposite: fear. Fear is unholy; fear keeps us from God; fear itself can become a false and devouring god.

I wonder how many of our sinful ways of being and doing can be traced back to our fear: our fear of failure, our fear of change, our fear of growth, our fear of all that is *other*. The fruits of our fear are bitter: violence, spiritual deadness, and contempt toward all whom we would push to the margins. I suspect that most of our sinful *isms* — racism, sexism, ageism — are the fruits of fear. — *My Soul in Silence Waits* by Margaret Guenther

When you make friends with fear, it can't rule you.
— *Traveling Mercies* by Anne Lamott

Courage is fear that has said its prayers.
— *Traveling Mercies* by Anne Lamott

"The light's going uncommon quick," said Rynelf.
"Back to the ship," muttered the men.
"I really think," said Edmund, "they're right. We can decide what to do with the three sleepers tomorrow. We daren't eat the food and there's no point in staying here for the night. The whole place smells of magic — and danger."
"I am entirely of King Edmund's opinion," said Reepicheep, "as far as concerns the ship's company in general. But I myself will sit at this table till sunrise."
"Why on earth?" said Eustace.
"Because," said the Mouse, "this is a very great adventure, and no danger seems to me so great as that of knowing when I get back to Narnia that I left a mystery behind me through fear."
— *The Voyage of the Dawn Treader* by C. S. Lewis

Lord Jesus, help me to live my life this day as a *son* rather than a *slave*. For I live as a slave when I start living in the fear of what might happen. I live as a slave when I live my life afraid that I do not have what it takes, that I don't measure up, that I am not enough, and that I am of no value. Then I become a slave not only to fear, but also to circumstances. I become a slave to comparison, a slave to competition, and a slave to affirmation, achievement, and applause.

That is when I must cling to the truth that I am no longer a slave but a son, your beloved son. You delight in me. When I truly believe this, only then is there any real hope of being truly free. Free to live as you live and free to love as you love. Lord Jesus, help me to love like you love today. By the power of your Spirit within me, remind me that I am your child and rid my heart of all that is not love. Amen.

—Jim Branch, January, 2016

Tears

I. Opening Prayer
O Lord my God, thank you that you keep track of all my sorrows. That you have collected my tears in your bottle. That you have recorded each one in your book. And that all the tears I've shed cannot begin to compare with the ones you shed for me. Amen.

II. Psalm 116

III. Daily Scripture Readings
Monday	John 11:17-44
Tuesday	Matthew 23:37-39
Wednesday	Matthew 26:36-46
Thursday	Hebrews 5:7-10
Friday	Luke 7:36-50
Saturday	2 Kings 20:1-6
Sunday	Psalm 56:8-13

IV. Readings for Reflection

V. Reflection and Listening: silent and written

VI. Prayer: for the church, for others, for myself

VII. Song   *I Need Thee*

VIII. Closing Prayer
Thank you, Lord Jesus that you wept. Thank you that you are a God who weeps — that our sorrow and sadness bring tears to your eyes as well. Thank you that you hold us, as well as all our tears, in the palm of your pierced hand. Amen.

Readings for Reflection-

What do you do with a God who weeps? Especially one who weeps over you and me, and our pain. What do you do with a God who is heartbroken over our hurt and our sadness? Maybe he weeps because he knows that somewhere deep inside we don't truly believe that he can redeem *this,* whatever *this* may be. Maybe he weeps over the fact that we do not really believe that he can, or will, bring life out of our unimaginable pain and brokenness. Or maybe his tears come from the fact that our circumstances have made us doubt the goodness of his heart. Who knows? The one thing that we do know is that God weeps for us, whatever the reason. It could be that the depths of his love and affection will not allow him to do otherwise.

God weeps because he knows us. He knows the depths of our hurt and our sadness and it breaks his heart. He weeps because he loves us so much that he cannot keep his hands off of us. That's why he came and entered into a sea of suffering and pain in the person of Jesus. Why on earth would he do that? I suppose it is because he just couldn't stay away. He couldn't stand far off, idly by, as his beloved children wept and hurt and struggled. So he came. And he wept.

—Jim Branch, May, 2014

Digory kept his mouth very tight shut. He had been growing more and more uncomfortable. He hoped that whatever happened, he wouldn't blub or do anything ridiculous.

"Son of Adam," said the Aslan. "Are you ready to undo the wrong that you have done to my sweet country of Narnia on the very day of its birth?"

"Well, I don't see what I can do," said Digory. "You see, the Queen ran away and—"

319

"I asked, are you ready," said the Lion.

"Yes," said Digory. He had had for a second some wild idea of saying "I'll try to help you if you'll promise to help about my Mother," but he realized in time that the Lion was not at all the sort of person one could try to make bargains with. But when he had said "Yes," he thought of his Mother, and he thought of the great hopes he had had, and how they were all dying away, and a lump came in his throat and tears in his eyes, and he blurted out:

"But please, please — won't you — can't you give me something that will cure Mother?" Up till then he had been looking at the Lion's great front feet and the huge claws on them; now, in his despair, he looked up at its face. What he saw surprised him as much as anything in his whole life. For the tawny face was bent down near his own and (wonder of wonders) great shining tears stood in the Lion's eyes. They were such big, bright tears compared with Digory's own that for a moment he felt as if the Lion must really be sorrier about his Mother than he was himself. — *The Magician's Nephew* by C. S. Lewis

Whenever you find tears in your eyes, especially unexpected tears, it is well to pay the closest attention.

They are not only telling you something about the secret of who you are, but more often than not God is speaking to you through them of the mystery of where you have come from and is summoning you to where, if your soul is to be saved, you should go next.
— *Whistling in the Dark* by Frederick Buechner

So much is distilled in our tears, not the least of which is wisdom in living life. From my own tears I have learned that if you follow your tears, you will find your heart. If you find your heart, you will find what is dear

to God. And if you find what is dear to God, you will find the answer to how you should live your life.
—*Windows of the Soul* by Ken Gire

"Tears hollow out places in the heart," wrote Gibran, "where joy can grow." To be emptied is to create a place that can be filled. "They that sow in tears..." says the psalmist, and which of us has no tears to sow? —*Living Prayer* by Robert Benson

Sometimes the tears are good tears, tears as a response to the mystery not only of human love but of human finitude, the transience of things; but more often than not, I suspect, the tears that are shed at weddings are not to be taken too seriously because they are mainly sentimental tears, and although I suppose that they do little harm, I would be surprised to hear that they ever did much good. To be sentimental is to react not so much to something that is happening as to your own reaction to something that is happening, so that when a person cries sentimentally, what he is really crying at very often is the pathos of his own tears. When we shed tears at a wedding, our tears are likely to have a great deal less to do with the bride and groom than with all the old dreams or regrets that the bride and groom have occasioned in us. In our sentimentality, we think, "How wonderful that they are going to live happily ever after," or "How terrible that they are never going to be so happy again," and then we relate it all to our own happiness or our own lost happiness and weep eloquently at ourselves. — *The Hungering Dark* by Frederick Buechner

Help me O God,
Give me the courage to cry.
Help me to understand that tears bring
    freshly washed colors arching across the soul

colors that wouldn't be there apart from the rain.
Help me to see in the prism of my tears,
    something of the secret of who I am.
Give me the courage
    not only to see what those tears are revealing
        but to follow where they are leading.
And help me to see,
    somewhere over the rainbow,
        that where they are leading me is home…
            —*Windows of the Soul* by Ken Gire

After prayer, the church needs to teach people what I call "the weeping mode." Weeping is different from beating up on ourselves. Weeping is a gentle release of water that washes, baptizes, and renews. Weeping leads to owning our complicity in the problem. Weeping is the opposite of blaming and also the opposite of denying. It leads to deep healing when inspired by the Spirit. The saints talked about weeping frequently, far more than I was ready for when I first started reading the mystics. They often referred to "the gift of tears."
—*Everything Belongs* by Richard Rohr

The Bible was written in tears and to tears it yields its best treasures. —*God Tells the Man Who Cares* by A. W. Tozer

The closest communion with God, I have begun to discover, comes through the shedding of my tears. If grapes and grain are not crushed, there can be no wine and bread. If my life is not crushed, there will not be the closest and most intimate communion with God.
—*Running on Empty* by Fil Anderson

I think a Christian is one who, along with Jesus, agrees to feel, to suffer the pain of the world. But we can't stop there. Tears come just as much with happiness. When it is an unearned happiness, when we know we did not deserve this goodness, we lose words. Tears are our only response. We perhaps have two eyes because reality is stereoscopic. When we see it fully, we have reason for both immense sadness and immense happiness — and both at the same time.

When faith reaches a certain intensity and the mystery becomes utterly overwhelming, often we can respond only with tears. — *Everything Belongs* by Richard Rohr

Trust

I. Opening Prayer

O Christ Jesus, when all is darkness and we feel our weakness and helplessness, give us the sense of your presence, your love, and your strength. Help us to have perfect trust in your protecting love and strengthening power, so that nothing may frighten or worry us, for, living close to you, we shall see your hand, your purpose, your will through all things.

—St. Ignatius

II. Psalm 31

III. Daily Scripture Readings

Monday	Psalm 62:1-12
Tuesday	John 14:1-4
Wednesday	Psalm 20:1-9
Thursday	Proverbs 3:5-6
Friday	Job 42:1-6
Saturday	Luke 22:31-38
Sunday	Psalm 37:1-11

IV. Readings for Reflection

V. Reflection and Listening: silent and written

VI. Prayer: for the church, for others, for myself

VII. Song   *Tis So Sweet to Trust in Jesus*

VIII. Closing Prayer

But I trust in you, O Lord, I say, "You are my God." My times are in your hands. Amen. —Psalm 31:14-15

Readings for Reflection-

Trust doesn't always come easy, especially when we are being called upon to trust in something or someone that we cannot see, much less control. That puts us in a very vulnerable and dependent position, and there are not many people I know that like being vulnerable or dependent. Maybe that's why we have such a hard time really trusting God. Oh we might say we trust him, but when it comes right down to it the way we live our lives usually tells us quite the opposite. In fact, we are much more apt to trust in our families or our friends or our careers or our own gifts and efforts more than we trust in God. But, as the Scriptures remind us over and over again, God is ultimately the only one who is completely trustworthy. Everything and everyone else will eventually let us down. Maybe all we really need to do is believe that it's true.

—Jim Branch, March, 2016

And remember, there are two things which are more utterly incompatible than even oil and water, and these two are trust and worry...When a believer really trusts anything, he ceases to worry about that thing which he has trusted. And when he worries, it is plain proof that he does not trust. — *The Christian's Secret of a Happy Life* by Hannah Whitall Smith

Take your stand on the power and trustworthiness of your God, and see how quickly all difficulties will vanish before a steadfast determination to believe. Trust in the dark, trust in the light, trust at night and trust in the morning, and you will find that the faith which may begin by mighty effort, will end sooner or later by becoming the easy and natural habit of the soul. —*The Christian's Secret of a Happy Life* by Hannah Whitall Smith

Your willingness to let go of your desire to control your life reveals a certain trust. The more you relinquish your stubborn need to maintain power, the more you will get in touch with the One who has the power to heal and guide you. And the more you get in touch with that divine power, the easier it will be to confess to yourself and to others your basic powerlessness. —*The Inner Voice of Love* by Henri J. M. Nouwen

The story was of a poor woman who had been carried triumphantly through a life of unusual sorrow. She was giving the history of her life to a kind visitor on one occasion, and at the close the visitor said, feelingly, "O Hannah, I do not see how you could bear so much sorrow!" "I did not bear it," was the quick reply; "the Lord bore it for me." "Yes," said the visitor "that is the right way. You must take your troubles to the Lord." "Yes," replied Hannah, "but we must do more than that; we must leave them there. Most people," she continued, "take their burdens to Him, but they bring them away with them again, and are just as worried and unhappy as ever. But I take mine, and I leave them with Him, and come away and forget them. And if the worry comes back, I take it to Him again; I do this over and over, until at last I just forget that I have any worries, and am at perfect rest." —*The Christian's Secret of a Happy Life* by Hannah Whitall Smith

The beginning of a path is always the most important. Miss the entrance, and you never walk the path. Perhaps the narrow gate that opens onto the route toward God, the gate that many Christians think they have walked through but never have, can be found in an idea so simple that we often miss its force:

You know you're finding God when you believe that
God is good no matter what happens.
We will know that we have found God when nothing
can shake our confidence in his unchanging goodness.
— *Finding God* by Dr. Larry Crabb

God's power, Presence, and love, then, come together to
establish a solid foundation on which to build trust.
Translated into practice, to trust means to be convinced
that God is fully aware of our circumstances, is present
in the midst of them, and is acting in wisdom, power,
and love to accomplish what is best for us. — *Rhythms of*
the Inner Life by Howard R. Macy

When I am not convinced that God is good, and when
I underestimate the seriousness of my struggle to believe
in his goodness, I will quietly — but with tight-lipped
resolve — take over responsibility for my own well-being.
— *Finding God* by Dr. Larry Crabb

During this week Judas and Peter present me with the
choice between running away from Jesus in despair or
returning to him in hope. Judas betrayed Jesus and
hanged himself. Peter denied Jesus and returned to him
in tears.

Sometimes despair seems an attractive choice, solving
everything in the negative. The voice of despair says, "I
sin over and over again. After endless promises to
myself and others to do better next time, I find myself
back again in the old dark places. Forget about trying to
change. I have tried for years. It didn't work and it will
never work. It is better that I get out of people's way, be
forgotten, no longer around, dead."

This strangely attractive voice takes all uncertainties
away and puts an end to the struggle. It speaks
unambiguously for the darkness and offers a clear-cut
negative identity.

But Jesus came to open my ears to another voice that says, "I am your God, I have molded you with my own hands, and I love what I have made. I love you with a love that has no limits, because I love you as I am loved. Do not run away from me. Come back to me — not once, not twice, but always again. You are my child. How can you ever doubt that I will embrace you again, hold you against my breast, kiss you and let my hands run through your hair? I am your God — the God of mercy and compassion, the God of pardon and love, the God of tenderness and care. Please do not say that I have given up on you, that I cannot stand you anymore, that there is no way back. It is not true. I so much want you to be with me. I so much want you to be close to me. I know all your thoughts. I hear all your words. I see all of your actions. And I love you because you are beautiful, made in my own image, an expression of my most intimate love. Do not judge yourself. Do not condemn yourself. Do not reject yourself. Let my love touch the deepest, most hidden corners of your heart and reveal to you your own beauty, a beauty that you have lost sight of, but which will become visible to you again in the light of my mercy. Come, come, let me wipe away your tears, and let my mouth come close to your ear and say to you, 'I love you, I love you, I love you.'"

This is the voice that Jesus wants us to hear. It is the voice that calls us always to return to the one who has created us in love and wants to re-create us in mercy. Peter heard that voice and trusted it. As he let that voice touch his heart, tears came — tears of sorrow and tears of joy, tears of remorse and tears of peace, tears of repentance and tears of gratitude.

It is not easy to let the voice of God's mercy speak to us because it is a voice asking for an always open relationship, one in which sins are acknowledged, forgiveness received, and love renewed. It does not offer us a solution, but a friendship. It does not take away our problems, but promises not to avoid them. It does not tell us where it all will end, but assures us that we will never be alone. A true relationship is hard work because loving is hard work, with many tears and many smiles. But it is God's work and worth every part of it.

O Lord, my Lord, help me to listen to your voice and choose your mercy. — *The Road to Daybreak* by Henri J. M. Nouwen

This is our Lord's will, that our prayer and our trust be both alike large. For if we trust not as much as we pray, we do not fully worship our Lord in our prayer, and also we tarry and pain ourselves. The cause is, I believe, that we know not truly that our Lord is Ground on whom our prayer springeth; and also that we know not that it is given us by the grace of His love. For if we knew this, it would make us to trust to have, of our Lord's gift, all that we desire. For I am sure that no man asketh mercy and grace with true meaning, but if mercy and grace be first given to him. — *Revelations of Divine Love* by Julian of Norwich

Wholeness

I. Opening Prayer
Gracious and loving God, you know the deep inner patterns of my life that keep me from being totally yours. You know the misformed structures of my being that hold me in bondage to something less than your high purpose for my life. You also know my reluctance to let you have your way with me in these areas. Hear the deeper cry of my heart for wholeness and by your grace enable me to be open to your transforming presence. Lord, have mercy. — *Invitation to a Journey* by M. Robert Mulholland Jr.

II. Psalm 122

III. Daily Scripture Readings

Monday	Mark 5:24-34
Tuesday	Psalm 23:1-6
Wednesday	Luke 24:36-53
Thursday	John 20:19-31
Friday	Deuteronomy 33:12
Saturday	Isaiah 26:1-15
Sunday	John 14:27

IV. Readings for Reflection

V. Reflection and Listening: silent and written

VI. Prayer: for the church, for others, for myself

VII. Song *Heal Us, Emmanuel*

VIII. Closing Prayer
My God, I wish to give myself to thee. Give me the courage to do so.

— Francois Fenelon

Readings for Reflection-

Few words in all of the Old Testament are as rich as the Hebrew word *shalom*. As a matter of fact, the translations of this one little word are varied and numerous, trying in vain to capture the fullness of the idea it is meant to communicate. The most common translation we have for the word is *peace*, but that does not seem to go far enough. Therefore, it is also translated *prosperity, tranquility, well-being, safety,* and *security*. Maybe the best word we have in the English language, however, that even comes close to capturing the true essence of *shalom* is the word *wholeness*. Because, at its core, *shalom* is about experiencing the creation intent of God. *Shalom* is life as God intended it to be. It is life before sin and brokenness entered the picture. *Shalom* is finding our way back into the garden where we were created to enjoy and experience God in his fullness as we "walk with him in the cool of the day." It is what our souls truly long for — deep communion, connection, and intimacy with our God.

— Jim Branch, September, 2006

Shalom , peace, is one of the richest words in the Bible. You can no more define it by looking up its meaning in the dictionary than you can define a person by his social security number. It gathers all aspects of wholeness that result from God's will being completed in us. It is the work of God that, when complete, releases streams of living water in us and pulsates with eternal life. Every time Jesus healed, forgave or called someone, we have a demonstration of *shalom*. — *A Long Obedience in the Same Direction* by Eugene Peterson

We strive for order, coherence, and wholeness in our lives. We want certainty. We long for *shalom*. Shalom is a peace that not only recalls all the pieces of one's life but sees how the parts fit together in a unified and glorious whole. Shalom involves rest and gratitude; it provides a balance and harmony where all things seem right. — *The Healing Path* by Dan Allender

The witness and vision of John's Gospel call us to enter more deeply into that mystery of the union between the living Jesus and the believer. We share the *shalom*, that vibrant word of peace and wholeness spoken in the locked room on Resurrection night. Our empty nets are filled from the lake; the fire and food are prepared for us on the beach. Our inner healing moves to a deeper place, and Jesus Christ gives us the mandate: "Feed my sheep." — *Feed My Shepherds* by Flora Slosson Wuellner

When you feel ready, think of Jesus' words to the disciples, "Peace [*shalom*] be with you" (John 20:19).
Focus on the word *peace.* It means wholeness and well-being. The presence of the living Christ is speaking and breathing well-being and wholeness in the very center of your fear, your vulnerable place. Stay in this living presence of the shalom as long as it seems right for you. Let your vulnerable, defended place breathe it in. — *Feed My Shepherds* by Flora Slosson Wuellner

Every summer, I go to the Boundary Waters, a million acres of pristine wilderness along the Minnesota-Ontario border. My first trip, years ago, was a vacation, pure and simple. But as I returned time and again to that elemental world of water, rock, woods, and sky, my vacation began to feel more like a pilgrimage to me — an annual trek to holy ground driven by spiritual need. Douglas Wood's meditation on the jack pine, a tree native to that part of the world, names what I go up north seeking: images of how life looks when it is lived with integrity.

Thomas Merton claimed that "there is in all things...a hidden wholeness." But back in the human world — where we are less self-revealing than jack pines — Merton's words can, at times, sound like wishful thinking. Afraid that our inner light will be extinguished or our inner darkness exposed, we hide our true identities from each other. In the process, we become separated from our own souls. We end up living divided lives, so far removed from the truth we hold within that we cannot know the "integrity that comes from being what you are."

My knowledge of the divided life comes first from personal experience: I yearn to be whole, but divided-ness often seems the easier choice. A "still, small voice" speaks the truth about me, my work, or the world. I hear it and yet act as if I did not. I withhold a personal gift that might serve a good end or commit myself to a project that I do not really believe in. I keep silent on an issue I should address or actively break faith with one of my own convictions. I deny my inner darkness, giving it more power over me, or I project it onto other people, creating "enemies" where none exist.

I pay a steep price when I live a divided life — feeling fraudulent, anxious about being found out, and depressed by the fact that I am denying my own selfhood. The people around me pay a price as well, for now they walk on ground made unstable by my divided- ness. How can I affirm another's identity when I deny my own? How can I trust another's integrity when I defy my own? A fault line runs down the middle of my life, and whenever it cracks open — divorcing my words and actions from the truth I hold within — things around me get shaky and start to fall apart.

But up north, in the wilderness, I sense the whole-ness "hidden in all things." It is in the taste of wild berries, the scent of sunbaked pine, the sight of the Northern Lights, the sound of water lapping the shore, signs of a bedrock integrity that is eternal and beyond all doubt. And when I return to a human world that is transient and riddled with disbelief, I have new eyes for the wholeness hidden in me and my kind and a new heart for loving even our imperfections.

In fact, the wilderness constantly reminds me that wholeness is not about perfection. On July 4, 1999, a twenty-minute maelstrom of hurricane-force winds took down twenty million trees across the Boundary Waters. A month later, when I made my annual pilgrimage up north, I was heartbroken by the ruin and wondered whether I wanted to return. And yet on each visit since, I have been astonished to see how nature uses devasta-tion to stimulate new growth, slowly but persistently healing her own wounds.

Wholeness does not mean perfection: it means embracing brokenness as an integral part of life. Knowing this gives me hope that human wholeness — mine, yours, ours — need not be a utopian dream, if we can use devastation as a seedbed for new life.
— *A Hidden Wholeness* by Parker J. Palmer

Peace I leave with you; my peace I give you. I do not give to you as the world gives. Do not let your hearts be troubled and do not be afraid. (John14:27)
So often in my life I feel like I am at the mercy of circumstances — anxious and afraid. It is so easy to get swept away in a whirlwind of fear and anxiety. But when I stop playing the victim, and fully recognize the offer that Jesus makes me, I realize that I do have the power and wherewithal to choose to live differently — in Christ. He offers me *his* peace. Not just any peace mind

you, but *his* peace. It is his gift to me and all I have to do is receive it.

Therein lies the problem. I don't always do that. I allow myself to get overwhelmed and overcome by what is around or within me and it is just a downward spiral from there. I think that's because, although I know in my head that Jesus offers me his peace, I have failed to receive it. Receiving involves more than just knowing in my head, it involves taking hold of that truth in my heart and making it my own. We do not truly receive any gift until we take hold of it and make it our own. And when we truly begin to do that with his peace, in prayer, anxiety and fear and insecurity seem to loosen their grip on us and we are able to breathe again.

"My peace I give to you," says Jesus. *"Therefore, do not let your hearts be troubled. You have another option. When your heart is troubled it is because you let it be. Receive my peace and your troubled heart can finally come to rest. Do not be afraid. Do not let your fears define you, but be defined by my love and my peace. That is who you are. Therefore, do not be swayed, or blown about, by fear, insecurity, or comparison. Don't allow people or things or circumstances to threaten or determine your worth. Live in my deep affection. Receive my peace this day. Take hold of it. Make it your own. Be free.*

—Jim Branch, May, 2016

Together

I. Opening Prayer

All praise and thanks to thee, most merciful God, for adopting us as thine own children, for incorporating us into thy holy Church, and for making us worthy to share in the inheritance of the saints in light. Grant us, we pray, all things necessary for our common life, and bring us all to be of one heart and mind within thy holy Church; through Jesus Christ our Lord. Amen.
— *The Book of Common Prayer*

II. Psalm 133

III. Daily Scripture Readings

Monday	Ecclesiastes 4:7-12
Tuesday	Hebrews 10:19-25
Wednesday	Romans 12:1-21
Thursday	Colossians 3:12-17
Friday	John 17:20-26
Saturday	Luke 10:25-37
Sunday	John 13:31-35

IV. Readings for Reflection

V. Reflection and Listening: silent and written

VI. Prayer: for the church, for others, for myself

VII. Song   *Blessed Be the Tie That Binds*

VIII. Closing Prayer

O God, fountain of love, pour love into our souls, that we may love those whom you love with the love you give us, and think and speak about them tenderly, meekly, lovingly; and so loving our brothers and sisters for your sake, may we grow in your love, and live in your love, that by living in your love we may live in you; for Jesus Christ's sake. —E. B. Pusey, quoted from *Classic Christian Prayers* by Owen Collins

Reading for Reflection-

There is this wonderful quality about being together in community that takes place whenever each individual takes whatever gifts he or she has been given and offers them to the body for the glory of God. The only way to describe it is that something magical happens. It is like *precious oil being poured out on everyone.* Somehow, mysteriously, abundance is created. The sum of the whole becomes much greater than the sum of the parts. It is sheer delight, for somehow, as the gifts are being given, they renew themselves, even as they are being poured out.

When we freely give to one another the things and the gifts that God has freely given to us, real community forms, and somehow new life is created both within us and among us. So let us, this very day, give what is *ours to give.* Let us pour precious oil on the heads of those who come into our paths, knowing that by doing so it will bring life to our souls and deep joy to the heart of our God.

—Jim Branch, February, 2014

How strange that we should ordinarily feel compelled to hide our wounds when we are all wounded! Community requires the ability to expose our wounds and weaknesses to our fellow creatures. It also requires the ability to be affected by the wounds of others… But even more important is the love that arises among us when we share, both ways, our woundedness.
—*A Different Drum* by M. Scott Peck

Let him who cannot be alone beware of community. Alone you stood before God when he called you; alone you had to answer the call; alone you had to struggle and pray.

But the reverse is also true: Let him who is not in community beware of being alone. Into the community you were called; in the community of the called you bear your cross, you struggle, you pray.

If you scorn the fellowship of the brethren, you reject the call of Jesus Christ, and thus your solitude can only be hurtful to you.

Only in the fellowship do we learn to be rightly alone and only in aloneness do we learn to live rightly in the fellowship. —*Life Together* by Dietrich Bonhoeffer

Two people, three people, ten people may be in living touch with one another through Him who underlies their separate lives. This is an astounding experience, which I can only describe but cannot explain in the language of science. But in vivid experience of divine Fellowship it is there. We know that these souls are with us, lifting their lives and ours continuously to God and opening themselves, with us, in steady and humble obedience to Him. It is as if the boundaries of our self were enlarged, as if we were within them and as if they were within us. Their strength, given to them by God, becomes our strength, and our joy, given to us by God, becomes their joy. In confidence and love we live together in Him. —*A Testament of Devotion* by Thomas Kelly

Community, then, cannot grow out of loneliness, but comes when the person who begins to recognize his or her belovedness greets the belovedness of the other. The God alive in me greets the God resident in you. When people can cease having to be for us everything, we can accept the fact they may still have a gift for us. They are partial reflections of the great love of God, but reflections nevertheless. We see that gift precisely and only once we give up requiring that person to be everything, to be God. We see him or her as a limited expression of an unlimited love. — *Turn My Mourning Into Dancing* by Henri J. M. Nouwen

Ultimately the body of Christ, so central in incarnational theology, is not the physical body of Jesus but the corporate body of those who gather around the Spirit, wherever it is found...Jesus exercises the only kind of leadership that can evoke authentic community — a leadership that risks failure (and even crucifixion) by making space for other people to act. When a leader takes up all the space and preempts all the action, he or she may make something happen, but that something is not community. Nor is it abundance, because the leader is only one person and one person's resources invariably run out. But when a leader is willing to trust the abundance that people have and can generate together, willing to take the risk of inviting people to share from that abundance, then and only then may true community emerge. — *Let Your Life Speak* by Parker J. Palmer

Without the discipline of community, solitude degenerates into self-absorption and isolation; without the discipline of solitude, community degenerates into codependency and enmeshment....The community of faith is where we learn the language of love. — *Journeymen* by Kent Ira Groff

It is best to live one's life with the support of a community which shares right values. When someone leaves such a community temporarily, let that person guard himself or herself. A human being is especially vulnerable when not supported by others. —*Always We Begin Again* by John McQuiston II

Never resign yourself to the scandal of the separation of Christians, all who so readily confess love for their neighbor, and yet remain divided. Be consumed with zeal for the unity of the Body of Christ. —*The Rule of Taize*

Accept with gratitude the companions God gives you to go with you on the way. Your task is to serve and upbuild one another as members of one body.

To the extent that you are filled with His Spirit and ready to die that others may live, to that extent will you grow in unity and reflect the face of Christ more and more clearly.

And to the extent that you are ready to die together that others may live will your community bear fruit for the coming of the Kingdom.

Then put aside ambition, and no longer concentrate on yourself. Be constantly converted to your companions and place yourself in God's hands.

Give instead of demanding, trust others instead of compelling their trust, serve instead of being served, bless instead of cursing. —*Rule for a New Brother* by H. van der Looy

Compassion

I. Opening Prayer:
Loving Father, teach me to love and care for those that
need you today. Those who are passed over and do not
feel love unless I love them for you. May Christ's love
for others be felt through me today. In your name and
by your power I pray these things. Amen. — *Disciplines
for the Inner Life* by Bob Benson and Michael W. Benson

II. Psalm 103

III. Daily Scripture Readings
Monday	Matthew 9:35-38
Tuesday	Micah 6:6-8
Wednesday	Luke 4:14-21
Thursday	Psalm 41:1-3
Friday	Matthew 25:31-46
Saturday	John 13:1-17
Sunday	Isaiah 58:6-12

IV. Readings for Reflection

V. Reflection and Listening: silent and written

VI. Prayer: for the church, for others, for myself

VII. Song   *Our God Reigns*

VIII. Closing Prayer
Our Father, here I am, at your disposal, your child, to
use me to continue your loving the world, by giving
Jesus to me and through me, to each other and the
world. Let us pray for each other as we allow Jesus to
love in us and through us with the love with which His
Father loves him. — *Seeking the Heart of God* by Mother
Teresa

Readings for Reflection-

The gospel of Matthew (6:39) tells us that *when Jesus saw the crowds, he had compassion for them, because they were harassed and helpless like sheep without a shepherd.* The word Matthew uses here is *splagchnizomai,* which means to me moved from the deepest parts of your being. That is what goes on in the heart of Jesus when he sees people in need, he is moved so deeply that he simply must *do* something to alleviate their suffering. That, I think, is the difference between pity and compassion. Pity is just a feeling, whereas compassion is a feeling that spurs us to action. And that is what Jesus asks of us, not to stop at a mere feeling, but to be moved all the way to action.

—Jim Branch, March, 2016

. . . Compassion—that sometimes fatal capacity for feeling what it is like to live inside another's skin, knowing that there can never really be peace and joy for any until there is peace and joy finally for all. *—A Room Called Remember* by Frederick Buechner

This is the Season of Love. What happens in us is the miracle of discovering our potential to care for others. And so, we become foot-washing, water-walking, healing, beatitude people. Our lives begin to bless. We are compelled to respond to the Word of God, to speak in the Holy Name, to live out our ministry of love.

We are fragile vessels whose love often gets tired. We need to be converted over and over again. And so, the healing act of our growth continues. We empty ourselves that we may be filled. We uproot that we may proclaim. We take off our masks. We call forth gifts. We bless. We wash feet. And somewhere between the shedding of our masks and the foot-washing, we discover that it is not so much what we do that touches

342

lives as who we are becoming. And so we rest in the truth that what is most important is not how much of ourselves we leave with others, but how much we enable others to be themselves. — *Seasons of Your Heart* by Macrina Wiederkehr

The hardest thing about really seeing and really hearing is when you really have to do something about what you've seen and heard.

— Frederick Buechner

If someone asked you if you were compassionate, you might readily say yes. Or at least, "I believe so." But pause to examine the word compassion and answering gets more complicated. For the word comes from roots that mean literally to "suffer with"; to show compassion means sharing in the suffering "passion" of another. Compassion understood in this way asks more from us than a mere stirring of pity or a sympathetic word.

To live with compassion means to enter others' dark moments. It is to walk into places of pain, not to flinch or look away when another agonizes. It means to stay where people suffer. Compassion holds us back from quick, eager explanations when tragedy meets someone we know or love. — *Turn My Mourning Into Dancing* by Henri J. M. Nouwen

You can't force the heart. Genuine compassion cannot be imposed from without. It doesn't happen simply by hearing a sermon on love, or being sent on a loving mission...Compassion, which is the very life of God within us, comes through slow and often difficult metamorphosis deep within the human soul. — *When the Heart Waits* by Sue Monk Kidd

343

And while God does not ask any of us to bring Christ into the world as literally as did Mary, God calls each of us to become a God bearer through whom God may enter the world again and again. — *The Godbearing Life* by Kenda Creasy Dean and Ron Foster

Compassion is hard because it requires the inner disposition to go with others to the place where they are weak, vulnerable, lonely, and broken. — *The Way of the Heart* by Henri J.M. Nouwen

A lot of giving and receiving has a violent quality, because the givers and receivers act more out of need than out of trust. What looks like generosity is actually manipulation, and what looks like love is really a cry for affection or support. When you know yourself as fully loved, you will be able to give according to the other's capacity to receive, and you will be able to receive according to the other's capacity to give. You will be grateful for what is given to you without clinging to it, and joyful for what you can give without bragging about it. You will be a free person, free to love. — *The Inner Voice of Love* by Henri J. M. Nouwen

No man ever receives a word from God without instantly being put to the test by it. We disobey and then wonder why we don't go on spiritually. — *My Utmost for His Highest* by Oswald Chambers

The question is not: How many people take you seriously? How much are you going to accomplish? Can you show results? But: Are you in love with Jesus? Perhaps another way of putting the question would be: Do you know the incarnate God? In our world of loneliness and despair, there is an enormous need for men and women who know the heart of God, a heart that forgives, that cares, that reaches out and wants to heal. In that heart there is no suspicion, no revenge, no resentment, and not a tinge of hatred. It is a heart that wants only to give love and receive love in response. It is a heart that suffers immensely because it sees the magnitude of human pain and the great resistance to trusting the heart of God who wants to offer consolation and hope. — *In the Name of Jesus* by Henri J. M. Nouwen

Try to imagine this scene. You are sitting at the table with Jesus and his friends on the night before he died. A confusing sorrow overshadows you. Yet, a mysterious hope has settled in your heart. Suddenly Jesus is standing in front of you. He looks into your eyes and immediately you are filled with an awareness of your tremendous worth.

> Supper was special that night
> There was both a heaviness and a holiness
> hanging in the air
> We couldn't explain the mood
> It was sacred, yet sorrowful.
> Gathered around that table
> eating that solemn, holy meal
> seemed to us the most important meal
> we had ever sat down to eat.
>
> We were dwelling in the heart of *mystery*
> Though dark the night
> Hope felt right
> as if something evil
> was about to be conquered.
> And then suddenly
> the One we loved startled us all
> He got up from the table
> and put on an apron.
> Can you imagine how we felt?

God in an apron!

Tenderness encircled us
    as He bowed before us.
He knelt and said,
    "I choose to wash your feet
    because I love you."

God in an apron, kneeling
I couldn't believe my eyes.
I was embarrassed
    until his eyes met mine
I sensed my value then.
He touched my feet
He held them in his strong, brown hands
He washed them
I can still feel the water
I can still feel the touch of his hands.
I can still see the look in his eyes.

Then he handed me a towel
    and said,
"As I have done
 so you must do."
Learn to bow
Learn to kneel.

Let your tenderness encircle
    everyone you meet
Wash their feet
    not because *you have to,*
    because you *want to.*

It seems I've stood two thousand years
    holding the towel in my hands,
"As I have done so you must do,"
    keeps echoing in my heart.

"There are so many feet to wash,"
   I keep saying
"No," I hear God's voice
   resounding through the years
"There are only my feet
What you do for them
   You do for me."
— *Seasons of Your Heart* by Macrina Wiederkehr

Love is one of the most misused words in our
language. It is unfortunate that a word so precious has
become so abused. Love is a Word that can become
flesh in each of our lives. This fleshed-out Word of Love
is a mystery. It is the Mystery of God living and acting
in our lives. It is the Mystery of God ministering
through our touch, and though our voice. It is God
seeing through our eyes.

Love is blind, we like to say, but *no*; Love is not blind.
The ego is blind. All it can see is itself. But Love is not
blind. Love is pure vision! God, seeing through us! The
more we will allow God to see though us, the more we
will notice a great healing taking place in our world.
— *Seasons of Your Heart* by Macrina Wiederkehr

Give Your Life Away

I. Opening Prayer

Take Lord, and receive all my liberty, my memory, my understanding, and my entire will, all that I have and possess. Thou hast given all to me. To Thee, O Lord, I return it. All is Thine, dispose of it wholly according to Thy will. Give me Thy love and thy grace, for this is sufficient for me.

—Ignatius of Loyola

II. Psalm 82

III. Daily Scripture Readings

Monday	Luke 9:12-17
Tuesday	Ezekiel 34:1-16
Wednesday	Isaiah 61:1-6
Thursday	2 Timothy 2:1-10
Friday	Luke 15:1-7
Saturday	Colossians 1:24-2:5
Sunday	Luke 14:1-14

IV. Readings for Reflection

V. Prayer: for the church, for others, for myself

VI. Reflection and Listening: silent and written

VII. Song   *For All the Saints*

VIII. Closing Prayer

Go forth now as God's servant. Remember God's presence often and draw strength from the knowledge that the One who calls and sends also sustains. Amen.
—*A Guide to Prayer*, Rueben P. Job and Norman Shawchuck

Readings for Reflection-

You give them something to eat. It seems that a significant amount of doing ministry involves figuring out what you've got and then figuring out how to give it and who to give it to. You see, God gave you something wonderfully unique and specific, something that only you can give. It may feel like only five loves and two fish among so many, but in his hands it is more than enough to satisfy a multitude and still have some left over. *"You give them something to eat,"* Jesus is saying. *"Because I gave you something that only you can give. First, give it to me, and then I will give it back to you in abundance. Only then will you be able to give it to them, whoever your 'them' may be. And in the giving of 'it' to 'them' you will find that there is enough to feed you as well."* Incredible!

There is one other small thing to notice in the text however, and it is really not small at all. Once we are willing enough and courageous enough to give Jesus our little loaves and fish, he does something really amazing with it. He takes *it*, then he blesses *it*, then he breaks *it*, and then he gives *it*. Now all of that sounds pretty great, except the breaking part. Because, it seems, in Jesus' economy we can't be multiplied enough to be given, we can only be broken enough to be given. It is in the breaking that the abundance comes. It is in the breaking that the multiplying occurs, just as it will be for each of us. If we really want to have something of depth and substance to give to those around us, it will usually involve some sort of breaking.

The funny thing is that the times when we are the most broken are usually the times when it feels like we have the least to give, but the opposite is actually true. It is when we are the most broken that we are most able to give something of substance and value to those in our lives and world. Because somehow, in the brokenness, it has stopped being about us and our ability to multiply ourselves and has begun being about God and his ability to multiply our little loaves and little fish with his strong and tender hands.

—Jim Branch, January, 2014

To suffer with another person does not mean to drown oneself in the other's suffering; that would be as foolish as jumping into a pool to save a sinking swimmer only to drown oneself. More to the point, I doubt that it is even possible to enter fully into another person's pain, for suffering is a profoundly solitary experience. To suffer with another person means to be there in whatever way possible, to share the circumstances of the other's life as much as one can — not to add to the world's pool of suffering, but to gain intimate understanding of what the other requires.

What we usually learn, once we are there, is that there is no "fix" for the person who suffers, only the slow painful process of walking through the suffering to whatever lies on the other side. Once there, we learn that being there is the best we can do, being there not as a cure but as a companion to the person who suffers on his or her slow journey. There is no arm's-length "solution" for suffering, and people who offer such only add to the pain. But there is comfort and even healing in the presence of people who know how to be with others, how to be fully there. — *The Active Life* by Parker Palmer

Put yourself completely under the influence of Jesus, so that he may think his thoughts in your mind, do his work through your hands, for you will be all-powerful with him to strengthen you. — *A Gift for God* by Mother Teresa

Christ has no body now on earth but yours;
yours are the only hands with which he can do his work,
yours are the only feet with which he can go about the

world,
yours are the only eyes through which his compassion
        can shine forth upon a troubled world.
Christ has no body now on earth but yours.

— Teresa of Avila

But real training for service asks for a hard and often
painful process of self-emptying. The main problem of
service is to be a way without being "in the way." And
if there are any tools, techniques and skills to be learned
they are primarily to plow the field, to cut the weeds
and clip the branches, that is, to take away the obstacles
for real growth and development. Training for service is
not a training to become rich but to become voluntarily
poor; not to fulfill ourselves but to empty ourselves; not
to conquer God but to surrender to his saving power.
All this is very hard to accept in our contemporary
world, which tells us about the importance of power and
influence. But it is important that in this world there
remain a few voices crying out that if there is anything
to boast of, we should boast of our weakness. Our
fulfillment is in offering emptiness, our usefulness in
becoming useless, our power in becoming powerless.
— *Reaching Out* by Henri J.M. Nouwen

The sight of the homeless woman hobbling down that
sidewalk in front of that playground was a window of
the soul. It showed me something of the sadness of
those whose life is the street. Something of the sidewalk
monotony of their lives. And the meandering tragedy of
a soul slowly walking itself to death. The picture of that
woman on the street was a window of the soul, and I
received at least something of what it had to offer.
    But what was given in return?
    There is more to windows of the soul than what we
receive there. Something also is required. Sometimes it

is a very small thing. Sometimes it is our very life. What is it God expects from us at those intersecting moments like the one at Rosewood and Croft?

> Is it not this I require of you as a fast:
> > to loose the fetters of injustice, to untie the knots of the yoke
> > to snap every yoke? and set free those who have been crushed?
> Is it not sharing your food with the hungry,
> > taking the homeless poor into your house,
> > clothing the naked when you meet them
> > and never evading a duty to your kinfolk?
> > (Isaiah 58:6-7 NEB)

It is how the Word of God dwelt among us. And how He dwells among us still. Except now it is our flesh He slips into. What else could it mean to be called the body of Christ, if it is not His feet we are becoming, His hands? If it is not going where His feet went and doing what His hands did, what is it?

> Whose eyes brim with compassion for the multitudes, if not ours?
> Whose arms will embrace the prodigals, if not ours?
> Whose hands will touch the lepers, if not ours?

—*Windows of the Soul* by Ken Gire

An old rabbi was once asked why so few people were finding God. He wisely replied that people are not willing to look that low. Jesus was born in a stable, and God is especially concerned for the poorest, the lowliest, the lost, and the neglected.

—*Liberation of Life* by Harvey and Lois Seifert

Would it be too much to say that ever since the Ascension, Jesus has sought other bodies in which to begin again the life he lived on earth? The church serves as this extension of the incarnation, God's primary way of establishing presence in the world. We are "AfterChrists," in Gerald Manley Hopkins's coinage:

352

...for Christ plays in ten thousand places,
Lovely in eyes, and lovely in limbs not His
To the Father through the features of men's faces.
— *The Jesus I Never Knew* by Philip Yancey

I gaze lovingly at my dinner plate filled with gifts from the earth. I am touched, overwhelmed at the truth that everything I eat has in some way had to die so I could live. It is the way of the earth, and I do not completely understand it. Ponder over the truth for a while. It may bring tears to your eyes. And if it does, I encourage you to welcome them. They could be healing.

I gaze more lovingly still. Gratitude overflows! I ask my heart a hard question: What is it in me that must die before I can truly give life to others? — *Seasons of Your Heart* by Macrina Wiederkehr

The more you are called to speak for God's love, the more you will need to deepen the knowledge of that love in your own heart. The farther the outward journey takes you, the deeper the inward journey must be. Only when your roots are deep can your fruits be abundant. The enemy is there, waiting to destroy you, but you can face the enemy without fear when you know that you are held safe in the love of Jesus. — *The Inner Voice of Love* by Henri J. M. Nouwen

Involved in Ministry

I. Opening Prayer

Dear Jesus,

Help us to spread your fragrance everywhere we go. Flood our souls with your Spirit and life. Penetrate and possess our whole being so utterly that our lives may only be a radiance of yours. Shine through us and so be in us that every soul we come I contact with may feel your presence in our soul. Let them look up and see no longer us but only You. Stay with us and then we shall begin to shine as you shine, so to shine as to be light to others. The light, O Jesus, will be all from you. None of it will be ours. It will be you shining on others through us. Let us thus praise you in the way you love best by shining on those around us. Amen. — *The Daily Prayer of Mother Teresa*

II. Psalm 145

III. Daily Scripture Readings

Monday	Matthew 5:13-15
Tuesday	1 Thessalonians 2:1-12
Wednesday	John 20:19-23
Thursday	Matthew 10:1-20
Friday	2 Corinthians 5:11-21
Saturday	Matthew 28:16-20
Sunday	Acts 8:26-40

IV. Readings for Reflection

V. Prayers: for the church, for others, for myself

VI. Reflection and Listening: silent and written

VII. Song   *Be Thou My Vision*

VIII. Closing Prayer

Almighty God, cause your good gifts to flow in and through my life and ministry this day and always. Amen. —*A Guide to Prayer* by Rueben P. Job and Norman Shawchuck

Readings for Reflection-

> *May what I do flow from me like a river,*
> *no forcing and no holding back,*
> *the way it is with children.*
>
> *Then in these swelling and ebbing currents,*
> *these deepening tides moving out, returning,*
> *I will sing you as no one ever has,*
>
> *streaming through widening channels*
> *into the open sea.*
> — *The Book of Hours* by Rainer Maria Rilke

The older I get the more I've come to believe that ministry is much less about *what we do* and much more about *who we are*. I think it is intended to be something that flows freely and pours forth from what God is doing in the depths of our hearts and souls, rather than something we have to manufacture or manipulate or create—thus no *contriving*, no *forcing*, no *holding back*.

I think that's why Jesus says that we *are* the salt of the earth and we *are* the light of the world. Salt and light do not have to work real hard to be salt and light, they just have to be what they were intended to be. They have to bring out the flavor of God within them, and illuminate the beauty of God around them.

It is the same with us. We're not called to *do* salt and light, we are called to *be* salt and light. Being salt and being light are the natural expressions of the life of God in us. If we are living in union with our God, if we are falling more and more in love with Jesus each day, it will pour forth from our lives and it will find its way to those in our world. Everyone will taste God's flavor uniquely in us. Everyone will see the beauty of God illuminated by us. All we have to *do* is to *be* our true, God-breathed, selves.

When we are not being who God made us to be — when we are forcing or when we are holding back — we are like salt that has lost its saltiness, or like a light that has been put under a bowl. And what good is that? So instead of constantly trying to figure out how to *do* ministry, from now on I think I'm going to think more about how to *be* who and what God has made me to be.

Lord Jesus, help us to be who and what you created us to be, for then, and only then, will we have any hope doing what you have called us to do. Amen.

—Jim Branch, January, 2016

More and more, the desire grows in me simply to walk around, greet people, enter their homes, sit on their doorsteps, play ball, throw water, and be known as someone who wants to live with them. It is a privilege to have the time and the freedom to practice this simple ministry of presence. Still, it is not as simple as it seems. My own desire to be useful, to do something significant, or be a part of some impressive project is so strong that soon my time is taken up by meetings, conferences, study groups, and workshops that prevent me from walking the streets. It is difficult not to have plans, not to organize people around the urgent cause, and not to feel that you are working directly for social progress. But I wonder more and more if the first thing shouldn't be to know people by name, to eat and drink with them, to listen to their stories and tell your own, and to let them know with words, handshakes, and hugs that you do not simply like them, but truly love them. —*Gracias!* by Henri J.M. Nouwen

356

The goal of education and formation of ministry is continually to recognize the Lord's voice, his face, and his touch in every person we meet. As long as we live, the Lord wants to reveal to us more of himself. As long as we minister, we can expect the Lord to make himself known to us in ways that we have not yet experienced. God himself became flesh for us so that we would be able to receive him every time we find ourselves serving another human being. —*Gracias!* by Henri J.M. Nouwen

The more I think about the meaning of living and acting in the name of Jesus, the more I realize that what I have to offer others is not my intelligence, skill, power, influence, or connections, but my own human brokenness through which the love of God can manifest itself. The celebrant in Leonard Bernstein's Mass says: "Glass shines brighter when it's broken...I never noticed that." This, to me, is what ministry and mission are all about. Ministry is entering with our human brokenness into communion with others and speaking a word of hope. This hope is not based on any power to solve the problems of those with whom we live, but on the love of God, which becomes visible when we let go of our fears of being out of control and enter into His presence in shared confession of weakness. —*Gracias!* by Henri Nouwen

The great paradox of ministry, therefore, is that we minister above all with our weakness, a weakness that invites us to receive from those to whom we go. The more in touch we are with our own need for healing and salvation, the more open we are to receive in gratitude what others have to offer us. —*Gracias!* by Henri J.M. Nouwen

The fundamental building blocks of the kingdom are relationships. Not programs, systems, or productivity.

But inconvenient, time-consuming, intrusive relationships. The kingdom is built on personal involvements that disrupt schedules and drain energy. When I enter into redemptive relationships with others, I lose much of my "capacity to produce desired results with a minimum expenditure of energy, time, money, or materials." In short, relationships sabotage my efficiency. A part of me dies. Is this perhaps what our Lord meant when He said we must lay down our lives for each other? — *Theirs is the Kingdom* by Robert D. Lupton

Transformation and intimacy both cry out for ministry. We are led through the furnace of God's purity not just for our own sake but also for the sake of others. We are drawn up into the bosom of God's love not merely to experience acceptance but also so we can give His love to others.

The world writhes under the pain of its arrogance and self-sufficiency. We can make a difference, if we will.

In earlier days, we tried to serve out of our spiritual bankruptcy, and we failed. We now know that ministry must flow out of abundance.

Bernard of Clairvaux writes, "If then you are wise, you will show yourself rather as a reservoir than a canal. For a canal spreads abroad water as it receives it, but a reservoir waits until it is filled before overflowing, and thus communicates, without loss to itself, its superabundant water. In the Church at the present day, we have many canals, few reservoirs." We have determined to be reservoirs. — *Prayer: Finding the Heart's True Home* by Richard J. Foster

Ministry is the least important thing. You cannot **not** minister if you are in communion with God and live in community. A lot of people are always concerned

about:" How can I help people? Or help the youth come to Christ? Or preach well?" But these are basically nonissues. If you are burning with the love of Jesus, don't worry: everyone will know. They will say," I want to get close to this person who is so full of God."
—Henri J.M. Nouwen in *Christianity Today*

The enthusiasm of (and for) the kingdom is missing because there is so little enthusiasm for the King.
— *The Key to the Missionary Problem* by Andrew Murray

The first verb Mark used to describe Jesus' action is "came." Jesus *came* to be with us. God's first move is to be among us — Immanuel, God is with us. God comes to us long before we come to God. We may think we are in pursuit of God, but in reality we are only responding to a God who has been pursuing us. — *Embracing the Love of God* by James Bryan Smith

The greatest news of all is that God is *with* his people, that he is truly present. What greater ministry, then, can be practiced than a ministry that reflects this divine presence? — *Gracias!* by Henri J.M. Nouwen

God came to us because He wanted to join us on the road, to listen to our story, and to help us realize that we are not walking in circles but moving towards the house of peace and joy. This is the great mystery of Christmas that continues to give us comfort and consolation: we are not alone on our journey. The God of love who gave us life sent us His only Son to be with us at all times and in all places, so that we never have to feel lost in our struggles but always can trust that He walks with us.
— *Gracias!* by Henri J.M. Nouwen

It is the nature of pastoral work to walk into an alien world, put our feet on the pavement, and embrace the *locale*. Pastoral work is geographical as much as it is theological. Pastors don't send memos, don't send generic messages, don't work from a distance: *locale* is part of it. It is the nature of pastoral work to be on site, working things out in the particular soil of a particular parish. — *Under the Unpredictable Plant* by Eugene H. Peterson

When Jonah began his proper work, he went a *day's journey into Nineveh*. He didn't stand at the edge and preach at them; he entered into the midst of their living — heard what they were saying, smelled the cooking, picked up the colloquialisms, lived "on the economy," not aloof from it, not superior to it. — *Under the Unpredictable Plant* by Eugene H. Peterson

God wants not only to be a God *for* us, but also a God *with* us. That happens in Jesus, the Emmanuel who walks with us, talks with us, and dies with us. In sending Jesus to us, God wants to convince us of the unshakable fidelity of the divine love. Still there is more. When Jesus leaves he says to us, "I will not leave you alone, but will send you the Holy Spirit." The Spirit of Jesus is God *within* us. Here the fullness of God's faithfulness is revealed. Through Jesus, God gives us the divine Spirit so that we can live a God-like life. The Spirit is the breath of God. It is the intimacy between Jesus and his Father. It is the divine communion. It is God's love active within us.

This divine faithfulness is the core of our witness. By our words, but most of all by our lives, we are to reveal God's faithfulness to the world. — *Here and Now* by Henri J.M. Nouwen

The main place you do the work of God is *as you go along*. It doesn't have to be in high-profile, important positions. It will happen, if it happens at all, in the routine, unspectacular corners of your life. *As you go along.* —*Love Beyond Reason* by John Ortberg

It seems to me that it is very likely the true essence of ministry has more to do with *being* to another than with some act or deed which we have come to believe we must be *doing* to, or for, them. Perhaps the deepest, kindest thing we can do for anyone is to just be there for them in such a way that all they are and all the gifts they possess will be released and affirmed. —*He Speaks Softly* by Bob Benson

We have it in us to be Christs to each other and maybe in some unimaginable way to God too—that's what we have to tell finally. We have it in us to work miracles of love and healing as well as to have them worked upon us. We have it in us to bless with him and forgive with him and heal with him and once in a while maybe even to grieve with some measure of his grief at another's pain and to rejoice with some measure of his rejoicing at another's joy as if it were our own. And who knows but that in the end, by God's mercy, the two stories will converge for good and all, and though we would never have had the courage or the faith or the wit to die for him any more than we have ever managed to live for him very well either, his story will come true in us at last. And in the meantime, this side of Paradise, it is our business (not, like so many, peddlers of God's word but as men and women of sincerity) to speak with our hearts (which is what sincerity means) and to bear witness to, and live out of, and live toward, and live by, the true word of his holy story as it seeks to stammer itself forth through the holy stories of us all. —*A Room Called Remember* by Frederick Buechner

Down

I. Opening Prayer

Lord, how great is our dilemma! In Thy Presence silence best becomes us, but love inflames our hearts and constrains us to speak.

Were we to hold our peace the stones would cry out; yet if we speak, what shall we say? Teach us to know that we cannot know, for the things of God knoweth no man, but the Spirit of God. Let faith support us where reason fails, and we shall think because we believe, not in order that we may believe.

In Jesus' name. Amen.

— *Knowledge of the Holy* by A. W. Tozer

II. Psalm 138

III. Daily Scripture Readings

Monday	Philippians 2:1-11
Tuesday	Jonah 1:1-2:10
Wednesday	John 21:15-19
Thursday	Mark 8:31-38
Friday	Mark 10:35-45
Saturday	Luke 22:7-30
Sunday	Matthew 5:1-12

IV. Readings for Reflection

V. Reflection and Listening: silent and written

VI. Prayer: for the church, for others, for myself

VII. Song   *How Great is Our God*

VIII. Closing Prayer

Lord Jesus, give us the grace and the strength and the courage to follow your invitation downward — to the place where there is only you and nothing else. In your name and for your sake we pray. Amen.

Readings for Reflection-

In our day and in our culture the language of *ascent* has indeed become a popular one. Success, productivity, power, independence, and competition seem to be held up, even in the Christian community, as characteristics to be valued and pursued. But when we listen carefully to the voice of Scripture and the words of our Savior, we begin to get a sense of a language and an attitude that is very different from that of the world around us. Jesus, in fact, used a completely different vocabulary to talk about life and faith. He used words like service, fruitfulness, humility, dependence, and compassion— most of which run directly against the grain of both the culture and the world. In fact, when it comes to the language of the Kingdom it seems that the word *descent* might actually be a more appropriate choice. Hence, if we really wish to follow Jesus' example and his teaching, we may find that the way actually leads downward.

—Jim Branch, September, 2006

From the heights we leap and go
To the valleys down below
Always answering to the call
To the lowest place of all
From the heights we leap and go
To the valleys down below
Sweetest urge and sweetest will
To go lower, lower still
—*Hinds' Feet On High Places* by Hannah Hurnard

The world says, "When you were young you were dependent and could not go where you wanted, but when you grow old you will be able to make your own decisions, go your own way, and control your own destiny." But Jesus has a different vision of maturity: it is the ability and willingness to be led where you would rather not go. Immediately after Peter has been commissioned to be a leader of his sheep, Jesus confronts him with the hard truth that the servant-leader is the leader who is being led to unknown, undesirable, and painful places. The way of the Christian leader is not the way of upward mobility in which our world has invested so much, but the way of downward mobility ending on the cross. This may sound morbid and masochistic, but for those who have heard the voice of the first love and said "yes" to it, the downward-moving way of Jesus is the way to the joy and the peace of God, a joy and peace that is not of this world. *— In the Name of Jesus* by Henri J. M. Nouwen

In Luke's gospel passage in which Jesus tells us, "It is an evil and adulterous generation that wants a sign" (Luke 11:29), he then says that the only sign he will give us is the sign of Jonah. As a good Jew, Jesus knew the graphic story of Jonah the prophet, who was running from God and was used by God almost in spite of himself. Jonah was swallowed by the whale and taken where he would rather not go. This was Jesus' metaphor for death and rebirth. Think of all the other signs, apparitions, and miracles that religion looks for and seeks and even tries to create. But Jesus says it is an evil and adulterous generation that looks for these things. That's a pretty hard saying. He says instead we must go inside the belly of the whale for a while. Then and only then will we be spit upon a new shore and understand our call. That's the only pattern Jesus promises us. Paul spoke of "reproducing the pattern" of

364

his death and thus understanding resurrection (Phil. 3:11). That teaching will never fail. The soul is always freed and formed in such wisdom. Native religions speak of winter and summer; mystical authors speak of darkness and light; Eastern religion speaks of yin and yang. Seasons transform the year; light and darkness transform the day. Christians call it the paschal mystery, but we are all pointing to the same necessity of both descent and ascent.

The paschal mystery is *the* pattern of transformation. We are transformed through death and rising, probably many times. There seems to be no other cauldron of growth and transformation.

We seldom go freely into the belly of the beast. Unless we face a major disaster like the death of a friend or spouse or loss of a marriage or job, we usually will not go there. As a culture, we have to be taught the language of descent. That is the great language of religion. It teaches us to enter willingly, trustingly into the dark periods of life. These dark periods are good teachers. Religious energy is in the dark questions, seldom in the answers. Answers are the way out, but that is not what we are here for. But when we look at the questions, we look for the opening to transformation. Fixing something doesn't usually transform us. We try to change events in order to avoid changing ourselves. We must learn to stay with the pain of life, without answers, without conclusions, and some days without meaning. That is the path, the perilous dark path of true prayer. — *Everything Belongs* by Richard Rohr

Years ago, someone told me that humility is central to the spiritual life. That made sense to me: I was proud to think of myself as humble! But this person did not tell me that the path to humility, for some of us at least, goes through humiliation, where we are brought low, rendered powerless, stripped of pretenses and defenses, and left feeling fraudulent, empty, and useless—a humiliation that allows us to regrow our lives from the ground up, from the humus of common ground.

The spiritual journey is full of paradoxes. One of them is that the humiliation that brings us down—down to ground on which it is safe to stand and to fall—eventually takes us to a firmer and fuller sense of self. When people ask me how it felt to emerge from depression, I can give only one answer: I felt at home in my own skin, and at home on the face of the earth, for the first time. —*Let Your Life Speak* by Parker J. Palmer

Everybody wants to be somebody. Since the dawn of history, human beings have been trying to move up the scale of importance. The clincher used by the serpent to tempt Adam and Eve was "when you eat of [the tree of good and evil], your eyes will be opened, and you will be like God, knowing good and evil" (Gen. 3:5). Henri Nouwen says that ever since then, we have been tempted to replace love with power. "The long painful history of the church is the history of people ever and again tempted to choose power over love, control over the cross, being a leader over being led." This is a theme running through the Bible, through human history and through our own psyche.

We should not be surprised nor excessively judgmental with James and John. Although their brashness may not be our style, the motive underlying their request is not strange: "Grant us to sit, one at your right hand and one at your left, in your glory." Shared glory, honored positions, closeness to powerful people-- these are popular means of being somebody. If we can't be the glory or the honored guest or the one with the power, then being close by is the next best thing. Some of the glory will make us shine. Some of the honor may spill over onto us.

Religion is fertile soil in which the seeds of ambition subtly grow. Being close to God has deadly dangers. Some of history's most dastardly deeds have been done by those who claimed to be sitting on God's right or left hand. It is easy for those of us who deal daily with holy things to be presumptuous. James and John apparently felt their closeness to Jesus gave them special entree. They prefaced their request for prominence with "Teacher, we want you to do for us whatever we ask of you."

It is easy to assume that relationship with God translates into entitlement. Career advancement, upward mobility, assignments or calls to bigger churches with larger salaries and more prominent leadership positions are popular expectations of clergy. Their competition for prestigious pulpits and powerful positions threatens their witness. Their drive for the honored and well-compensated positions contributes to the weakening of congregations located in mission fields. Small, impoverished congregations become temporary stepping stones in the pursuit of prominent places.

Insights from the social sciences fill contemporary books on effective leadership. But although the social sciences provide helpful tools for understanding the dynamics of leadership, they must not be foundational for leadership in the church. Without a firm theological foundation, leadership is only a sophisticated means of upward mobility through institutional advancement. Much of the material I read sounds more like James and John pursuing prominence than Jesus calling us to a life of servanthood and downward mobility; it has more to do with the pursuit of power than the implications of leadership as the power of love.

Jesus' response to James and John challenges popular assumptions about greatness, power and prominence: "Are you able to drink the cup that I drink, or be baptized with the baptism that I am baptized with?" The other disciples were angry, perhaps afraid that James and John would be given positions which they had sought. But Jesus said to all the disciples, "Whoever wishes to become great among you must be your servant, and whoever wishes to be first among you must be a slave of all. For the Son of Man came not to be served but to serve, and to give his life as a ransom for many."

The cup from which Jesus drank is self-emptying love, the giving of one's own life for others. The baptism with which he was baptized is a burial of the old world with its power games and the rising of God's reign of justice, generosity and joy. This is downward mobility.

The world's image of greatness is hierarchical, with the greatest at the pinnacle of the pyramid and God hovering over the top. The closer one gets to the pinnacle, the closer one is to greatness and to the image of God. Success, upward mobility and being served are signs of faithfulness to a hierarchical god.

The way of Jesus leads in another direction. Nouwen writes: "The way of the Christian leader is not the way of upward mobility in which the world has invested so much, but the way of downward mobility ending on the cross.... It is not a leadership of power and control, but a leadership of powerlessness and humility in which the suffering servant of God, Jesus Christ, is made manifest."

Giving our lives "as a ransom for many" involves making ourselves available to others in response to the One who laid down his life for us. It is offering our total being — our hope and our despair, our doubts and our faith, our fear and our courage, our ambition and our humility.

James and John at least knew where true greatness lay. They may not have understood what they were asking when they asked to be seated on the right hand and left hand of Jesus, the victorious Christ. They were, however, asking the right person. They suspected that Jesus was the One who would "come into glory," although they did not understand the full implication of their request.

The disciples' request to be positioned near Christ reflects the ambivalence of the human spirit. On the one hand there is the drive to be somebody, a drive often expressed in substituting power for love. On the other hand there is the lure of Incarnate Love, whose power is manifested in weakness. Following the Christ toward downward mobility and giving oneself to others is authentic greatness. — *The Call to Downward Mobility* by Kenneth L. Carder from *The Christian Century*

Humility means staying close to the ground (*humus*), to people, to everyday life, to what is happening with all its down-to-earthness. — *The Contemplative Pastor* by Eugene H. Peterson

I love the fact that the word *humus* — the decayed vegetable matter that feeds the roots of plants — comes from the same root that gives rise to the word *humility*. It is a blessed etymology. It helps me understand that the humiliating events of life, the events that leave "mud on my face" or that "make my name mud," may create the fertile soil in which something new can grow. — *Let Your Life Speak* by Parker J. Palmer

God has been teaching me a lot about humility lately; some through prayer and scripture, and some through hard experience. He is teaching me about the great value of being unnoticed, unseen, and unnecessary. He has actually been teaching me about these things for years, but finally, I think (and hope) I am beginning to embrace what he is trying to do in me. Madeleine L'Engle once wrote: *"When we are self-conscious, we cannot be wholly aware; we must throw ourselves out first."* It seems that this *throwing ourselves out* is what the work of humility is all about, in order that we might be fully aware of God and what he desires and what he is up to within and around us.

Humility is such a good and beautiful — and terrible — thing. It creates such open, receptive soil in our souls. It opens our ears and our hearts to God's voice because it keeps us from being so full of our own. Humility brings about freedom and wholeness because it releases us from the burden of constantly having something to prove. It empties us of *self* and creates space for God to move and to act by preparing our souls to receive whatever he might desire to plant in us.

It is a *dying* that makes way for a *living*. It is an *emptying* that makes space for a *filling*. It is an *absence* that makes us aware of a *presence*. It is a *sorrow* that brings about a *joy*. It is a *letting go* that leads to a *taking hold*. And I have a suspicion that this work of humility God is doing within me is not so much a season as it is a destination — calling me to a new way of being.

Eugene Peterson said it this way: "*When God became human in Jesus, he showed us how to be complete human beings before him. We do it the way Jesus did it, by becoming absolutely needy and dependent on the Father. Only when we stand emptied, stand impoverished before God can we receive what only empty hands can receive. This is the poverty of spirit in which Jesus blesses us (Matt. 5:3).*

Lord Jesus, let humility do its work in me: *emptying* me of self, *opening* my ears to your voice, *softening* my heart to those around me, and *allowing* me to be — and to love — more like you each day. Amen.

— Jim Branch, September, 2015

Calling

I. Opening Prayer

Help me, O God,
To listen to what it is that makes my heart glad
   and to follow where it leads.
May joy, not guilt,
    Your voice, not the voices of others,
    Your will, not my willfulness,
      be the guides that lead me to my vocation.
Help me to unearth the passions of my heart
   that lie buried in my youth.
And can help me to go over that ground again and again
   until I can hold in my hands,
     hold and treasure,
       Your calling on my life…
— *Windows of the Soul* by Ken Gire

II. Psalm 25

III. Daily Scripture Readings

Monday	John1:35-51
Tuesday	Luke 5:1-11
Wednesday	Luke 19:1-10
Thursday	Jeremiah 1:1-19
Friday	Luke 5:27-32
Saturday	Acts 9:1-31
Sunday	1 Samuel 3:1-11

IV. Readings for Reflection

V. Reflection and Listening: Silent and Written

VI. Prayer: for the church, for others, for myself

VII. Song   *All for Jesus*

VIII. Closing Prayer

Go forth as God's servant. Remember God's presence often and draw strength from the knowledge that the One who calls and sends also sustains. Amen. — *A Guide to Prayer* by Rueben Job and Norman Shawchuck

Readings for Reflection-

pieces by Jim Branch

a piece at a time is how it comes
and where
does
                it
                        all
              fit?
and how?

can i see the picture again? so i'll know.
if not i'll have no clue of where each one fits   or me.
making sense of the pieces
without the picture
                      seems an impossible task
false assumptions
              rabbit trails
                  wrong turns
now i see it
no i don't

waiting…
          for the next piece to be given
waiting…
for all to fall into place   in time
doubting…
          in the midst of the jumble
can i see the picture again? so i'll know.

i need to know to my depths the beauty of it all
i need to know the beauty of the pieces   and trust
because a piece at a time is how it comes

Your unique presence in your community is the way
God wants you to be present to others. Different people
have different ways of being present. You have to know
and claim your way. That is why discernment is so
important. Once you have an inner knowledge of your
true vocation, you have a point of orientation. That will
help you decide what to do and what to let go of, what
to say and what to remain silent about, when to go out
and when to stay home, who to be with and who to
avoid.

When you get exhausted, frustrated, overwhelmed,
or run down, your body is saying that you are doing
things that are none of your business. God does not
require of you what is beyond your ability, what leads
you away from God, or what makes you depressed or
sad. God wants you to live for others and to live that
presence well. Doing so might include suffering,
fatigue, and even moments of great physical or
emotional pain, but none of this must ever pull you
away from your deepest self and God. — *The Inner Voice
of Love* by Henri J.M. Nouwen

Maybe that means that the voice we should listen to
most as we choose a vocation is the voice that we might
think we should listen to least, and that is the voice of
our own gladness. What can we do that makes us
gladdest, what can we do that leaves us with a strong
sense of sailing true north and of peace, which is much
of what gladness is? Is it making things with our hands
out of wood or stone or paint on canvas? Or is it making
something we hope like truth out of words? Or is it
making people laugh or weep in a way that cleanses

their spirit? I believe that if it is a thing that makes us truly glad, then it is a good thing and it is our thing and it is the calling voice that we were made to answer with our lives. — *The Hungering Dark* by Frederick Buechner

I wish that I might emphasize how a life becomes simplified when dominated by faithfulness to a few concerns. Too many of us have too many irons in the fire. We get distracted by the intellectual claim to our interest in a thousand and one good things, and before we know it we are pulled and hauled breathlessly along by an over-burdened program of good committees and good undertakings. I am persuaded that this fevered life of church workers is not wholesome. Undertakings get plastered on from the outside because we can't turn down a friend. Acceptance of service on a weighty committee should really depend upon an answering imperative within us, not merely upon a rational calculation of the factors involved. The concern-oriented life is ordered and organized from within. And we learn to say *No* as well as *Yes* by attending to the guidance of inner responsibility. Quaker simplicity needs to be expressed not merely in dress and architecture and the height of tombstones, but also in the structure of a relatively simplified and co-ordinated life-program of ministry responsibilities. And I am persuaded that *concerns* introduce that simplification, and along with it that intensification which we need in opposition to the hurried, superficial tendencies of our age. — *A Testament of Devotion* by Thomas Kelly

Am I keeping the line clear between what I am committed to and what people are asking me? Is my primary orientation God's grace, his mercy, his action in creation and covenant? And am I committed to it enough that when people ask me to do something that will not lead them into a more mature participation in

374

these realities, I refuse? — *The Contemplative Pastor* by Eugene Peterson

Vocare, to call, of course, and a man's vocation is a man's calling. It is the work that he is called to in this world, the thing that he is summoned to spend his life doing. We can speak of a man's choosing his vocation, but perhaps it is at least as accurate to speak of a vocation's choosing the man, of a call's being given and a man's hearing it, or not hearing it. And maybe that is the place to start: the business of listening and hearing. A man's life is full of all sorts of voices calling him in all sorts of directions. Some of them are voices from inside and some of them are voices from outside. The more alive and alert we are, the more clamorous our lives are. Which do we listen to? What kind of voice do we listen for? — *The Hungering Dark* by Frederick Buechner

There is always one moment in childhood when the door opens and lets the future in. — *The Power and the Glory* by Graham Greene

To do the work I am given to do, I am going to need to do some homework. I am going to need to do some thinking and wondering and studying about my gifts and my talents. I am going to need to be sure that what I do with my hands actually comes from and nurtures my heart. I am going to have to examine its effects upon others and how it fits into the kingdom that has already come. And I am going to have to be clear about why I am doing it and my hopes and my dreams. —*Living Prayer* by Robert Benson

We skip down the hallways of our youth, you and I, stopping now and then to catch our breath. And every now and then we catch something else. A glimpse of the future. *Our* future. A glimpse we caught when we came across a window suddenly flung open in front of us, its gossamer curtains lifted by the breeze redolent with the future, filling our lungs with refreshing air and our heart with hopeful dreams.

At that window we hear something like somebody calling our name, only in a language we can't quite understand, so we don't recognize who it is who is calling us or to where we are being called.

But we recognize the name.

Even in a foreign language, names translate closely to the original. Whoever it is calling us is calling us by our true name. Whispering to us a secret. Telling us who we are. And showing us what we will be doing with our lives if only we have eyes to see, the ears to hear, and the faith to follow. —*Windows of the Soul* by Ken Gire

I am always amazed when I read the story of Matthew, the wealthy tax collector—a man who had it made. Sure, Matthew was hated and feared by many, but he had it all—power, great wealth, and the support of the state. Jesus walked by and casually said to Matthew, "Follow me." Ridiculous. Who in Matthew's position would respond to some vagabond? But Matthew does exactly that! He immediately left his wealth and power and followed Jesus. What happened? I'll tell you what happened. Matthew was called. Every bone in his body, every part of his being stood on tiptoe when the Master spoke those words. "Follow me!" Matthew's ears tingled with excitement, his heart thundered with anticipation, his mind was filled with electricity. He had been called. He didn't know it until that moment, but he had been waiting all his life to hear those words.

May God capture our unspoken dreams. May Jesus speak those words that make our soul stand on tiptoe.

May each of us find our calling in Jesus. — *The Back Door*, Mike Yaconelli

...It was as though someone gave me permission to do what I most wanted to do. "I felt something deep in me relax," I later wrote in my journal, "and say yes." There was no audible voice, nothing dramatic save the starry sky, but some deep part of me knew what I was to be about. — *Awake My Soul* by Timothy Jones

Frederick Buechner has written that we spend our lives in search. We search, he says,"for a self to be, for other selves to love, and for work to do." And I believe that it is possible for the fruit of that search for work to do to be aligned with what God dreamed we would be when we were whispered into being. — *Between the Dreaming and the Coming True* by Robert Benson

Deep in our hearts, we all want to find and fulfill a purpose bigger than ourselves. Only such a larger purpose can inspire us to heights we know we could never reach on our own. For each of us the real purpose is personal and passionate: to know what we are here to do. Soren Kierkegaard wrote in his journal: "The thing is to understand myself, to see what God really wants me to do; the thing is to find the truth which is true for me, to find the idea for which I can live and die." — *The Call* by Os Guinness

When we are younger and are wrestling with choices about the future, we are very often asked, and ask ourselves: "What are you going to do when you grow up?" It is the wrong question. What we are going to *do* is not who we *are*.

When it was time for me to make choices, I should have been wrestling with another question. I should have been asking, "Who am I going to *be* when I grow up?" What I then went on to do with that should have been a reflection of who I was to be, a reflection of the word that was whispered into me. I should have been looking for work to do that would sustain and nurture who I am (who I *be*, if you will). I was then, and am still, the only person on earth who has any clue at all what was whispered into me in the depths of my mother's womb. Everyone else is just guessing, and their guesses are a lot less well informed than mine. God whispered the word *Robert* into *me*, and no one else. If I cannot hear that word, no one can. If I do not hear that word, no one will. If I do hear it and fail to act upon it, no one will be the word called *Robert* that God spoke.

Rabbi Zusya, one of the great wisdom teachers of the Hebrew tradition, once said, "In the world to come I shall not be asked: *Why were you not Moses?* I shall be asked: *Why were you not Zusya?*"

The will of the One who sent us is that we be the one who was sent. What we do is meant to be lived out of the context of discovering and becoming the person we are. — *Between the Dreaming and the Coming True* by Robert Benson

Most of us go through life praying a little, planning a little, jockeying for position, hoping but never being quite certain of anything, and always secretly afraid that we will miss the way. This is a tragic waste of truth and never gives rest to the heart.

There is a better way. It is to repudiate our own wisdom and take instead the infinite wisdom of God. Our insistence upon seeing ahead is natural enough, but it is a real hindrance to our spiritual progress. God has charged Himself with full responsibility for our eternal happiness and stands ready to take over the management of our lives the moment we turn in faith to Him. — *The Knowledge of the Holy* by A.W. Tozer

. . . I think the secret to being reasonably good at whatever it is that eventually calls you and draws you to it, whatever becomes your life's work, is for you to be in love with the little things that it takes to do it. That you love to do those things over and over until you can do them every time that they need to be done, intuitively and gracefully and passionately. That there will be very few days when you win or lose based on some heroic effort that you muster up to save the day, but there will be lots of days when it is the little things that will make all the difference. — *The Game: One Man, Nine Innings, a Love Affair with Baseball* by Robert Benson

> *Some time when the river is ice ask me*
> *mistakes I have made. Ask me whether*
> *what I have done is my life. Others*
> *have come in their slow way into*
> *my thought, and some have tried to help*
> *or to hurt: ask me what difference*
> *their strongest love or hate has made.*
>
> *I will listen to what you say.*
> *You and I can turn and look*
> *at the silent river and wait. We know*
> *the current is there, hidden; and there*
> *are comings and goings from miles away*
> *that hold the stillness exactly before us.*
>
> *What the river says, that is what I say.*
> —William Stafford, "Ask Me"

"Ask me whether what I have done is my life." For some, those words will be nonsense, nothing more than a poet's loose way with language and logic. Of course what I have done is my life! To what am I supposed to compare it?

But for others, and I am one, the poet's words will be precise, piercing, and disquieting. They remind me of moments when it is clear — if I have eyes to see — that the life I am living is not the same as the life that wants to live in me. In those moments I sometimes catch a glimpse of my true life, a life hidden like a river beneath the ice. And in the spirit of the poet, I wonder: What am I meant to do? Who am I meant to be?

I was in my early thirties when I began, literally, to wake up to questions about my vocation. By all appearances, things were going well, but the soul does not put much stock in appearances. Seeking a path more purposeful than accumulating wealth, holding power, winning at competition, or securing a career, I had started to understand that it is indeed possible to live a life other than one's own. Fearful that I was doing just that — but uncertain about the deeper, truer life I sensed hidden inside me, uncertain whether it was real or trustworthy or within reach — I would snap awake in the middle of the night and stare for long hours at the ceiling.

Then I ran across a Quaker saying, "Let your life speak." I found those words encouraging, and thought I understood what they meant: "Let the highest truths and values guide you. Live up to those demanding standards in everything you do." Because I had heroes at the time who seemed to be doing exactly that, this exhortation had incarnate meaning for me — it meant living a life like that of Martin Luther King Jr. or Rosa Parks or Mahatma Ghandi or Dorothy Day, a life of high purpose.

So I lined up the loftiest ideal I could find and set out to achieve them. The results were rarely admirable, often laughable, and sometimes grotesque. But always they were unreal, a distortion of my true self — as must be the case when one lives from the outside in, not inside out. I had simply found a "noble" way to live a life that was not my own, a life spent imitating heroes instead of listening to my heart.

Today, some thirty years later, "Let your life speak" means something else to me, a meaning faithful both to the ambiguity of those words and to the complexity of my own experience: "Before you tell your life what you intend to do with it, listen for what it intends to do with you. Before you tell your life what truths and values you have decided to live up to, let your life tell you what truths you embody, what values you represent."
— *Let Your Life Speak* by Parker Palmer

You ask whether your verses are good. You ask me. You have asked others before. You send them to magazines. You compare them with other poems, and you are disturbed when certain editors reject your efforts. Now (since you have allowed me to advise you) I beg you to give up all that. You are looking outward, and that above all you should not do now. Nobody can counsel and help you, nobody. There is only one single way. Go inward. Search for the reason that bids you write; find out whether it is spreading out its roots in the deepest places of your heart, acknowledge to yourself whether you would have to die if it were denied you to write. This above all—ask yourself in the stillest hour of your night: must I write? Delve into your heart for a deep answer. And if this should be affirmative, if you may meet this earnest question with a strong and simple "I must," then build your life according to this necessity; your life even into its most indifferent and slightest hour must be a sign of this urge and testimony to it.
— *Letters to a Young Poet* by Rainer Maria Rilke

I believe in all that has never yet been spoken.
I want to free what waits within me
so that what no one has dared to wish for

may for once spring clear
without my contriving.

If this is arrogant, God, forgive me,
but this is what I need to say.
May what I do flow from me like a river,
no forcing and no holding back,
the way it is with children.
Then in these swelling and ebbing currents,
these deepening tides moving out, returning,
I will sing you as no one ever has,

streaming through widening channels
into the open sea.
— *The Book of Hours* by Rainer Maria Rilke

tilt-a-whirl by Jim Branch

back and forth
to and fro
here then there
round and round
where will it finally stop?
    and when?
how will i know when to get off?
when my world comes to rest once again?
when i've stopped spinning?
    stopped being so dizzy and restless
    stopped swaying and swinging
    settled in to what this life will be
i'm ready to get off
get my feet back on solid ground
but the ride is not over yet
so for now i just hang on

Direction

I. Opening Prayer

God be in my head, and in my understanding;
God be in mine eyes, and in my looking;
God be in my mouth, and in my speaking;
God be in my heart, and in my thinking;
God be at mine end, and at my departing.
—Sarum Primer, 16th century

II. Psalm 17

III. Daily Scripture Readings

Monday	Jeremiah 6:16
Tuesday	Jeremiah 33:1-9
Wednesday	Proverbs 3:1-6
Thursday	Isaiah 43:14-21
Friday	Isaiah 30:15-21
Saturday	Jeremiah 18:1-6
Sunday	Proverbs 4:20-27

IV. Readings for Reflection

V. Reflection and Listening: silent and written

VI. Prayer: for the church, for others, for myself

VII. Song   *All My Days*

VIII. Closing Prayer

O heavenly Father, in whom we live and move and have our being: We humbly pray thee so to guide and govern us by thy Holy Spirit, that in all the cares and occupations of our life we may not forget thee, but may remember that we are ever walking in thy sight; through Jesus Christ our Lord. Amen. —*The Book of Common Prayer*

Readings for Reflection-

"Thus says the Lord, 'Stand at the crossroads and look; ask for the ancient paths, ask where the good way is, and walk in it, and you will find rest for your souls.'"

Stand. What an interesting place to start. In other words, seeking God's direction starts by stopping. Just stand. Be still. Be present, fully present. Be present first to God within you and then to God around you. Or, in other words, *show up.* Show up with God and show up with others. That's where it all begins.

Next comes *look.* Stand at the crossroads and look. Pay attention. Look for God. Look deeply for him in whatever, or whoever, might be in front of you at the moment. Look past the surface. Look into the depths of your heart and soul, as well as your world. Search. Seek. Seek him in all things, you never know who or what he might use to speak to you.

Then comes *ask.* Specifically, *ask* God. Ask God, "What are you up? What are you up to within me? What are you up to around me? What are you up to in this circumstance? What are you up to in the life of the person in front of me?" Ask.

Ask for the ancient paths. The ancient paths are those well-worn paths that lead straight to the heart of God. Those paths that multitudes of other saints, poets, and pilgrims have traveled well before us. In fact, whenever you see someone walking deeply and intimately with God you need to take note because that person has found these ancient paths, and watching them can show you the way into the heart of God. They include things like solitude, silence, prayer, and Scripture. All of these things are part of the *good way.*

And finally, once you have stood and looked and asked, it is time to move. *Walk in it* is the phrase Jeremiah uses. Walk in the good way, whatever that may mean. For once we have received our direction and

384

guidance from God, it is time to *enter into* whatever he is doing. It is time to *move toward him,* and his work, whatever that may be. Sometimes it will mean speaking a word he has given us to speak, and at others it will mean keeping our mouths shut. Sometimes it will mean simply being present, and others it will mean reaching out to embrace. But whatever it is, you can be sure of its power, substance, and authenticity because it has come directly from his heart and not merely your own.

And the beautiful result of it all is that *you will find rest for your soul.* What a promise! And isn't that what we all most deeply long for?

—Jim Branch, September, 2014

The journey is not to be completed in a day, and the path leading to its end is twisted and invisible, but we can help them see the next small, often deceptively simple steps. — *Holy Listening* by Margret Guenther

Tend only to the birth in you and you will find all goodness and consolation, all delight, all being and all truth. Reject it and you reject goodness and blessing. What comes to you in this birth brings with it pure being and blessing. But that you seek or love outside of this birth will come to nothing, no matter what you will or where you will it.

—Meister Eckhart

We desperately need men and women at our side who have disciplined their minds to think *God*: who God is and what he is doing in and among us; what it means to be created and chosen by God and how we get in on what he intends for us. — *The Wisdom of Each Other* by Eugene Peterson

Spiritual direction takes place when two people agree to give their full attention to what God is doing in one (or both) of their lives and seek to respond in faith. More often than not for pastors these convergent and devout attentions are brief and unplanned; at other time they are planned and structured conversations. Whether planned or unplanned, three convictions underpin these meetings: (1) God is always doing something: an active grace is shaping this life into a mature salvation; (2) responding to God is not sheer guesswork: the Christian community has acquired wisdom through the centuries that provides guidance; (3) each soul is unique: no wisdom can simply be applied without discerning the particulars of this life, this situation. — *Working the Angles* by Eugene H. Peterson

Everybody should know this truth that no one is gifted with such prudence and wisdom as to be adequate for himself in the guidance of his own spiritual life. Self-love is a blind guide and fools many. The light of our own judgment is weak and we cannot envision all of the snares and errors to which we are prone in the life of the spirit. — *A Treatise of Spiritual Life* by John Cardinal Bona

Sometimes Spiritual Direction is a little like bird-watching — waiting quietly and noticing what appears. We desire a prayerful place and quality in our time together. We try to pay attention to how the Holy Spirit is with us now — in the present. — *Holy Invitations* by Jeanette Bakke

I see myself more as a guide or companion. "Director" sounds too active. I prefer "spiritual companion." Companion in Latin is *cum panis*, which means "with bread." This suggests that I'm also on the journey. I have not yet arrived.

We are, in some ways, bread for one another's journeys. I try to create comfortable space so that the seeker can feel safe to explore and ask questions. Encouragement and reverent presence is important. Many come in darkness, feeling abandoned by God and by others. I encourage them to lean into the darkness rather than fight it. And to lean into their own deep hunger and longing for God. The darkness can be of value. If not for the darkness, would there be the seeking, the hunger? It is only in the darkness we see the stars. — an interview with Macrina Wiederkehr from *The Mars Hill Review*, Fall 1997

Perhaps one of the main tasks of the Christian spiritual guide is to help men and women discover precisely in the actual messy situations of their daily lives, the way in which, without their being aware of it, Jesus has chosen to give himself to them, and how they are to "go forth and bear fruit" as a result of that choice (John 15:16). — *The Art of Spiritual Guidance* by Carolyn Gratton

Those to whom spiritual guidance is entrusted should only lay bare faults as God prepares the heart to see them. One must learn to watch a fault patiently, and take no external measure until God begins to make it felt by the inward conscience. Nay, more: one must imitate God's own way of dealing with the soul, softening rebuke, so that the person rebuffed, feels as if it was rather self-reproach, and a sense of wounded love, than God rebuking. All other methods of guidance, reproving impatiently, or because one was vexed at infirmities, smack of earthly judgments, not the correction of grace. It is imperfection rebuking the imperfect: it is a subtle, clinging self-love, which cannot see anything to forgive in the self-love of others. The greater our own self-love, the more severe critics we shall be. Nothing is so offensive to a haughty, sensitive, self-conceit as the self-conceit of others. But, on the contrary, the love of God is full of consideration, forbearance, condescension, and tenderness. It adapts itself, waits, and never moves more than one step at a time. The less self-love we have, the more we know how to adapt ourselves to curing our neighbor's failings of that kind; we learn better never to lance without putting plenty of healing ointment to the wound, never to purge the patient without feeding, never to risk an operation save when nature indicates its safety. One learns to wait years before giving a salutary warning; to wait till Providence prepares suitable external circumstances, and grace opens the heart. If you persist in gathering fruit before it is ripe, you simply waste your labor.

— *The Royal Way of the Cross* by Francois Fenelon

Joy and Celebration

I. Opening Prayer
Our Father, giver of all gifts, You love and choose us, your least ones. Increase our humility so that we might rejoice in the generosity of Your love and be mindful that the good in us comes from You, Creator, Redeemer, and Giver of Life, now and forever. Amen.

— Macrina Wiederkehr

II. Psalm 66

III. Daily Scripture Readings
Monday	John 15:9-17
Tuesday	Nehemiah 8:1-12
Wednesday	Philippians 4:4-9
Thursday	Exodus 15:1-21
Friday	Isaiah 55:6-12
Saturday	Revelation 19:6-9
Sunday	Luke 15:20-32

IV. Readings for Reflection

V. Reflection and Listening: silent and written

VI. Prayer: for the church, for others, for myself

VII. Song   *Joyful, Joyful, We Adore Thee*

VIII. Closing Prayer
O God, quicken to life every power within me, that I may lay hold of eternal things. Open my eyes that I may see; give me acute spiritual perception; enable me to taste Thee and know that Thou art good. Make heaven more real to me than any earthly thing has ever been.
— *The Pursuit of God* by A.W. Tozer

Readings for Reflection-

There is something growing within me, day by day. With each passing year it takes root more deeply in my soul. It is something that did not seem possible in my earlier days, due to my tendency to climb and to strive and to achieve. But now, probably as a result of age and attrition, and hopefully even a little maturity, there is finally room within me for its presence. The tiny seed is beginning to sprout, or maybe I am just now beginning to notice it.

It is the fruit of gratitude, it seems. Or maybe it is the other way around. Whatever the case, it is causing me to see differently and to live differently — less frustrated and more open. It is causing me to slow down, to stop, to reflect, to savor, and to appreciate. It is the birth of *joy*. What a surprise and delight! Thanks be to God!

—Jim Branch, March, 2016

Only the one who has experienced it can know what the love of Jesus Christ is. Once you have experienced it, nothing else in the world will seem more beautiful or desirable. — *The Signature of Jesus* by Brennan Manning

Celebration gives us the strength to live in all the other Disciplines. The other Disciplines faithfully pursued bring us deliverance from those things that have made our lives miserable for years, which in turn evokes increased celebration. Thus is formed and unbroken circle of life and power. — *Celebration of Discipline* by Richard Foster

One aspect of choosing life is choosing joy. Joy is life-giving, but sadness brings death. A sad heart is a heart in which something is dying. A joyful heart is a heart in which something new is being born.

I think that joy is much more than a mood. A mood invades us. We do not choose a mood. We often find ourselves in a happy or depressed mood without knowing where it comes from. The spiritual life is a life beyond moods. It is a life in which we choose joy and do not allow ourselves to become victims of passing feelings of joy or depression.

I am convinced that we can choose joy. Every moment we can decide to respond to an event or a person with joy instead of sadness. When we truly believe that God is life and only life, then nothing need have the power to draw us into the sad realm of death. To choose joy does not mean to choose happy feelings or an artificial atmosphere of hilarity. But it does mean the determination to let whatever takes place bring us one step closer to the God of life. — *The Road to Daybreak* by Henri J. M. Nouwen

It is impossible to receive Christ and not to receive His joy. For His joy **IS** joy! It is the delirious music of those who have been delivered. —*Walking with the Saints* **by** Calvin Miller

Christian joy is essentially the enjoyment of God, the fruit of communion with Him. — *The Practice of Godliness* by Jerry Bridges

The joy that Jesus offers His disciples is His own joy, which flows from His intimate communion with the One who sent Him. It is a joy that does not separate happy days from sad days, successful moments from moments of failure, experiences of honor from experiences of dishonor, passion from resurrection. This joy is a divine gift that does not leave us during times of illness, poverty, oppression, or persecution. — *Lifesigns* by Henri J.M. Nouwen

Do not look for rest in any pleasure, because you were not created for pleasure: you were created for JOY. And if you do not know the difference between pleasure and joy you have not yet begun to live. — *Seeds of Contemplation* by Thomas Merton

Joy ignores suffering or laughs at it or even exploits it to purify itself of its greatest obstacle, selfishness. — *Seeds of Contemplation* by Thomas Merton

Joy dwells with God; it descends from Him and seizes the spirit, soul, and body, and where this joy has grasped a man it grows greater, carries him away, opens closed doors…The joy of God has been through the poverty of the crib and the distress of the cross; therefore it is insuperable, irrefutable. — *True Patriotism* by Dietrich Bonhoeffer

Joy is essential to spiritual life. Whatever we may think or say about God, when we are not joyful, our thoughts and words cannot bear fruit. Jesus reveals to us God's love so that his joy may become ours and that our joy might become complete. Joy is the experience of knowing that you are unconditionally loved and that nothing — sickness, failure, emotional distress, oppression, war, or even death — can take that love away. — *Here and Now* by Henri J.M. Nouwen

The difference between shallow happiness and deep, sustaining joy is sorrow. Happiness lives where sorrow is not. When sorrow arrives, happiness dies. It can't stand pain. Joy, on the other hand, rises from sorrow and therefore can withstand all grief. Joy, by the grace of God, is the transfiguration of suffering into endurance, and of endurance into character, and of character into hope — and the hope that has become our joy does not (as happiness must for those who depend upon it) disappoint us.

In the sorrows of the Christ — as we ourselves experience them — we prepare for Easter, for joy. There can be no resurrection from the dead except first there is death! But then, because we love him above all things, his rising is our joy. And then the certain hope of our own resurrection warrants the joy both now and forever. — *Reliving the Passion* by Walter Wangerin Jr.

Joyful persons do not necessarily make jokes, laugh, or even smile. They are not people with an optimistic outlook on life who always relativize the seriousness of a moment or event. No, joyful persons see with open eyes the hard reality of human existence and at the same time are not imprisoned by it. They have no illusion about the evil powers that roam around, "looking for someone to devour" (1 Peter 5:8), but they also know that death has no final power. They suffer with those who suffer, yet they do not hold on to suffering; they point beyond it to an everlasting peace. — *Lifesigns* by Henri J.M. Nouwen

There is a distinct difference between joy and happiness. Happiness is mostly circumstantial; when suffering comes, happiness hits the road. But joy is much deeper, more substantial. Joy is not dependent on conditions being favorable. In fact, joy is something that is able to endure the presence of pain and still abide. The word joy comes from the Greek word *chara* which means *a deep and sustaining gladness*. This gladness is able to see the bigger picture and to trust in the sacred heart of the One who can bring beauty from ashes and victory from the jaws of defeat.

So when James (1:2-4) tells us to *count it all joy when we face trials of many kinds,* he is not telling us we need to be happy about it. He is telling us to trust in the end result. He is telling us that beneath the sorrow or the suffering or the pain is always a Hand that is working in us to make us more and more into the people he desires for us to be. This joy holds an unfailing trust in his unfailing love; trust that regardless of the situation or the circumstances, he is always up to something good. Thanks be to God. — *Journey to the Cross* by Jim Branch

Celebration is a part of the heart of God. We were created to celebrate and to be celebrated. You can see it in a beautiful spring day, as all of creation comes to life and celebrates the glory of its Creator. You can catch hints of it when you are captured by the transcendence of a song or overcome by the magnificence of a painting. You can taste it as you witness excellence on the athletic field or as you dance in revelry at the winning of a championship. It is what we were made for. It is the image we were made in. So when we celebrate, or are celebrated, may we always be aware of the celebration of God that is going on around us and within us.

—Jim Branch, March, 2016

394

Home

I. Opening Prayer:

Thank you, Lord Jesus, that one day you will make all things new. Thank you that one day you will do away with sorrow and suffering and pain, and you yourself will dwell with us in joy for all eternity. O how we long for that day. O how we yearn to be *home*. Come, Lord Jesus! Amen.

II. Psalm 126

III. Daily Scripture Reading

Monday	Revelation 21:1-7
Tuesday	John 13:31-14:4
Wednesday	Zephaniah 3:14-20
Thursday	Luke 23:32-43
Friday	Revelation 21:9-27
Saturday	1 Corinthians 15:50-58
Sunday	Revelation 2:17

IV. Readings for Reflection

V. Reflection: silent and written

VI. Prayers for the Church, Others, and Myself

VII. Song   *Jesus Let Us Come to Know You*

VIII. Closing Prayer

Dear Lord Jesus,

Thank you that here and there you have shown me glimpses of heaven, however briefly. Now and then you have sent me echoes of it, however faintly. And that once in a while you have allowed it to touch me, however gently. Those glimpses, those echoes, those touches have awakened my longing for home, and for each one of those awakenings, I thank you.

Thank you that I have a room in your Father's house. A place just for me. Thank you for all you have done to ready it for my arrival. For all the longings that lead me there and for all the reminders that let me know that this is not my home, I thank you, O Lord. Remind me often, for so often I forget, that the very best of homes here on earth is just a shadow of the home waiting for me in heaven. —*Moments with the Savior* by Ken Gire

Readings for Reflection:

We live our entire lives, from the minute we are born until the day we die, with a longing for *home*. Not our physical home mind you, although that indeed gives us a taste of it, but our *true home*. Our home within the heart of our God. The God who made us to live in the intimacy and affection of the Trinity. Our home where there is no more fear, no more hiding, no more proving, no more performing, no more tears, and no more pain. It is the place, or more accurately the state, where we are completely safe and secure. It is the home that finally allows us the freedom to breathe, the freedom to rest, the freedom to be. I don't know about you, but I can't wait.

—Jim Branch, March, 2016

John says someday God will wipe away your tears. The same hands that stretched the heavens will touch your cheeks. The same hands that formed the mountains will caress your face. The same hands that curled in agony as the Roman spike cut through will someday cup your face and brush away your tears. Forever. —*The Applause of Heaven* by Max Lucado

I'll be home soon. The plane will land. I'll walk down the ramp and hear my name and see my children's faces. I'll be home soon.

You'll be home soon, too. You may not have noticed it, but you are closer to home than ever before. Each moment is a step taken. Each breath is a page turned. Each day is a mile marked, a mountain climbed. You are closer to home than you've ever been.

Before you know it, your appointed arrival time will come; you'll descend the ramp and enter the City. You'll see the faces that are waiting for you. You'll hear your name spoken by those who love you. And, maybe, just maybe — in the back, behind the crowds — the One who would rather die than live without you will remove his pierced hands from his heavenly robe and. . . applaud.
— *The Applause of Heaven* by Max Lucado

The Christian doctrine of suffering explains, I believe, a very curious fact about the world we live in. The settled happiness and security which we all desire, God withholds from us by the very nature of the world: but joy, pleasure, and merriment He has scattered broadcast. We are never safe, but we have plenty of fun, and some ecstasy. It is not hard to see why. The security we crave would teach us to rest our hearts in this world and pose an obstacle to our return to God: a few moments of happy love, a landscape, a symphony, a merry meeting with our friends, a swim or a football match, have no such tendency. Our Father refreshes us on the journey with some pleasant inns, but will not encourage us to mistake them for *home*. — *The Problem of Pain* by C.S. Lewis

It seems that most of my life is sacrificed protecting and enhancing a home that is supposedly not my home.
— *Bold Love* by Dan Allender

This life ought to be spent by us only as a journey towards heaven.

—Jonathan Edwards

The longing for home is a dominant theme in Lewis's writings (C. S. Lewis). All art is about coming home. All music, all drama, all literature is about coming home. All psychology, too. As well as theology. —*The Divine Embrace* by Ken Gire

There would be different pastors along the way [at our church], none of them exactly right for us until a few years ago when a tall African-American woman named Veronica came to lead us. She has huge gentle doctor hands, with dimples where the knuckles should be, like baby's fists. She stepped into us, the wonderful old worn pair of pants that is St. Andrews, and they fit. She sings to us sometimes from the pulpit and tells us stories of when she was a child. She told us this story just the other day: When she was about seven, her best friend got lost one day. The little girl ran up and down the streets of the big town where they lived, but she couldn't find a single landmark. She was frightened. Finally a policeman stopped to help her. He put her in the passenger seat of his car, and they drove around until she finally saw her church. She pointed it out to the policeman, and then she told him firmly, "You could let me out now. This is my church, and I can always find my way home from here."

And that is why I have stayed so close to mine — because no matter how bad I am feeling, how lost or lonely or frightened, when I see the faces of the people at my church, and hear their tawny voices, I can always find my way home. —*Traveling Mercies* by Anne Lamott

Everything is designed to bring us home, if only we would work with it. — Max Pearse, quoted in *A Traveler Toward the Dawn*

We need to be at home with ourselves, with others, with our God. When we discover our center and our connectedness, we come closest to sharing in the creating and forgiving power of God. Then we are always at home, no matter where we are, because God reveals his love by creating the home within me, within you, within all. — *Gathering the Fragments* by Edward J. Farrell

There are two realities to which you must cling. First, God has promised that you will receive the love you have been searching for. And second, God is faithful to that promise.

So stop wandering around. Instead, come home and trust that God will bring you what you need. Your whole life you have been running about, seeking the love you desire. Now it is time to end that search. Trust that God will give you that all-fulfilling love and will give it in a human way. Before you die, God will offer you the deepest satisfaction you can desire. Just stop running and start trusting and receiving.

Home is where you are truly safe. It is where you can receive what you desire. You need human hands to hold you there so you don't run away again. But when you come home and stay home, you will find the love that will bring rest to your heart — *The Inner Voice of Love* by Henri J. M. Nouwen

Bibliography

Ainsworth, Percy C. "Petition and Communion," *Weavings*, Volume XXII, Number 4, (July/August 2007). Used with permission.

Allender, Dan. *Bold Love*. Colorado Springs: NavPress, 1992.
———. *The Healing Path: How the Hurts in Your Path Can Lead You to a More Abundant Life*. Colorado Springs: Waterbrook, 2000.

Anderson, Fil. Excerpt(s) from *Running on Empty*: *Contemplative Spirituality For Overachievers* by Fil Anderson, copyright © 2004 Fil Anderson. Used by permission of WaterBrook Multnomah, an imprint of the Crown Publishing Group, a division of Penguin Random House LLC. All rights reserved.

Anderson, Keith R. and Randy D. Reese *Spiritual Mentoring*: *A Guide for Seeking and Giving Direction*. Downers Grove, IL: Intervarsity Press, 1999.

Ashbrook, R. Thomas. *Mansions of the Heart*: *Exploring the Seven Stages of Spiritual Growth*. San Francisco: Jossey-Bass, 2009.

Baillie, John. *A Diary of Private Prayer*. New York: Charles Scribner's Sons, 1949.

Baker, Howard. *Soul Keeping*: *Ancient Paths of Spiritual Direction*. Colorado Springs: NavPress, 1998.

Bakke, Jeannette. *Holy Invitations: Exploring Spiritual Direction*. Grand Rapids, MI: Baker Books, 2000.

Barnes, M. Craig. *Extravagant Mercy*. Grand Rapids, MI: Baker Books,
———. *Hustling God*. Grand Rapids, MI: Zondervan, Used by permission of Zondervan. www.zondervan.com.
———. Taken from *Sacred Thirst* by M. Craig Barnes

Copyright © 2001 by M. Craig Barnes. Used by permission of Zondervan. www.zondervan.com.

Benner, David G. *Sacred Companions: The Gift of Spiritual Friendship & Direction*. Downers Grove, IL: Intervarsity Press, 2002.

benShea, Noah. *Jacob's Journey*: Wisdom to Find Your Way; Strength to Carry On. Albuquerque, NM: Number Nine Media, LLC, 1991.

Benson, Bob. *Disciplines for the Inner Life*. Nashville: Thomas Nelson, 1989. Used with permission.
———. *He Speaks Softly: Learning to Hear God's Voice*. Dallas: Word Books, 1985. Used with permission.
———. *See You at the House*. Nashville: Thomas Nelson, 1986. Used with permission.

Benson, Robert. From *Between the Dreaming and the Coming True: The Road Home to God* by Robert Benson, copyright © 1996 by Robert Benson. Used by permission of Tarcher, an imprint of Penguin Publishing Group, a division of Penguin Random House LLC.
———. *The Game: One Man, Nine Innings, A Love Affair with Baseball*. Copyright © 2001 by Robert Benson. Used by permission of Tarcher, an imprint of Penguin Publishing Group, a division of Penguin Random House LLC.
———. *A Good Life: Benedict's Guide to Everyday Joy*. Brewster, MA: Paraclete Press, 2004.
———. From *Living Prayer* by Robert Benson, copyright © 1998 by Robert Benson. Used by permission of Tarcher, an imprint of Penguin Publishing Group, a division of Penguin Random House LLC.
———. *Venite: A Book of Daily Prayer*. Copyright © 2000 by Robert Benson. Used by permission of Tarcher, an imprint of Penguin Publishing Group, a division of Penguin Random House LLC.

Bernard, Mary Ann. "Resurrection." From Rueben Job and Norman Shawchuck, eds., *A Guide To Prayer*. Nashville: The Upper Room, 144.

Bernanos, Georges. *A Diary of a Country Priest*. New York: Carroll & Graf, 1935, 1965.

Boa, Kenneth. *That I May Know God: Pathways to Spiritual Formation*. New York: Multnomah, 1998.

Bonhoeffer, Dietrich. *Life Together*. Two brief excerpts from *Life Together* by Dietrich Bonhoeffer and translated by John Doberstein. English translation copyright © by Harper & Brothers, copyright renewed 1982 by Helen S. Doberstein. Reprinted by permission of HarperCollins Publishers.
———. *True Patriotism: Letters, Lectures, and Notes, 1939–45*. New York: Harper and Row, 1973.
———. *The Way to Freedom*. New York: Collins, 1966.

Branch, Jim. *Becoming*. New York: CreateSpace Independent Publishing, 2013.
———. *Beginnings*. New York: CreateSpace Independent Publishing, 2012.
———. *Being With Jesus: A Thirty-Day Journey*. New York: CreateSpace Independent Publishing, 2014.
———. *Pieces II*. New York: CreateSpace Independent Publishing, 2012.
———. *Watch and Wait*. New York: CreateSpace Independent Publishing, 2015.

Bridges, Jerry. *The Practice of Godliness*. Colorado Springs: NavPress, 2014.

Brother Lawrence. *The Practice of the Presence of God*. New Kensington, PA: Whitaker House, 1982.

Browning, Elizabeth Barrett. *Aurora Leigh*. London: Oxford University Press, 1993.

Brunner, F. Dale. *Theology, Notes, and News*, October 1999.

Buechner, Frederick. Excerpts from p. 13, 37, 56, 106, 147, 152 from *A Room Called Remember: Uncollected Pieces* by Frederick Buechner. Copyright © 1984 by Frederick Buechner. Reprinted by permission of HarperCollins Publishers.

————. Excerpts from p. 27, 31–32, 92, 104 from *The Hungering Dark* by Frederick Buechner. Copyright © 1969 by Frederick Buechner. Reprinted by permission of HarperCollins Publishers.

————. Excerpts from p. 47–48, 48, 81, 99, 112 from *The Magnificent Defeat* by Frederick Buechner. Copyright © 1966 by Frederick Buechner. Reprinted by permission of HarperCollins Publishers.

————. Excerpts from pp. 45, 105–106 from *Telling Secrets* by Frederick Buechner. Copyright © 1991 by Frederick Buechner. Reprinted by permission of HarperCollins Publishers.

————. Brief excerpts from p. 23, 78 from *Telling the Truth* by Frederick Buechner. Copyright © 1977 by Frederick Buechner. Reprinted by permission of HarperCollins Publishers.

————. Brief excerpt from p. 117 from *Whistling in the Dark* by Frederick Buechner. Copyright © 1988, 1993 by Frederick Buechner. Reprinted by permission of HarperCollins Publishers.

————. Brief excerpts from p. 39, 87 from *Wishful Thinking: A Seekers ABC* by Frederick Buechner. Revised and Expended. Copyright © 1973, 1993 by Frederick Buechner. Reprinted by permission of HarperCollins Publishers.

Calvin, John. *Heart Aflame: Daily Readings from Calvin on the Psalms.* Phillipsburg, NJ: P&R Publishing, 1999.

Candler, Dana. *Deep Unto Deep: The Journey of the Embrace.* Kansas City, MO: Forerunner Publishing, 2004.

Card, Michael. *The Walk.* Copyright © 2006 by Michael Card and used by permission of Discovery House, Grand Rapids, Michigan 49512. All rights reserved.

Carder, Kenneth L. Copyright © 1997 by the *Christian Century*. "The Call to Downward Mobility" by Kenneth L. Carder is reprinted by permission from the October 8, 1997, issue of the *Christian Century*.

Carreto, Carlo. *The God Who Comes.* Maryknoll, NY: Orbis, 1974.
———. *Letters from the Desert.* Maryknoll, NY: Orbis, 1972.

Chambers, Oswald. *My Utmost for His Highest.* Uhrichsville, OH: Barbour, 1963.

Chesterton, G. K. *Orthodoxy.* Chicago: Moody, 2009.

Claypool, John R. *Tracks of a Fellow Struggler: Living and Growing through Grief.* New Orleans: Insight Press, 1974, 1995.

Collins, Owen. *Classic Christian Prayers: A Celebration of Praise and Glory.* New York: Testament, 2003.

Cornell, George. *The Untamed God.* New York: Harper & Row, 1975.

Crabb, Larry. *Finding God.* Copyright © 1995 Lawrence J. Crabb, Jr. Used by permission of Zondervan. www.zondervan.com.
———. *Encouragement: The Key To Caring.* Copyright © 1990 Lawrence J. Crabb, Jr. Used by permission of Zondervan. www.zondervan.com.

Cronk, Sandra. "Dark Night." *Weavings*, Volume XXIV, Number I, January/February 2009, p. 15–19.

De Caussade, Jean-Pierre. *The Sacrament of the Present Moment.* Excerpts from pp. 63, 65, 70 from *The Sacrament of the Present Moment* by Jean-Pierre De Caussade. English translation copyright © 1981 by William Collins Songs & Co. Ltd. Introduction copyright © 1982 by Harper & Row,

Publishers, Inc. Reprinted by Permission of HarperCollins Publishers.

De Foucauld, Charles. *Meditations of a Hermit.* New York: Orbis, 1981.

De Mello, Anthony. *Awareness: The Perils and Opportunities of Reality.* New York: Doubleday, 1992.

De Saint-Exupery, Antoine. *The Little Prince.* New York: Harcourt Brace, 1943.

De Waal, Esther. *Living with Contradiction.* Harrisburg, PA: Morehouse, 1989, 1997.

Dean, Kenda Creasy and Ron Foster. *The Godbearing Life: The Art of Soul Tending for Youth Ministry.*

Eagan, John S.J. *A Traveler Toward the Dawn.* Excerpt from *A Traveler Toward the Dawn: The Spiritual Journey of John Eagan* edited by William J. O'Malley, SJ (Loyola Press, 1990). Used with permission by Loyola Press. www.loyolapress.com.

Farrell, Edward J. *Free to Be Nothing.* Collegeville, MN: Liturgical Press, 1991.
———. *Gathering the Fragments: A Gospel Mosaic.* New York: Alba House, 1999.
———. *Prayer is a Hunger.* Mt. Pleasant, SC: Dimension Books, 1972.

Fenelon, Francois. *Let Go—The Spiritual Letters.* New Kensington, PA: Whitaker House, 1973.
———. *The Royal Way of the Cross.* Brewster, MA: Paraclete, 1982.

Fenhagen, James. *Invitation to Holiness.* Two brief excerpts as submitted from *Invitation to Holiness* by James C. Fenhagen. Copyright © 1985 by James C. Fenhagen. Reprinted by permission of HarperCollins Publishers.

Fonseca, Michael. *Living in God's Embrace: The Practice of Spiritual Intimacy*. Notre Dame, IN: Ave Maria Press, 2000.

Foster, Richard. *Celebration of Discipline*. Brief quotes from pp. 108, 201 from *Celebration of Discipline, 25th Anniversary Edition* by Richard J. Foster. Copyright © 1978, 1988, 1998 by Richard J. Foster. Reprinted by permission of HarperCollins Publishers.
————. *Prayer: Finding the Heart's True Home*. Excerpts from pp. 2, 3–4, 168 from *Prayer: Finding the Heart's True Home* by Richard J. Foster. Copyright © 1992 by Richard J. Foster. Reprinted by permission of HarperCollins Publishers.

Gilliland, Glaphre. *When the Pieces Don't Fit: God Makes the Difference*. Grand Rapids, MI: Zondervan, 1984.

Gire, Ken. *The Divine Embrace*. Carol Stream, IL: Tyndale, 2003.
————. *Moments with the Savior*. Copyright © 1998 Ken Gire. Used by permission of Zondervan. www.zondervan.com.
————. *The Reflective Life*. © 1998 Ken Gire. *The Reflective Life* is published by David C. Cook. All rights reserved.
————. *The Weathering Grace of God: The Beauty God Brings from Life's Upheavals*. Ventura, CA: Vine, 2001.
————. Taken from *Windows of the Soul* by Ken Gire. Copyright © 1996 by Ken Gire Jr. Used by permission of Zondervan. www.zondervan.com.

Gratton, Carolyn. *The Art of Spiritual Guidance*. New York: Crossroad, 1992.

Greene, Graham. *The Power and the Glory*. New York: Penguin, 1991.

Griffin, Emilie. *Clinging—The Experience of Prayer*. Wichita, KS: Eighth Day, 2003.

Groff, Kent Ira. *Journeymen: A Spiritual Guide for Men (and for Women Who Want to Understand Them)*. Nashville: Upper Room, 1999.

Guenther, Margaret. *Holy Listening: The Art of Spiritual Direction.* Lanham, MD: Rowman & Littlefield, 1992.
———. *My Soul in Silence Waits: Meditations on Psalm 62.* Lanham, MD: Cowley Publications, 2000.

Guinness, Os. *The Call: Finding and Fulfilling the Central Purpose of Your Life.* Nashville: Thomas Nelson, 2003.

Guyon, Jeanne. *Experiencing the Depths of Jesus Christ.* Nashville: Thomas Nelson, 2000.

Hackenberg, Rachel. "Barefoot." Used with permission. www.rachelhackenberg.com.

Hammarskjold, Dag. Excerpt(s) from *Markings* by Dag Hammarskjold, translated by W.H. Auden and Leif Sjoberg, translation copyright © 1964, copyright renewed 1992 by Alfred A. Knopf, a division of Penguin Random House LLC and Faber & Faber Ltd.. Used by permission of Alfred A. Knopf, an imprint of the Knopf Doubleday Publishing Group, a division of Penguin Random House LLC. All rights reserved.

Hermes, Kathryn J. *The Journey Within: Prayer as a Path to God.* Cincinnati, OH: St. Anthony Messenger Press, 2004.

Houselander, Caryll. *The Risen Christ: The Forty Days after the Resurrection.* New York: Scepter Publishers, 2007.

Howatch, Susan. *Absolute Truths.* New York: Ballantine, 1994.

Howell, James C. *Servants, Misfits, and Martyrs.* Nashville: Upper Room, 1999.

Hurnard, Hannah. *Hinds' Feet On High Places.* Uhrichsville, OH: Barbour, 1940, 2000.

Chariton, Igumen. *The Art of Prayer: An Orthodox Anthology.* New York: Faber and Faber, 1966.

James, Steven. *A Heart Exposed: Talking to God with Nothing to Hide.* Grand Rapids, MI: Revell, a division of Baker, 2009.

Job, Rueben P. and Norman Shawchuck. *A Guide to Prayer for All Who Seek God.*
————. *A Guide to Prayer for Ministers and Other Servants.*

Jones, E. Stanley. *The Way.* Minneapolis, MN: Summerside Press, 1946, 2011.

Jones, Timothy. *Awake My Soul: Practical Spirituality for Busy People.* Colorado Springs: WaterBrook, 2000.

Julian of Norwich. *Revelations of Divine Love.* New York: Penguin, 1998.

Jung, C. G. and Sir Herbert Read, ed. *Psychology and Religion: West and East (The Collected Works of C. G. Jung, Volume 11.* New York: Princeton University Press, 1975.

Karnes, Caroline McKinney. *Storm Dance.* Used by permission.

Karon, Jan. *At Home in Mitford.* Copyright © 1994 by Jan Karon. Used by permission of Viking Books, an imprint of Penguin Publishing Group, a division of Penguin Random House LLC.

Keating, Thomas. *Awakenings.* New York: Crossroad Publishing, 1990.

Kelly, Thomas R. *A Testament of Devotion.* Excerpts from pp. 3, 8, 11–12, 14, 18, 26, 43–44, 47, 59, 66, 84, 92, 95–96 from *A Testament of Devotion* by Thomas R. Kelly. Copyright © 1941 by Harper & Row Publishers, Inc. Renewed 1969 by Lois Lael Kelly Stabler. New introduction copyright (c) 1992 by HarperCollins Publishers Inc. Reprinted by permission of HarperCollins Publishers.

Kelsey, Morton T. *The Other Side of Silence: Meditation for the Twenty-First Century*. New York: Paulist Press, 1976.

Kidd, Sue Monk. *When the Heart Waits: Spiritual Direction for Life's Sacred Questions*. New York: HarperCollins, 1990.

Lamott, Anne. Excerpt(s) from *Traveling Mercies: Some Thoughts On Faith* by Anne Lamott, copyright © 1999 by Anne Lamott. Used by permission of Pantheon Books, an imprint of the Knopf Doubleday Publishing Group, a division of Penguin Random House LLC. All rights reserved.

Leech, Kenneth. *True Prayer: An Invitation to Christian Spirituality*. New York: Morehouse Publishing, 1980, 1995.

Lewis, C. S. *A Grief Observed.* Copyright © 1961 C.S. Lewis Pte. Ltd. Extracts reprinted by permission.
———. *A Horse and His Boy*. Copyright © 1954 C.S. Lewis Pte. Ltd. Extracts reprinted by permission.
———. *The Last Battle.* Copyright © 1952 C.S. Lewis Pte. Ltd. Extracts reprinted by permission.
———. *Letters to Malcolm*. Copyright © 1963 C.S. Lewis Pte. Ltd. Extracts reprinted by permission.
———. *The Magician's Nephew.* Copyright © 1955 C.S. Lewis Pte. Ltd. Extracts reprinted by permission.
———. *Mere Christianity*. Copyright © 1952 C.S. Lewis Pte. Ltd. Extracts reprinted by permission.
———. *The Problem of Pain.* Copyright © 1940 C.S. Lewis Pte. Ltd. Extracts reprinted by permission.
———. *The Silver Chair.* Copyright © 1953 C.S. Lewis Pte. Ltd. Extracts reprinted by permission.
———. *The Voyage of the Dawn Treader*. Copyright © 1952 C.S. Lewis Pte. Ltd. Extracts reprinted by permission.
———. *The Weight of Glory*. Copyright © 1949 C.S. Lewis Pte. Ltd. Extracts reprinted by permission.

Loder, Ted. *Guerrillas of Grace.* Copyright © Ted Loder, admin. Augsburg Fortress. Reproduced by permission.

Lucado, Max. Taken from *The Applause of Heaven* by Max Lucado. Copyright © 2011 Max Lucado. Used by permission of Thomas Nelson. www.thomasnelson.com.

———. *In the Grip of Grace*. Nashville: Thomas Nelson, 1996.

Lupton, Robert D. *Theirs is the Kingdom: Celebrating the Gospel in Urban America.* New York: HarperCollins, 1989.

Macy, Howard R. *Rhythms of the Inner Life: Yearning for Closeness with God.* Newberg, OR: Red Nose Fun Publishing, 1988, 2012.

Manning, Brennan. *The Furious Longing of God.* Copyright © 2009 Brennan Manning. *Furious Longing of God* is published by David C. Cook. All rights reserved.

———. *The Rabbi's Heartbeat.* Colorado Springs: NavPress, 2003.

———. *Ruthless Trust.* Brief excerpt from p. 147 from *Truthless Trust* by Brennan Manning. Copyright © 2000 by Brennan Manning. Reprinted by permission of HarperCollins Publishers.

———. Excerpts from *The Signature of Jesus* by Brennan Manning, copyright © 1996 by Brennan Manning. Used by permission of WaterBrook Multnomah, an imprint of the Crown Publishing Group, a division of Penguin Random House LLC. All rights reserved.

Marechal, Paul. *Dancing Madly Backwards: A Journey into God.* New York: Crossroad Publishing, 1982.

Marmion, Columba. *Union with God: Letters of Spiritual Direction.* Bethesda, MD: Zaccheus Press, 1957, 2006.

Martin, Charles. *Chasing Fireflies: A Novel of Discovery.* Nashville: Thomas Nelson, 2008.

———. *Unwritten.* New York: Center Street, 2013.

May, Gerald G. *The Awakened Heart.* Excerpts from pp. 1, 91, 93, 96–97, 104, 106, 124, 163, 176 from *The Awakened Heart* by Gerald G. May, MD. Copyright © 1991 by Gerald G. May. Reprinted by permission of HarperCollins Publishers.

————. *The Dark Night of the Soul.* Brief excerpt from p. 73 from *The Dark Night of the Soul* by Gerald G. May, MD. Copyright © 2004 by Gerald G. May. Reprinted by permission of HarperCollins Publishers.

McGrath, Alister. Excerpts from *The Journey* by Alister McGrath, copyright ©2000 by Alister McGrath. Used by permission of Doubleday, an imprint of the Knopf Doubleday Publishing Group, division of Penguin Random House LLC. All rights reserved.

McQuiston, John II. *Always We Begin Again.*

McCullough Donald W. *The Trivialization of God: The Dangerous Illusion of A Manageable Deity.* Colorado Springs: NavPress, 1995.

Merton, Thomas. *Life and Holiness.* New York: Abbey of Gethsemani, 1963, 1966.

————. *New Seeds of Contemplation.* Copyright ©1961 by The Abbey of Gethsemani, Inc. Reprinted by permission of New Directions Publishing Corp.

————. *Seeds of Contemplation.* New York: Abbey of Gethsemani, 2007.

————. *Thoughts in Solitude.* New York: Farrar, Straus and Giroux, 1999.

Miller, Calvin. *The Singer.* Downers Grove, IL: Intervarsity Press, 1975.

————. *Walking with the Saints.* Nashville: Thomas Nelson, 1995.

Miller, Donald. *A Million Miles in a Thousand Years.* Copyright © 2011 Donald Miller. Used by permission of Thomas Nelson. www.thomasnelson.com.

Mogabgab, John S. Editor's Introduction. *Weavings*, November/ December 2005.

———. *Weavings*, March/April 2008. "Editor's Introduction," *Weavings: A Journal of the Christian Spiritual Life*, Vol. XXIII, No. 2 (Nashville, TN: The Upper Room, 2008), 2–3. Used by permission.
———. *Weavings*, July/August 2003, 2. "Editor's Introduction," *Weavings: A Journal of the Christian Spiritual Life*, Vol. XXIII, No. 2 (Nashville, TN: The Upper Room, 2008), 2–3. Used by permission.

Mollenkott, Virginia Ramey. *Speech, Silence, Action!: The Cycle of Faith*. Nashville: Abingdon Press, 1980.

Mother Frances Dominica. *Prayer*. Chicago: Amate Press, 1981.

Mother Teresa and Brother Roger. *Seeking the Heart of God*. New York: HarperOne, 1993.

Mother Teresa. *A Gift for God.* Brief excerpts from pp. 37, 70 from *A Gift for God: Prayers & Meditations* by Mother Teresa of Calcutta. Copyright © 1975, 1996 by Mother Teresa Missionaries of Charity. Reprinted by permission of HarperCollins Publishers.
———. *No Greater Love*. Novato, CA: New World Library, 1995.

Mueller, George. *The Autobiography of George Mueller.* New Kensington, PA: Whitaker House, 1984.

Mulholland M. Robert Jr. *For the Sake of Others.* Transforming Community #8
———. *Invitation to a Journey*. Taken from *Invitation to a Journey* by M. Robert Mulholland Jr. Copyright © 1993 M. Robert Mulholland Jr. Used by permission of InterVarsity Press, P.O. Box 1400, Downers Grove, IL 60515, USA. www.ivpress.com. M. Robert Mulholland, Jr., Transforming Center Blog, March 7, 2016. www.transformingcenter.org.

Murray, Andrew. *The Key to the Missionary Problem*. Fort Washington, PA : CLC Publications, 1981.

Norris, Kathleen. *The Cloister Walk*. New York: Riverhead Books, a division of Penguin, 1996.

Nouwen, Henri J. M. and John S. Mogabgab, ed. "A Spirituality of Waiting." *Weavings Reader*. Nashville: Upper Room, 1993.

————. "July 15: Being Broken" from *Bread for the Journey: A Daybook of Wisdom and Faith* by Henri J.M. Nouwen. Copyright © 1997 by Henri J.M. Nouwen. Reprinted by permission of HarperCollins Publishers.

————. Excerpts from pp. 18–19, 20, 73, 82, 148 from *Gracias! A Latin American Journal* by Henri J.M. Nouwen. Copyright © 1983 by Henri J.M. Nouwen. Reprinted by permission of HarperCollins Publishers.

————. Excerpt(s) from *The Genesee Diary* by Henri Nouwen, copyright © 1976 by Henri J.M. Nouwen. Copyright renewed © 2004 by Sue Mosteller, CSJ, executrix of the Estate of Henri J.M. Nouwen Used by permission of Doubleday, an imprint of the Knopf Doubleday Publishing Group, a division of Penguin Random House LLC. All rights reserved.

————. *Here and Now* by Henri Nouwen (Crossroad, 2006). Reprinted by arrangement with The Crossroad Publishing Company. www.crossroadpublishing.com.

————. *In the Name of Jesus* by Henri Nouwen (Crossroad, 1992). Reprinted by arrangement with The Crossroad Publishing Company. www.crossroadpublishing.com.

————. Excerpt(s) from *The Inner Voice of Love* by Henri Nouwen, copyright © 1996 by Henri Nouwen. Used by permission of Doubleday, an imprint of the Knopf Doubleday Publishing Group, a division of Penguin Random House LLC. All rights reserved.

————. Brief excerpt from p. 57 from *Letters to Marc About Jesus* by Henri J.M. Nouwen . Copyright © 1987, 1988 by Henri J.M. Nouwen. English translation Copyright © 1988 by Harper & Row, Publishers, Inc. and Darton, Longman & Todd, Led. Reprinted by permission of HarperCollins Publishers.

————. *Turn My Mourning Into Dancing: Moving Through Hard Times with Hope.* Nashville: W Publishing Group, 2001.

————. Excerpts from pp. 27–28, 34, 52–53 from *The Way of the Heart* by Henri J.M. Nouwen. Copyright © 1981 by Henri J.M. Nouwen. Reprinted by permission of HarperCollins Publishers.

————. *With Open Hands.* Notre Dame, IN: Ave Maria Press, 1972, 1995, 2005.

————. *The Wounded Healer: Ministry in Contemporary Society.* New York: Bantam Doubleday, 1972.

O'Connor, Elizabeth. *Journey Inward, Journey Outward.* New York: HarperCollins, 1975.

Oden, Marilyn Brown. *Abundance: Joyful Living in Christ.* Nashville: Upper Room, 1980.

Ortberg, John. Taken from *The Life You've Always Wanted* by John Ortberg Copyright © 1997, 2002 by John Ortberg. Used by permission of Zondervan. www.zondervan.com.

————. *Love Beyond Reason.*

Owens, Virginia Stem. *And the Trees Clap Their Hands.* Used by permission of Wipf and Stock Publishers. www.wipfandstock.com

————. *Looking For Jesus.*

Packer, J.I. *Knowing God.* Downers Grove, IL: InterVarsity Press, 1993.

Palmer, Parker J. *A Hidden Wholeness*: *The Journey Toward an Undivided Life.* Copyright © 2009 Parker J. Palmer. Reproduced with permission of John Wiley & Sons, Inc.

————. *Let Your Life Speak: Listening for the Voice of Vocation.* Copyright © 1999 Parker J. Palmer. Reproduced with permission of John Wiley & Sons, Inc.

————. Brief excerpt from pp. 84–85 from *The Active Life: A Spirituality of Work, Creativity, and Caring* by Parker

Palmer. Copyright © 1990 by Parker J. Palmer. Reprinted by permission of HarperCollins Publishers.

Paulsell, William O. "Ways of Prayer: Designing a Personal Rule." *Weavings* (Sept./Oct. 1987).

Peck, M. Scott. *A Different Drum: Community Making and Peace.* New York: Touchstone, 1987.

Pennington, M. Basil *Living in the Question.* © M. Basil Pennington, *Living in the Question,* Bloomsbury Continuum, an imprint of Bloomsbury Publishing Inc. Used with permission.
———. *Breaking Bread: The Table Talk of Jesus.* New York: Harper & Row, 1986.
———. *Seeking His Mind.* Brewster, MA: Paraclete Press, 2002.

Peterson Eugene H. *Working the Angles: The Shape of Pastoral Integrity.* Grand Rapids, MI: Wm. B. Eerdmans, 1987.
———. *A Long Obedience in the Same Direction: Discipleship in an Instant Society.* Downers Grove, IL: InterVarsity, 2000.
———. *Five Smooth Stones for Pastoral Work.* Grand Rapids, MI: Wm. B. Eerdmans, 1992. Used with permission.
———. *Under the Unpredictable Plant.* Grand Rapids, MI: Wm. B. Eerdmans, 1994.
———. *The Wisdom of Each Other: A Conversation Between Spiritual Friends.* Grand Rapids, MI: Zondervan, 1998.
———. *Subversive Spirituality.* Grand Rapids, MI: Wm. B. Eerdmans, 1997.
———. *The Contemplative Pastor: Returning to the Art of Spiritual Direction.* Grand Rapids, MI: Wm. B. Eerdmans, 1989.

Powell, John. *A Reason to Live! A Reason to Die!* Boston: Argus, 1975.

Prevallet, Elaine M. *Reflections on Simplicity*. Wallingford, PA: Pendle Hill Pamphlet #244, 1982, 3–4. Used with permission.

Puls, Joan. *Every Bush Is Burning: A Spirituality for Our Times*. New London, CT: Twenty-Third Publications, 1985.

Quoist, Michael. *Prayers of Life*. New York: Gil and MacMillan, 1965.

Rahner, Karl. *Encounters with Silence*. South Bend, IN: St. Augustine Press, 1999.

Richard, Rolle and Richard Misyn, trans. *The Fire of Love*. Grand Rapids, MI: CCEL, 2010. www.ccel.org.

Rilke, Rainer Maria. *Book of Hours*. "Ich bin auf der Welt.../I'm too alone in the world...", "Ich glaube an Alles.../I believe in all that has never yet been spoken...", "Und doch, obwohl ein jeder.../And yet, though we strain...", "Ich finde dich in allen.../I find you there in all these things...", from *Rilke's Book of Hours: Love Poems to God* by Rainer Maria Rilke, translated by Anita Barrows and Joanna Macy, translation copyright © 1996 by Anita Barrows and Joanna Macy. Used by permission of Riverhead, an imprint of Penguin Publishing Group, a division of Penguin Random House LLC.
———. *Letters to a Young Poet*. New York: W.W. Norton, 1993.

Rohr, Richard. *Everything Belongs* by Richard Rohr (Crossroad, 2003). Reprinted by arrangement with The Crossroad Publishing Company. www.crossroadpublishing.com.
———. *Simplicity* by Richard Rohr (Crossroad, 2004). Reprinted by arrangement with The Crossroad Publishing Company. www.crossroadpublishing.com.

Schweitzer, Albert, Marvin Meyer & Kurt Bergel, eds. *Reverence for Life: The Ethics of Albert Schweitzer for the*

Twenty-First Century. New York: Syracuse University Press, 2002.

Seifert, Harvey and Lois. *Liberation of Life: Growth Exercises in Meditation and Action*. Nashville: Upper Room, 1976.

Shannon, William H. *Silence on Fire: The Prayer of Awareness*. New York: Crossroad, 1991.

Shepherd, J. Barrie. Copyright © 1986 by the *Christian Century*. "Incarnating" by J. Barrie Shepherd is reprinted by permission from the December 10, 1986, issue of the *Christian Century*.

Shrigley, G. A. Cleveland, ed. *Daily Prayer Companion: A Prayer for Every Day in the Year*. New York: Foster and Stewart Publishers, 1947.

Smith, Hannah Whitall. *The Christian's Secret of a Happy Life*. Grand Rapids, MI: Revell, a division of Baker, 1952.

Smith, James Bryan. *Embracing the Love of God: The Path and Promise of Christian Life*. New York: HarperOne, 2008.

Sproul, R. C. *Grace Unknown: The Heart of Reformed Theology*. Grand Rapids, MI: Baker, 1997.

Strong, Mary. *Letters of the Scattered Brotherhood*. Brief excerpt from p. 129 from *Letters of the Scattered Brotherhood* by Mary Strong. Copyright 1948 by Harper & Brothers, renewed © 1975 by George W. Penny, Jr. Reprinted by permission of HarperCollins Publishers.

Strunk, Orlo Jr. *Selections from the Writings of Dietrich Bonhoeffer*. Nashville: The Upper Room, 1967.

Sutera, Judith. *The Work of God: Benedictine Prayer*. Collegeville, IN: Liturgical Press, 1997.

Taylor, Howard and Geraldine Taylor. *Hudson Taylor's Spiritual Secret.* Chicago: Moody, 1989, 2009.

Teresa of Avila. *Interior Castle.* New York: Dover, 1976, 2007.
———. *The Way of Perfection.* New York: Dover, 1946, 2012.

Thompson, Marjorie J. *Soul Feast.* Louisville, KY: Westminster John Knox Press, 1995, 2005, 2014.
———. *The Way of Forgiveness: Participants Book.* Nashville: Upper Room, 2002.

Tournier, Paul. *Reflections on Life's Most Crucial Questions.* New York: Harper & Row, 1976.

Townsend, Stuart and Keith Getty. *Speak, O Lord.* Dayton, OH: Lorenz Publishing, 2008.

Tozer, A. W. *God Tells the Man Who Cares: God Speaks to Those Who Take the Time to Listen.* Camp Hill, PA: Wing Spread Publishers, 1993.
———. *Knowledge of the Holy.* Excerpts from pp. 1, 6, 63, 93, 97, 107 from *The Knowledge of the Holy: The Attributes of God: Their Meaning in the Christian Life* by A.W. Tozer. Copyright © 1961 by Aiden Wilson Tozer. Reprinted by permission of HarperCollins Publishers.
———. *The Pursuit of God.* Excerpt taken from *Pursuit of God* by A.W. Tozer © 2014, published by Aneko Press. Used with permission.

Tuoti, Frank X. *Why Not Be a Mystic?* New York: Crossroad, 1995.

Underhill, Evelyn. *The House of the Soul and Concerning the Inner Life.* : Winston Press, 1984.
———. *The Spiritual Life.*

van der Looy, H. *Rule for a New Brother.*

Wangerin, Walter Jr. *Preparing for Jesus*. Copyright © 1999 Walter Wangerin Jr. Used by permission of Zondervan. www.zondervan.com.
————. *Reliving the Passion*.

Westerhoff, John III and John D. Eusden. *The Spiritual Life: The Foundation for Preaching and Teaching*. Louisville, KY: Westminster John Knox Press, 1994.

Wiederkehr, Macrina. *Abide*. Copyright 2011 by Order of Saint Benedict. Published by Liturgical Press, Collegeville, Minnesota. Reprinted with permission.
————. Excerpted from *Behold Your Life* by Macrina Wiederkehr. Copyright 1999 by Ave Maria Press, P.O. Box 428, Notre Dame, IN 46556. Used with permission of the publisher.
————. "Harvest of God." Taken from A *Tree Full of Angels*. The full title of the poem is "The Harvest of God: Feasting on Your Theophanies." Used with permission.
————. Interview from *The Mars Hill Review*, Fall 1997. This copyrighted article was originally published in Mars Hill Review, a 200-page journal of essays, studies and reminders of God. For more information, please visit www.marshillreview.com.
————. Excerpts from pp. 7, 9–10, 15, 70–71, 76, 78–80, 91, 134, 188 from *Seasons of Your Heart: Prayers and Reflections* by Macrina Wiederkehr. Copyright © 1991 by Macrina Wiederkehr. Reprinted by permission of HarperCollins Publishers.
————. Excerpt from pp. 11–12 from *The Song of the Seed* by Macrina Wiederkehr. Copyright © 1995 by Macrina Wiederkehr. Reprinted by permission of HarperCollins Publishers.
————. Excerpts from pp. xiii, 26–27, 51, 78, 154–155 ("The Harvest of God: Feasting on Your Theophanies") from *A Tree Full of Angels* by Macrina Wiederkehr. Copyright © 1988 by Macrina Wiederkehr. Reprinted by permission of HarperCollins Publishers.

Wiesel, Elie. Excerpt from *Night* by Elie Wiesel, translated by Marion Wiesel. Translation copyright © 2006 by Marion Wiesel. Reprinted by permission of Hill and Wang, a division of Farrar, Straus and Giroux, LLC. Used with permission.

Willard, Dallas. *Renovation of the Heart: Putting on the Character of Christ*. Colorado Springs: NavPress, 2012.

Wilson, Patricia F. *Quiet Spaces: Prayer Interludes for Women*. Nashville: Upper Room, 2002.

Wright, Wendy M. *The Time Between: Cycles and Rhythms in Ordinary Time*. Nashville: Upper Room, 1999.

Wuellner, Flora Slosson. *Feed My Shepherds: Spiritual Healing and Renewal for Those in Christian Leadership* by Flora Slosson Wuellner. Copyright 1997. Used by permission of Upper Room Books. www.books.upperroom.org.

Yaconelli, Mike. "The Back Door." *The Door* (March/April, 1994).

Yancey, Philip. *The Jesus I Never Knew*. New York: Zondervan, 2002.

Made in the USA
Middletown, DE
16 January 2022

58812203R00234